Transformational Dog Training

Transformational Dog Training
Bring Out the Best in Your Dog by Bringing Out the Best in Yourself

Brian Bergford

Dedication

To the love of my life: Gina, my wife and best friend.
Thank you for believing in me and being the most
loving and remarkable person I have ever known.

Acknowledgments

I wish to express my deepest thanks to the many people who contributed to this work. Everyone in my life has, in some special way, influenced me, which has shaped my experience and therefore the content of this book. I am thankful to an endless list of individuals, but in the interest of brevity I will highlight a few who were instrumental to the creation of *Transformational Dog Training*.

First, I must express thanks to my beautiful bride, Gina. I love you. Without your faith in me—and patient nudging—I never would have embarked on this journey. Your love, kindness, and boundless support mean more than you will ever know. You've helped me grow. You've made me stronger. You've picked me up many times, spoken to my heart, and been the best helpmate anyone could ever ask for.

To Aimee Sadler: I am forever grateful to you and cherish your friendship. You are one of the most inspiring people I have ever met. Years ago when I desperately needed a dog-training mentor, connecting with you was truly a godsend. I had no idea how much I would learn. Your generosity amazes me. I am always in awe of your exquisite leadership and ability as a training and behavior expert. Watching your organization, Dogs Playing for Life, change the face of sheltering and the lives of countless dogs and people is an honor. To be able to contribute in my little way is a privilege.

I remember being starstruck when I met Martin Deeley years ago. Everybody knew about him and what an accomplished dog trainer he was. What I didn't know was how much I would grow to admire and respect him. His humility and heart are my favorite things about him. Thank you, Martin, for being so gracious when I approached you about reading this book (despite the disarray of that early draft). Your encouragement helped me press on when I felt riddled with doubt about whether to see this project through.

Writing a book is no small feat, but editing one is an act of brilliance. Erin Brown, you are incredible. Thank you for sifting through the rubble and bringing out the best in my writing. You brought clarity and refinement to the text while preserving my author's voice. I am so glad I found you. Your skill, patience, and care are most appreciated.

To my friends and family: I love you and am blessed to have you in my life. I thank God every day for being surrounded by supportive and uplifting people. Thank you for loving me and sharing your warmth, smiles, encouragement, grace, and laughter through the years. Here's to many more.

And here's to everyone else who has inspired me throughout the years—the mentors, training professionals, coaches, teachers, and many others who model excellence and an uncompromising commitment to the highest good. Watching you is exhilarating; it quickens my spirit and compels me to become the best I can be.

Finally, I want to acknowledge and honor all of the dogs and dog owners I have had the pleasure of working with. You have been my greatest teachers. Thank you for your trust and the invaluable lessons you've taught me through the years. This book is my attempt to demonstrate my appreciation and indebtedness to you—I sincerely hope it impacts your life in a significant and positive way.

Foreword

With so many books on the shelf regarding both dog training and personal development, I wondered at first why Brian wrote *Transformational Dog Training*. As I got further into it, I began to realize not only had I transformed dogs' lives through training but also they had transformed mine through the relationship we built together. The relationship/partnership I built with dogs stimulated my love of the countryside, shooting, and wildlife. We never thought about what we were achieving as we walked together as a pack through fields and forests. We never thought about the sense of fulfillment when we did wonderful retrieves or won competitions. I walked miles, I experienced extreme weather, and conquered fears because of my dogs and with my dogs.

Although we talk of leadership, I prefer to call it a partnership. My dog and I possess skills and natural abilities. On occasions my dog will take leadership because he knows better than I. Other times I take leadership because I know better than he. And at times we experiment together to achieve a common aim. I had to be fit to keep up with my dogs, both in mind as well as body. My dogs had to be fit to achieve what I asked of them. The true relationship with a dog is a bonding of the physical, mental, and spiritual. You have to "be" with each other, and to do that you have to "be" with yourself and your dog; to be able to read and understand each other through the slightest communication and to know your dog as well as you know yourself. You both test yourself not on what you ask of each other but what each of you ask of yourself. A true relationship is more than love and affection. It is a complex togetherness that few achieve, yet with effort anyone can attain this worthwhile goal.

In this book, Brian Bergford explains how he created the relationship not only with his dogs but also inside himself. When dogs and owners come together to be the one special dog and one special owner in their lives, they obtain a peace that transcends all. My dogs have given me inner peace and enabled me to reach greater heights than I would otherwise have reached. I like to think I have done the same for them. They have been my true partners. My dogs are my life, and I believe I am also theirs.

Martin Deeley

Co-Founder and Executive Director, International Association of Canine Professionals
Director, International School for Dog Trainers

Contents

Introduction

With a multitude of great dog training literature already available, why yet another book on the subject? After all, there are plenty of books outlining training and behavior modification techniques that provide step-by-step instructions for dog owners seeking good advice and helpful tips. Yet I couldn't shake the feeling that this book *needed* to be written. I had something fundamentally important to share that was initially difficult to explain—it was more of an intuition. All I knew was that I noted that something was missing in the training that was causing communication breakdowns and serious issues between people and their pets. Dog ownership in the United States is on the rise, and those owners spend billions of dollars on training, with the worthy goal of having well-behaved and obedient companions. So it's disappointing to see such a tremendous amount of frustration, confusion, and lackluster results despite people's best efforts.

Then I discovered the missing link that had puzzled me. The power to enjoy a better relationship with man's best friend is now more accessible than ever and can be harnessed by those who understand and apply the principles found in *Transformational Dog Training*. As this book was nearing completion I gave a friend the synopsis. After a thirty-second overview she smiled and said, "So it's a self-development book for dog owners." I nodded. She had summed it up perfectly.

The role of personal growth, stability, and the way we live and interact daily with our dogs is largely ignored or merely alluded to in most of the current dog training literature. The few books that touch on this critical issue are typically written with a flawed assumption that owners know how to make personal changes that will allow their dogs to overcome dysfunction. Thus, people are left without specific action plans they can apply to overcome personal challenges that contribute to their dogs' "issues." *Transformational Dog Training* is a refreshing departure, taking you and your canine companion on an amazing journey. You are given an empowering practical framework for applying dog training and behavior modification principles with your dog, as well as specific mental tactics for use in your own life to experience the kind of peace and balance that supports training progress and ensures lasting results. It's about bringing out the best in your dog by bringing out the best in yourself. It's turning around the question "Is this the right dog for me?" and asking, "Am I the right person for this dog?"

This notion of personal growth in the context of dog training may seem a bit odd upon first glance, but upon further reflection, we recognize that training is a partnership and the dog is only half of that equation. Most of us have dogs so we can experience and enjoy a healthy, genuine connection with them. If there is dysfunction in our relationships with our dogs or in their behavior (or both) and we want to improve it, we cannot afford to ignore the role we play. We must know *how* to make those changes in our lives that will be reflected in our dogs' behavior and—most importantly—have a willingness implement them.

My pastor has reminded many that "It's cheaper to pay attention than to pay alimony." While this statement is obviously directed toward married couples, the principle is applicable to many areas of life. With respect to our dogs, it's cheaper to pay attention than to pay vet bills after your dog attacks another because you haven't properly socialized him; it's cheaper to pay attention than to pay court fees because you didn't train your dog well when he was young and he bit your neighbor; and it's certainly cheaper to pay attention to how you *live* with your dog than having to pay the price of unbearable heartache from a broken relationship with him.

When we spend the time, energy, and money necessary to train our dogs properly, taking into account individual needs and making sure that we are creating balance in our own lives as well, we reap the rewards of a healthy, functional relationship with a dog that is welcome anywhere. This book will provide you with a greater depth of understanding about the most relevant dog-training and personal-development principles as well as practical tools to build that one-of-a-kind bond you've always desired to have with your dog.

There's a huge difference between dog training and *Transformational* dog training: the latter being decidedly more daring because we accept the fact that powerful relational dynamics are at work and we can't have true dog training success without also training ourselves. *Transformational Dog Training* is no mere series of techniques or a fixed school of thought. It is a constantly evolving personal journey requiring significant courage as we challenge ourselves to stretch and become more. Growth and awareness are at the heart of this very personal journey, but our dogs are with us every step of the way, learning and growing right beside us. Through observing their behavior, which is heavily influenced by our own, we will begin to see that our dogs provide candid mirrors that reflect our way of being and provide us with real-time feedback about our states of mind, whether or not we are in balance, and areas that need adjustment.

By having personal stability and a firm grasp of training principles, we can help our dogs experience the most significant, lasting, and meaningful change possible. Creating this type of change in our dogs reaches far beyond addressing surface-level nuisance behaviors. It touches the core of who they are and cultivates inner peace. Most of us would love to help our dogs realize this level of stability. The question is whether we're willing to be the agents of change, and the prerequisite is having the guts to engage in self-examination while embarking on a simultaneous journey with our dogs of personal transformation. Such a path is wrought with challenge and adventure. It will be an exhilarating time and also the source of your greatest struggle as you come to grips with the realization that you and your dog have higher levels of unrealized potential.

Moving beyond your comfort zone can feel like a threat, and change naturally involves venturing into the unknown which gives rise to fear. Staying where you are, even if it's not healthy, feels safe—you know what to expect. As the saying goes, most people are more comfortable with old problems than they are with new solutions. It's ironic that people expend so much energy avoiding reaching out into the unknown when it's the one thing that will give them an opportunity to grow and experience great breakthroughs.

It's only through cultivating an appetite for something greater or to solve an important problem that we are moved to step outside the old familiar realms. Your dog can be the catalyst that awakens this desire within you. Investing in his well-being and happiness can be the springboard to engage your fears and embark on an exciting new journey. No longer passive observers of other people's lives through reality shows, you are fully immersed in your own adventure that is sure to have its share of fear, wonder, excitement, suspense, letdowns, and ultimate, satisfying victory.

Transformational Dog Training examines overarching training and psychological principles and then breaks them down into practical steps that guide you along the way. But remember, it is still very much *your* journey, and it's not a true adventure if there is no fear, danger, or breaching the unknown. This is exactly where you can summon the power to break through self-imposed mental barriers that may have been impeding personal progress for years.

As you and your dog venture out, you may be stretched beyond what you thought was possible, but if you are willing to travel the path, you will enter into a place of profound joy and genuine peace. An ancient proverb admonishes, "The journey of a thousand miles begins with a single step." Lay claim to your true power and freedom today by taking that single, bold step with your faithful companion.

For the greatest transformation, I suggest you read one chapter per week and apply the exercises and information for a full seven days before moving on to the next chapter. Transformational change cannot be rushed. Much can be accomplished in a relatively short period, but all of the principles and practices require a certain amount of time to permeate our lives. Your success with Transformational dog training depends upon applying the principles *as you read* instead of plodding through the text without immersing yourself in the process. Group training classes are typically six sessions long, and I've intentionally designed this book to correspond with that timeframe. Genius doesn't lie in knowing the information; it lies in an individual's dedication and ability to apply the information. Action and experience is what separates those who grow and reap the benefits of transformational change from those who can make sense of the material but don't realize the changes they desire. My prayer is that you'll quicken to action, work wholeheartedly to realize the life you've always longed for, and cherish every moment of the journey ahead.

Chapter One

What Is Your Dog's Design? What's Yours?

You're sitting alone, high up on a ridge that overlooks lush valleys and rolling hills. The sun is warm on your skin and a gentle breeze chases away the heat, making the temperature perfect for a summer afternoon hike in the mountains. When you started your trek a couple hours prior, many thoughts ran through your mind about your week, meetings at work, and what activities each of your family members had been doing. As you climbed farther along the path, the river of thoughts slowed as your attention shifted to the sights and sounds of your surroundings.

Arriving at the top of the trail, your mind has shed its typical banter. Now you are admiring the unmistakable beauty and peace of this place. The sun trickles through gaps between tree leaves above the rock you're sitting on as the branches sway in the breeze rustling along the mountainside. A cloud emerges from behind a towering peak off in the distance. The wind brushes the cloud over the back side of the slope and it rises above the mountain's crest before gently settling along the front of the ridge. A panorama of opulence spreads out below you: rivers and streams sparkle as they nourish the landscape now teeming with brilliant hues of green. Everything seems to make sense up here. All is in order as the birds chirp and small animals scurry about gathering food and exploring their mountaintop world. Nature's soundtrack plays steadily in the background, but you're struck by the profound silence. So much is going on, yet it all fits together so effortlessly.

What is it about being in natural outdoor settings that captures our attention and refreshes us in a magical way? Why does it feel so right? So peaceful? Everything is functioning in its perfect role.

Every bird, every creature, every tree, every blade of grass is doing exactly what it was designed to do, interacting seamlessly. The grandeur of the scene before you is possible because of the orchestration of fully functioning components working together. Rivers flow, eagles soar, flowers bloom, and horses graze the valley floors.

Now imagine a very different picture with eagles trying to swim the rivers while horses stalk bears in the brush. Ridiculous? Absolutely. But perhaps it illustrates why the mountaintop feels so right, but our normal, everyday lives feel awkward and forced. The fact is that most of us are out of alignment with our true design. We struggle and strain to be the best at things that aren't in keeping with our natures. As a consequence, we experience a nagging unease deep within. We become our own worst enemy.

Our dogs are no exception. Each of them has a specific design, and when they fulfill that destiny, they thrive. When they don't have their core needs met, they compensate in other ways, and the ensuing frustration often manifests itself in neurotic behaviors and destructive tendencies.

The first order of business in experiencing a rewarding life for ourselves and our dogs is to seek out and understand our respective designs. While it is good for each of us to move outside our comfort zones periodically, we should never leave our design zones. Our mountaintop experience demonstrates the importance of design, so let's explore it more thoroughly so that we might align ourselves and our dogs with our intended purpose.

Your Dog's Design

Does Breed Matter?

Hundreds, some say thousands, of different dog breeds exist in the world. Over the years, dogs have been selectively bred to enhance certain characteristics. Some breeds are geared toward retrieving and others are used to help herd animals. Some people desire a certain type of dog and train them competitively for a specific sport or utility. For most of us, though, we just want a terrific companion to share our lives. After all, we don't take the family Newfoundland with us to the local reservoir every morning so she can ride along in the fishing boat and haul in the nets; and when was the last time you sent your dachshund into the fields to track down a ferocious badger and fearlessly tussle with it in the burrow before dragging it out, kicking and screaming, to you, her proud and beaming owner? (I hope your answer to this question is "never," by the way).

Yet, what do people always ask when they learn that you own a dog? "What *kind* of dog do you have?" It's as if the answer will tell them everything they need to know. Sure, it gives them an idea of how large or small he is and what he might look like, but dogs aren't destined to live within the lines of a breed standard. We'd like to think that Weimaraners will be great hunting dogs, when, in fact, many of them will prove to be hunting flunkies. We believe that our new Labrador puppy will be the perfect family dog; after all, labs are very loving toward family and great with children, right? Fast-forward six months: that cute little lab pup is maturing into an ill-tempered child-toppler, guarding her food from your five-year-old. Yikes!

Despite human efforts to breed for specific and predictable traits, it's all very unpredictable. For example, I have met several cattle dogs that point. Seeing them in action makes most pointer junkies quite jealous. The takeaway is that dogs are individuals. If you amassed a large sample of purebred pointers, you would statistically see higher levels of pointing behavior than in a similarly sized sample of cattle dogs. But again, breed isn't the most accurate measure for evaluating or classifying any *single* dog. To complicate things further, many mixed breeds' genetic makeups are staggeringly complex. Oftentimes, people looking for a new dog search for a particular breed or type of dog. However, when you're looking for a companion dog (as opposed to a working one), you're normally looking for a combination of traits that aren't ascribable to any one breed or group. For example, let's say you want to bring a new dog into your family. Let's also assume that your family consists of four children, you have a busy schedule, and you entertain a lot. Your "wish list" for a new dog might look something like this:

- Easy-going, non-rambunctious
- Loving; enjoys cuddling on the couch
- A coat with shorter hair and minimal shedding
- Medium-size build
- Some type of brindle or merle markings
- Enjoys playing fetch
- Gentle with children
- Welcoming of new guests in the home and not too protective
- Already housebroken
- Confident and relaxed in new situations and in public

Looking over this list, it is evident that there's no particular breed of dog that meets all of these criteria. You're actually looking for an *individual* dog that is a good fit for your lifestyle and will be a satisfied and content member of your family. Breed then, especially with respect to shelter and rescue animals if you're adopting, isn't the most useful indicator of what you can expect from a dog. Keep this in mind and ask pertinent questions about a dog's observed behavioral characteristics and disposition when deciding on a companion.

Am I saying that breed is not important? No. It's just not of *primary* importance. Dogs are dogs, just as people are people, and while individuals are of differing descents, regions of the world, neighborhoods, cultures, political and religious persuasions, etc., we are all human beings first and foremost. When we lose sight of this fact, we stop treating one another with dignity and respect.

A Dog's Basic Needs

Despite our outer differences, people have the same inner longings. Abraham Maslow identified in 1943 the human hierarchy of needs. He taught that to self-actualize and reach our potential, our basic needs (such as eating and drinking, assurance of personal safety, a sense of belongingness, love and of feeling esteemed) must be met. Without these in place first, self-actualization is impossible.

Similarly, every dog, regardless of size or breed, has inborn, universal needs. Cesar Millan championed the formula of "Exercise, Discipline, and then Affection" to help people understand how to fulfill dogs' most deeply ingrained, basic needs. He emphasized that breed is secondary in importance with respect to a more basic and common unifying tie among dogs: they're animals of the same species, *Canis familiaris*, and have a hierarchy of needs that must be met if they are to actualize their potential. If the first thing we see is a dog's breed, we have missed the boat. Seeing them as an animal and dog first may seem trivial, but psychologically speaking, it carries profoundly different implications for how we ultimately treat them. Cesar refers to this order as "Animal, Species [dog], Breed, and then Name." He also points out that most people think of them in reverse order, starting with their dog's name and having a hard time even referring to them as an animal. But when we learn to value them for what they are, we gain the perspective necessary to provide for their needs more fully.

Ask yourself: Do I understand and am I truly fulfilling my dog's most basic needs, or do I just want to hurry up and get her "trained" so she will behave better and be easier to live with? If you put your dog's needs first, she'll pay you back a million times over and meet your needs as well. She will be better behaved because she will live with less tension, frustration, and pent-up energy. So put first things first. Focus on the basics.

Vince Lombardi, one of the most celebrated football coaches of all time, began each new year of his players' training camps by holding up a football and declaring, "Gentlemen, this is a football." Of course they knew it was a football, but he wanted to remind them that to do anything great, whether in football or in business or in the game of life, one must master the basics. Building upon any other type of foundation might last a short time but will eventually crumble. Following is one of my favorite stories to illustrate this principle:

One day a teacher wanted to demonstrate for her students a lesson on the importance of priorities. She set a gallon-sized glass jar on a table at the front of the classroom and put in as many large rocks as she could. She then asked her students if the jar was full.

They answered yes.

She noted their reply and then reached behind her, grabbed a bucket of gravel, and began pouring it into the glass jar. The gravel sifted through the large rocks and filled in the gaps until no more gravel could fit. She asked the question again: "Is the jar full?"

Having jumped the gun already, the class was hesitant and said no, even though they weren't exactly sure how anything more could fit.

Their teacher brought out a bucket of sand and began pouring it into the jar. Her class watched as the sand settled around the large rocks and the gravel. Again, she asked, "Is the jar full?"

Her students answered no, all quite interested to see how anything more could possibly fit into the jar.

She smiled. "Good." She produced a pitcher of water and poured it into the glass jar until the water reached the brim. Then she presented her class with the key question: "What is the purpose of this lesson?"

One of her students blurted, "There's always more room!" The rest of the class nodded their heads in support.

The teacher continued. "That's a good guess, but it's the wrong answer. The purpose of this lesson is to teach you to always put the big things in first."

Her students learned an important lesson that day about priorities. If they put the big things in first, they could always fit the less important things around them. But if they always put the little things in first, they would never have room for those things that are most important.

Mastering the basics and "putting them in the jar" first is the essence of all greatness. With respect to our dogs, we have a responsibility to ensure that their basic needs are always met. Upon such a foundation, we can add all kinds of fun activities and training to further their education and fill in the gaps. But always remember this: education doesn't *create* stability, balance, or peace of mind (the big rocks in the jar). Rather, it sharpens, supports, and refines those things. Training is a critical component of your dog's life; a most necessary catalyst that rounds out everything else you do with her but can be detrimental if overemphasized as a "fix all." Haven't you met some incredibly well-educated people that are completely out of balance? While education is imperative, common sense and fortitude must form the bedrock of an individual's upbringing, human or canine.

Evaluate your daily routine with your dog. Are you giving her ample exercise? Does she go on walks with you every day? Does she live with a consistent structure and have a strong sense of boundaries? Does she *earn* access to the special activities you share with her, like playing fetch, going to the dog park, getting praise, and enjoying down time? Giving your dog access to these things without her earning them absolutely cannot build self-esteem. A dog that doesn't work for what she gets inevitably becomes spoiled (expects something for nothing) and exhibits negative behavior patterns. She might become pushy, hyperactive, destructive, and exhibit poor social skills with other dogs, or she may appear lackluster and timid. On the flip side, a dog that earns access to the great things in her life will be more content and even-keeled. She'll also be much easier to live with.

Every dog has an inborn energy level and needs a certain amount of exercise and mental stimulation to achieve balance. You might think that giving your dog more exercise will make your job harder over time because her body will adapt and require more and more stimulation to achieve the same result, but this isn't the case. For every dog, there is an optimal level of exercise and it's all about finding the right amount for her. Sure, if your dog is out of shape, she's going to adapt over time to the demands of exercise and will be able to take on more activity. But this cycle doesn't carry on forever. At some point, she will reach her optimal cadence of physical and mental activity. If you dip below this level for too long, she will begin to exhibit behavioral problems; she'll become stir-crazy. If you stay above her optimal cadence for too long, she will exhibit signs of fatigue and lose her natural enthusiasm and zest and potentially develop injuries. You don't want to much or too little. Find the balance.

One important caveat: If you drain physical energy *without* simultaneously challenging the mind, you will only build drive in your dog and run into problems. She'll have incredible physical stamina and more energy to carry out shenanigans. When dogs have to engage their brains *and* their bodies, a synergy is created and satisfaction is the outcome. Be sure you're making her think and not just move.

Something else to keep in mind is the type of exercise that forms the core of your dog's regimen. Throwing a tennis ball for half an hour until she is physically exhausted is not the way to go. This is a form of exercise, sure, but it is a game—a reward. Rewards must be earned, ideally through participating in exercise that requires focus and concentration *first*. Having her chase a ball does not create the same benefits (i.e. relaxation and contentment) that come from healthy, structured exercise. Chasing a tennis ball or doing "happy laps" around the back yard while chasing squirrels builds and strengthens a frenetic prey drive and overexcited state of mind. If, however, you provide her with access to daily outings such as swimming, hikes, runs, or trotting alongside you on bike rides, etc., she will channel her physical and psychological energy into tasks that bring contentment instead of creating obsessions. Then throwing the tennis ball or Frisbee becomes a well-deserved and healthy outlet that rounds out her need for physical activity and fun.

Discovering Your Dog's Special Abilities

Once your dog has sufficient outlets for her basic needs, it's time to delve into the exciting task of uncovering her special abilities. As we've seen, picking a dog because of her breed(s) isn't the most effective way to choose the perfect pet for your family, but having some knowledge about her breed(s) can be very useful in giving you clues about her intended design and unique capabilities. One place to go for clues is your dog's breed standard(s). Reading about the purposes for which your dog was bred can supply you with information about her particular design characteristics. If you've ever seen a German shorthaired pointer working alongside a hunter out in the field, or a Belgian Malinois working in Ring Sport, you've seen a thing of beauty. There's nothing quite like watching the pure joy and elegance of a dog doing exactly what she was meant to do.

Sled dogs doing what they were meant to do… and loving it!

So what does this mean for you and your dog? Let's say you own an Australian Shepherd. You religiously share a brisk walk with her twice a day, establish appropriate boundaries both inside and outside the home, and give her plenty of love. But a few issues remain unresolved. She displays some neurotic barking and spinning, overexcitement and "mouthiness" toward pe especially noticeable when guests come over.

Knowing that Aussies were bred for activities such as herding, you'll want to identify some outlets for her. One option is to seek out a local herding operation where your dog can do some actual sheep herding work. Herding is the most authentic option, but if it's not feasible due to budget, time, or geographical constraints, you still have options. One possibility would be to enroll her in a class for Treibball, or "Urban Herding" as it's sometimes called. Treibball is a sport that combines herding and obedience work. The object is for the dog to target and "herd" large, inflatable balls into a goal by pushing them around with her nose. The dog is given cues from her handler about which balls to move, in which direction, and in what order. Other options for your Aussie might include agility, Frisbee, or Flyball. The point is to explore these options. You might find the perfect match and have a much happier dog for it! Be creative. You can even develop variations of these activities to do with your dog at home.

When dogs are doing what they were designed to do, it boosts their confidence and satisfies them in a way that nothing else can. You'll be amazed at how many of your dog's "issues" will subside or disappear entirely with adequate constructive outlets. Dogs need jobs. If you don't give your dog a job, she'll invent one of her own. Better to come home to what I call a "happy-tired" dog, than to one who's exhausted herself by disemboweling your brand-new Italian leather couch while you were at work.

Aggression and Dominance

In my mind, *aggression* wins the award for the most grossly overused term in the dog world. This word is thrown around to describe many dogs and behaviors, almost *none* of which truly are. Aggression is a very specific attribute that is feared by most people. I am one of the few weirdos who enjoys rehabilitating aggressive dogs. I have realized two primary benefits as a result of specializing in this. First, I understand aggression so it doesn't make me apprehensive; and, second, I can more accurately identify when aggression is present and when it's not (which is most of the time). Most dogs diagnosed with aggression are anything but; they may have outbursts or exhibit aggressive behavior, but it's not their true nature. Dogs are a social species, and aggression is not an adaptive quality within a pack that has to work together. As Chad Mackin puts it: "It doesn't make sense to hurt someone you have to hunt with tomorrow."

Aggressive episodes are usually symptoms of a different problem. If you suspect you have an aggressive dog, make sure to seek out a *qualified* professional with expertise in this area. Please note that such a professional may or may not be *certified*. Some top trainers have extensive credentials and half the alphabet behind their names, while others have none. Do your research and take your time in selecting a trainer that's a good fit for both you and your dog. Finding the right professional is critical, because if your dog is misdiagnosed, you may end up treating her for something that isn't there. Furthermore, not treating the correct underlying issue may result in a perfect storm that elicits aggressive responses in your dog. A good place to start your search for a local professional is the training directory on the International Association of Canine Professionals (IACP) Website.

The second most overused term in the dog world is *dominance*. The subject of dominance is highly controversial. Many discrepancies exist, especially among professionals, about the nature of dominance. Many of these differences boil down to semantics. Before we dive into this subject, let me ask you a question: Is it good for a dog to be dominant? Take a moment to think about the word's connotations. Do you picture a dog that is pushy? Is she snarky with other dogs? Does she fight with other dogs? Does she jump up on people? Does she try to intimidate people? Is she a little temperamental in the home? It may come as a surprise that none of these behaviors are characteristic of a dominant dog.

Dominance is a great thing. Most of the time when people describe a dog as being dominant, they say things like, "If she doesn't get her way, she gets upset and starts to act dominant toward us." But just as very few dogs are actually aggressive, fewer still are truly dominant.

Let's do an exercise. Read the list below and attach a label to describe a dog that possesses these qualities (the label could be something like "happy-go-lucky," "mellow," etc.):

- Even-tempered
- Faces new situations with a healthy curiosity
- Great with family and respectful of all its members
- Protective only in the face of legitimate danger
- Socially savvy and imperturbable
- A great teacher (other dogs learn from her and benefit from being in her presence)
- Easy-going but willing to correct other dogs when necessary
- Quick to move on after facing unpleasant or uncomfortable situations
- Solicits play from other dogs and has a knack for engaging wallflowers
- Does not fight with other dogs; de-escalates conflict peacefully but will defend herself if necessary

What labels came to mind? For me, the best label I could attach to a dog fitting these descriptions is "dominant." True dominance is characterized by a calm, centered, and even-keeled but appropriately assertive dog that maintains the peace within a pack.

A dominant dog is similar to the kind of people who walk into a room and are respected by everyone but not out of fear or intimidation. They just have natural leadership qualities and project positive energy. They don't feel the need to exert their superiority because they don't feel superior to anyone else. They're who they are and they're quite content with that. They have a way of bringing very different people together. Furthermore, they provide direction for the group and inspire confidence. They diffuse conflict whenever possible by being fair and diplomatic and focusing on similarities instead of differences. They settle disputes by physical means only when all other options have been exhausted.

Very few dogs are truly dominant. For one thing, it is far more taxing on a dog to be a leader than a follower, as it requires genetically more robust physiological and psychological systems. Being in charge of ensuring group well-being and survival is anything but a stress-free job. True dominance, in my experience, is present in about 1 percent of dogs. Certainly, there is a dominance spectrum along which dogs fall, with some dogs displaying a stronger propensity for dominance than others. However, a dominant dog in the truest sense is a rare and wonderful find.

I naturally love dominant dogs in my work because they can play a mentor role to other dogs that are in the process of being rehabilitated. Dominant dogs have great instincts and make sound decisions in virtually any situation they face, so they can usually tell me exactly what another dog needs to move forward and become more stable. One potential drawback of dominant dogs is that they place specialized demands on their owners. They are very confident and must have people in their lives who can match their energy level and provide crystal-clear direction. If they don't live with firm, fair, and emotionally stable leaders, they can easily become very difficult to live with. The demands they naturally place on their owners make them too much dog for the majority of people.

Often when people describe their dogs as dominant, they're describing a dog that is pushy and out of balance due to a lack of proper outlets and clearly defined expectations. In short, the dog has learned to be a poser and a bully. Dominance and leadership are skills that people can learn. In dogs, however, it's more an inborn quality that's either present or absent. So the pushy dogs who like to throw their weight around have issues, but dominance isn't the culprit. Dominance isn't a problem; it's a positive attribute. You can always identify a poser, because her presence and actions lack authenticity. She'll strut into a group of dogs like she has it all together and may try to intimidate others. As we've already seen, however, this is not a quality of a dominant dog. In fact, it's quite the opposite. Dominant dogs don't have anything to prove. They just *are*.

Four-Legged Children

Our dogs are so much more than just animals that live with us. They are undoubtedly part of our families. They have a special place in our hearts and have gone from filling roles that are strictly functional in nature (hunting, guarding, vermin control, etc.) to being loyal and trusted friends. For many people, however, their dogs start to be thought of and treated as though they are kids. This dysfunctional doctrine is the root of a great deal of the instability and behavioral challenges that eventually force people to contact a dog trainer for help. The problems can be as mild as whining and jumping up, or as serious as biting a child in the face and attacking other dogs at the park.

The technical term for projecting human characteristics and attributes onto animals and other nonhuman things is "anthropomorphism." When working with clients, I will often utilize this concept to compare their dogs' behaviors with common human thought processes and actions. I find that this helps many people gain a better understanding of where their dogs are coming from, because it is something they can relate to. Anthropomorphism can be a useful tool in gaining perspective and insight into what our dogs are going through. For example, I might explain to a mother of four that her older dog is snapping because he feels overwhelmed and sometimes needs a break from the new puppy, just as she might need a few minutes at the end of the day to decompress without having to manage her children.

The real danger arises when the lines begin to blur and we no longer appropriately differentiate dogs and their tendencies from our own. A good example is a dog that guards her owner from other people in the home and is referred to as "jealous." Jealousy is a trait of the *human* psyche. What the dog is actually displaying is a form of resource guarding, which is entirely different. The motive and the mechanisms of jealousy and resource guarding are worlds apart. If we are unaware of or in denial of this fact, we will unwittingly attempt to rectify the situation from a human perspective, and our efforts will backfire, damaging our relationships with our dogs and making the situation worse. In striving to understand our dogs, it is imperative that we remember one very critical fact: they are dogs. If we see them as our children and constantly think of them in human terms, we are no longer respecting their nature. We must acknowledge our dogs as a different species, educate ourselves about their unique makeup, and treat them in a befitting manner.

Imagine for a moment that the roles of dogs and humans were suddenly reversed and we lived in a world where dogs owned people (some would quip that this is already the case). Now imagine that those dogs decided their humans were their puppies and needed to be treated like and act like dogs. We'd have to walk around on all fours (the equivalent of carrying dogs around like babies). I don't even want to think about how they'd expect us to greet each other . . . yikes! While this is humorous to consider, ask yourself what it would be like to be forced to live like a dog. Words like *humiliating* and *demeaning* come to my mind. Many people in such a world would eventually become completely defunct. They would surrender their dignity, no longer having any way of relating to people and themselves in a natural way. In evaluating dogs at my center, I have many times uttered to members of my team: "She doesn't even know she's a dog anymore." Typically I am referring to an absence of normal social skills and total confusion in the dog's mind as to how to behave when put into a natural situation. She can make due in the home where she's treated like a child, but if she's treated like a dog, she acts like a cow staring at a new gate.

It is good to keep some basic things in mind as we interact with our dogs, lest we be tempted to misinterpret their intentions or hold them to a set of unsuitable expectations. First, as much as we'd like to think our dogs understand what we're explaining to them, they don't speak English. When we "teach" them words, we are merely building associations between certain sounds and actions or objects in the environment. Their native language is energy and intention. Second, our dogs weren't put on this earth to take care of us and fulfill our needs; they were put here to be respected and cared for. The good news is when we do our part first, they always repay the favor. Third, our dogs aren't secretly trying to dominate us or scheming to take over the world (only cats are doing that). And last, our dogs are not what we want them to be—they are what they *are*, and the true measure of our love for them is whether we are willing to accept and honor that fact.

So far we've discussed discovering, developing, and respecting our dogs' design. When we honor their nature, they can grow into their potential, living happy and content. It's also true that when we honor our own natures, we reap the very same rewards. This all begins with recognizing our unique makeups and then appreciating and celebrating the differences.

Your Design

The mass of men lead lives of quiet desperation.

Henry David Thoreau

We have explored the purposes for which our dogs were created, but what about us? What about your purpose? Far too many people go through life with a subtle but certain emptiness; despite many wonderful qualities and accomplishments, they seem a bit hollow, lacking a substantial center, like a planet with no gravity, and nothing to anchor them. It's like they have no peace. They might be involved in lots of activities, but when the dust settles, being around them feels a bit like being in a ghost town.

Haven't you also met people who exude an unmistakable inner peace? These people know who they are, what they were designed to do, and they function in their roles with grace. When you're in their presence, you simultaneously feel energized and profoundly tranquil. It's inspiring. It's also quite effortless for these people because they're not trying too hard. It's just who they are.

The key concept here is *authenticity*: a common thread woven throughout every facet of their lives. It's embedded within their fabric and adds color to their every endeavor. These people are leaders and influencers, the human equivalent of a dominant dog. It seems that no matter what activity they're engaged in, their demeanor is calm, cool, and collected.

Bad Art and the Scoreboard

Dictionary.com defines identity as "the condition of being oneself or itself, and not another." The sheer number of advertisements and symbols constantly vying for our attention and appealing to our sense of self is overwhelming. Daily we are barraged with messages that prod us to assert ourselves and show the world who we are. Some people are defined by their favorite sports teams, their jobs, and even political and personal views. Sure, we may not define ourselves by any one of these things in isolation, but over time we become a composite of our assembled likes, dislikes, beliefs, and interests.

Indeed, many of us feel compulsively driven to lock in our identity, mistakenly grasping for the security we think a fixed sense of self will provide us. What we fail to realize is that we are chasing a mirage, and the closer we get to settling on one form, we notice we are missing something and the identity mirage disappears. So what do we do? We wait around until another one appears on the horizon and chase after it, because maybe this will be the one we can latch on to that brings the stability we're looking for. But consider these facts:

- Each of us is evolving
- There is no static self
- We are constantly being reinvented

Our "self" is as ever changing as our physical bodies. Research has shown that every cell in our bodies will be replaced every seven years. Many parts of the body, such as the skin, are replaced more quickly, often over the course of just a few days.

My observation is that people who cultivate that illusive quality of inner peace do not struggle with trying to tie their identity to anything external; they are in touch with the essence of who they are. In other words, they are internally driven and motivated. However, most of us are taught and measured against external values and standards. When we're young, our parents, teachers, peers, and others place great importance on polarizing models.

When I was in elementary school, I was labeled as being either "sufficient" or "insufficient" in different academic subjects.

etty sure that in art class I received my fair share of
icient" report cards. After all, you can create only so many
poorly crafted pieces of pottery before the art teacher starts saying,
"Oh, Brian, I think it's just *fantastic*." Even a seven-year-old can
pick up on sarcasm.

People assign labels to us based upon the results of our efforts,
and we're either allowed to feel good about ourselves or we must
cope with the shame and disappointment of substandard
performances. When we're old enough, we take over this role and
reward ourselves with a pat on the back when we do well, while
self-flogging for bad choices and performances.

This habit of labeling ourselves and our efforts as successful
or unsuccessful can lead us into a couple of traps. The first pushes
us into straining to achieve and trying too hard. Our stress
hormones soar under the strict demands we place on ourselves.
After all, we have to do a good job; our self-image depends on it.
And the worst part of it is that each success and its accompanying
relief is short-lived. Before long, we're back in the throes of the
next assignment, and to compound our stress, we remind ourselves
that we have a track record of wins that must be maintained. It's a
self-perpetuating cycle, and burnout is the inevitable outcome of
this trap.

The second trap we can fall prey to is characterized by a
pattern of apathy and ambivalence. This allows us to sidestep trap
number one, only to crash and burn in another. The ambivalence
cycle has us saying that we don't care about something in order to
spare the disappointment of failure. One obvious snare is that deep
down we *do* care. We want to do a good job. But our pride and
sense of self cannot bear yet another blow as we gaze upon the
scoreboard of life. It's much easier to cover it up with a huge
banner of "I don't care" than to be constantly reminded of the
dismal score. The worst thing about this scenario isn't that we are
lying to others; it's that we've developed a pattern of lying to
ourselves. This trap is also a self-perpetuating cycle, and the

inevitable outcome is withdrawal from others and detachment from our true selves and what we value most.

I fell into both of these traps in art class as a kid. In the beginning, I really wanted to do a great job. I wanted to be seen as talented and artistic. Subconsciously, this would feed my ego by causing others to see me in a positive light, which I thought would somehow validate my worth as a person. I had a "success" or two early on and tried even harder on the projects that followed, which became increasingly stressful and unrealistic to maintain, and I hit a couple of snags with pieces of artwork that my teacher or classmates did not receive well. After enough instances of my all-out-effort producing subpar results, I thought to myself, *This just isn't worth it.* So I puffed out my chest and declared that art wasn't important to me. I knew deep down that it wasn't true, but at least I had developed an out for myself and any future creations that didn't measure up.

Needless to say, neither of these approaches were healthy. Did that stop me? No way. I grew older and fell into countless variations of these traps. Sound familiar? Has your boss ever given you a project that became your baby? Think about the project's progression. Did you work tirelessly in the quest for another win that you could pin on your scoreboard? If you did, you probably allowed yourself to feel good about your achievement and at some level believed yourself to be a better person for it. Or did you take the opposite approach and start the project with some enthusiasm but ultimately succumb to blaming a coworker for her failure in completing her part of the project, thus letting yourself off the hook to avoid the self-image blow of a failed attempt?

Basing our self-image on what we have or haven't accomplished is a trap either way. We need an authentic center. We must learn to program our minds with a self-image built on what we were created to be and to do, and from that platform launch our efforts. We will *act* our best when we are connected with our true selves. People will always judge us by what we do (or what they perceive we do); that's how the world works. But the purest measure of who we truly are is our essence and what dwells within our hearts.

I Know Who You Are, But What Am I?

There's no denying that we Americans love sports and we love to win. Just last night I was watching a March Madness tournament game. I never cease to be amazed by the crazy things sports fans will do to show support for their teams and to get on TV. I saw grown men wearing fluorescent wigs, with shirtless, painted bodies, jumping up and down and screaming like crazy people. It was intense. Most of us may not go to such extremes to show our team loyalty, but have probably been to a few tailgate parties or occasionally yelled at the referee on TV who just made a horrible call that cost our favorite team the game.

Competition can be a wonderful thing. It can motivate us to do things that we would never do by ourselves. It can inspire great performances. But it also impels us to base our personal value on how we compare with others, and comparison cannot tell us who we really are. I heard a wise man once say, "You should always be yourself, because everybody else is already taken."

In seeking to find a balance in our lives, we have to look beyond comparison with other people. We're individuals, after all, so how can our identities possibly be rooted in how well we measure up to someone else's idea of who we should be? It's illogical. To make things worse, one of comparison's greatest traps is that we inevitably compare our weaknesses to others' strengths. Comparison is a perfect recipe for depression. Once in a while I'll flip through a magazine showcasing celebrities, and with each turn of the page, I feel worse about myself. Looking at airbrushed portrayals leaves me asking, *How can anyone be that good looking? How can they be so talented? Look at me: I'm not great at any of that stuff! Was someone on God's assembly line drinking on the job when I rolled through?* It's enough to make a person crazy.

The first step in dismantling the power comparison wields over us is to recognize that we're neither better nor worse than anyone else. Our very own Declaration of Independence calls us to recognize that all people are created equal. This isn't to say that we are equal in talents. It doesn't propose that people have equal physical or mental abilities. It simply points to the fact that none of us has any greater *intrinsic* value than the next person. Typically, people say they agree with such a statement, but their daily actions belie the principle. We don't have to look very hard to find people (perhaps ourselves) on power and ego trips, jockeying for position and playing silly games to either assert superiority or grasp for equality with others; these actions and attitudes expose an insidious, ego-based, false identity.

A comparison-based identity places us in a perpetual state of defensiveness, ever vigilant to identify with outward achievements that supposedly validate our worth and guard against criticism and the possibility of failure. We even get a little "boost" when those around us stumble and fall. We overreact to situations because we take everything personally. Someone makes an innocent inquiry, and we assume they're questioning us, so we hurl a curt response in retaliation for the ding to our egos.

Anytime we tie our value to what other people think, say, or do, we've *given* them the power to define us. That's power we should never give to anyone. If you were the only person on earth (and it's true that you are the only you!), your identity couldn't be rooted in comparisons. It couldn't be measured by some artificial scoreboard society dictates you maintain. It couldn't be derived from anything . . . except that intangible *something* we feel at our core but have a hard time describing—that something we were created to be or do.

We've looked at the problems inherent with basing our personal value on external labels like "success" and "failure," and deriving our identity from comparison with others. We've seen that each of these paradigms leads us in a downward spiral and leaves us empty-handed, with a contrived and hollow sense of self, and that there is no authenticity to be found in these caverns we all too often find ourselves lost within. We are so much more than the sum of our "wins" and "losses." Scoreboards can tell us nothing about who we truly are—only what we did in the past. The saying "We are 'human beings' not 'human doings'" is one of my favorites because it is so very apropos and true.

So what do we do with the scoreboards? Bury them. And wake up and become acutely aware of the destructive nature of deriving our personal value from false ideals, choosing instead to find an authentic identity that doesn't sway with every wave of emotion and circumstance.

The Source

> *Let me tell you why you're here.*
> *You're here because you know something.*
> *What you know you can't explain, but you feel it.*
> *You've felt it your entire life, that there's*
> *something wrong with the world.*
> *You don't know what it is, but it's there,*
> *like a splinter in your mind, driving you mad.*
>
> Morpheus, *The Matrix*

We interact with people every day. Some we describe as athletic or outgoing or intelligent or funny. These are attributes. But when it comes to a person's identity, it's impossible to fully know, because it lies within the realm of the heart and spirit. Sure, their behaviors give us clues, but the closest we can hope to get is being in tune with their presence—with their energy signature, if you will. This is not a cerebral thing; it is an intuitive process and must be felt.

That being said, we *can* come to know our own identities.

It's very much human nature to classify things, and that includes how we view ourselves and others. Probably the most common way we categorize ourselves is by identifying with our professions. "I'm a school teacher," some say, while others identify themselves as salespeople or business owners. Somehow, though, none of these labels reveal who we are. They are insufficient descriptors, because who we are as individuals in terms of personality and levels of consciousness is in continual flux. I am not the same person I was ten years ago. I have learned new things, grown through experiences, and changed so much that I would venture to say if I met my ten-year-younger self, we may not get along particularly well.

On the other hand, our spiritual DNA is with us throughout our whole lives. Some people call it the soul. Its label is not so important; rather, our unique, underlying, unifying essence breathed into us by our Creator is what we yearn to know and understand, and what we might refer to as our true "identity." When we are intimately acquainted with it, we feel whole and develop clarity of meaning and purpose. When we don't have a firm connection to it, we continually experience a haunting void. The slippery part is that who we are extends far beyond a simple label, and the intangible nature of it at first glance may seem touchy-feely and distant, but it doesn't need to feel so esoteric.

The condition of being in love may help make this concept far easier to relate to. While measurable physical, hormonal, and cognitive changes are present in a person who has fallen in love, anyone who has been in love knows it goes much deeper than just those things. Being in love is not something that will ever fit within scientific measurement or be adequately expressed with words. One of my favorite metaphors is that words are like a cup: they are not the truth, but they contain the truth. They are only a description of something real. Sonnets of love from the pen of a master like Shakespeare may be eloquent but are no substitute for the experience. The roots of love go deeper.

The physical world is no exception. The building blocks of the physical world are invisible to the naked eye. Atoms are units of matter that have mass but are made up of subatomic particles that often have *no* mass. As science has delved into the realm of quantum physics, scientists have discovered even more baffling issues, such as instances when these particles have no location, or are in multiple locations at once. Then there's the problem of conscious observation as a requisite for the very *existence* of certain particulate matter and how it is expressed. When we dive into the nature of the physical world, we find that its foundation is made up of non-physical components without a particular location or sometimes multiple locations at the same time, often requiring observation to manifest them in the physical world. It's fascinating and mind-boggling.

This is a grossly oversimplified discourse to very complex scientific inquiries. The point isn't to get lost in the minutia of the details but to grasp an overarching principle: Everything that we experience in the material world is a manifestation of nonmaterial energy and vibrations and what is perhaps best described as an organizing intelligence. The lines certainly blur here between the physical realm and what many refer to as the spiritual realm. Spiritual doesn't have to mean religious. It is a helpful concept to consider, though, in wrapping our heads around such abstract concepts. After all, most people believe that humans are three-part beings: mind, body, and spirit. Identity would fall into the third category: the nonphysical, non-tangible realm of the spirit. The spirit is never something we understand, because understanding is done with the mind. Rather, it's something we experience; something we feel. The question remains: How do we grasp the source of our nature from which we spring?

We must come to *know* it.

The Knowing

Know thyself.

Plato

By accepting the nonphysical nature of our world, and our identities in particular, we also accept that it cannot be explained in strictly physical terms with traditional measurements and scientific classifications. Just as water flows from a kitchen faucet but certainly isn't the water's source, the source of our identity is rooted at a deeper level that transcends intellectual understanding. So we look past the mere appearances of our basic human nature so that we can *know* ourselves to the very core. We become determined to home in on our identities and are able to do this to the extent we can see through different eyes. These are not eyes of the mind or body but of the spirit.

There's a feeling even beyond emotions that accompanies "the knowing." Let's recall the example of being in love. When you're in love, you know it in your gut, plain and simple. It's not logical; it can be described but not explained. We may say that we "get butterflies in the stomach" whenever we see the person we love, but it goes much deeper. When we're in love, we feel it at the level of the soul. If we can learn to know our identities at this level, we can access the power and peace we yearn for and we become tremendously comfortable in our own skin. The question is: How do we go about doing that?

MEDITATION

Seeking to get in tune with the quiet core of our true selves, we have to block all extraneous distractions and mental clutter that clamors for our attention. Meditation is an indispensable method for quieting our minds in order to dive beneath the surface of our daily experiences. When done properly, meditation results in a state and feeling akin to those peaceful moments we occasionally encounter while completely relaxed in the midst of nature, when the cares of the outer world have fallen to the wayside. Stepping away from our compulsive busyness, we become wholly present, immersed in the calmness of the moment—at peace with ourselves. The meditation process accomplishes all of this, and it answers the following question: What's left over when I shed every distraction and move beyond mental and physical sensation? Tucked within that question is, Who am I, and from what source do I spring?

Most of us live fully associated with our minds and thoughts, and yet the answer that emerges through meditation is not a thought or even a physical sensation, but an inexplicable knowing of your nature and identity, accompanied by a peace that settles on you. You will find that the heart of your identity beats softly but is unmistakably present. It speaks to you out of the silence. It forms the bedrock upon which everything else is built, giving you greater depth, substance, and a decidedly quiet confidence that will enable you to stay grounded and weather the storms of life . . . to the extent you are *firmly connected* with it.

If consistently practiced, meditation guides you to know and feel the essence of who you really are. Awareness also expands through the process as you realize you are connected to an infinite field of potentiality beyond yourself. You begin to see the "self" as a localized expression of creation, similar to one of many moons reflecting the light of nearby suns in an incomprehensibly vast universe. However, unlike moons that reflect, the light of consciousness radiates *through* you. You are a conduit. As your connection to the Source of consciousness is strengthened, the more truly awake and powerful you become. Meditation provides a gateway to knowledge of your "self" and, more important, for moving beyond it.

I found that I could create stillness of mind by finding a quiet place devoid of outside distractions, sitting comfortably, closing my eyes, and then directing my attention into my senses, which are present-moment entities, especially my breathing, making sure to keep it slow, relaxed, and deep. When sustained for a sufficient length of time (the exact amount will be a little different for everybody and can vary day-to-day), staying relaxed in body and quieting the mind gives you access to a higher form of consciousness. As you experience God in the stillness of the now, you come to know yourself, too. You also tap into an unlimited reservoir of creative potential where, through prayer (focused thought) you deliberately plant the seeds of your heart's desires, and these form the root of what you will see manifested in your life.

Consummate balance and harmony is established through the seamless integration of the mind, body, and spirit, and meditation is the medium by which you connect (or reconnect) with God, the source of your power and essence.

The physical world cannot offer you lasting peace and joy. To confirm this truth, one need only think back through life and the emptiness inevitably waiting at the end of all worldly pursuits and accomplishments. Temporary pleasure and happiness is just that: temporary. Lasting joy and peace is yours for the taking but can be accessed only by transcending the corporeal world. This is the fundamental message communicated by all great sages throughout human history, and while their specific religious persuasions might differ, the underlying spiritual principles are exactly the same.

I believe each of us perceives the truth that there is a nontangible spiritual plane, yet only some of us actively pursue spiritual wisdom. Those of us who do are drawn in by its unshakable gravity and find its many mysteries fascinating. Perhaps most intriguing is the realization that the answers to such mysteries reside within. Interestingly, intense physical exercise (particularly if it is prolonged and rhythmic in nature) can have a similar effect to meditation practices and is one of the reasons I believe some individuals do so much of it: It's the one thing that clears their minds, settles their bodies, and brings them closer to their power center. It's the nearest thing to an authentic spiritual experience they regularly encounter, and most of them don't recognize it's their divine natures and desires that propel them.

Meditation: an age-old practice for creating balance and alignment.

In this chapter we have discussed at length the importance of getting to the very heart of who we are, yet the method for doing it is quite simple. We start by becoming aware of—and then stripping away—everything that binds us to an external-based self-image (labels, failures, accomplishments, upbringing, unexamined opinions and beliefs, etc.) and then silencing our minds and bodies in order to tap into our true essence. If such fundamentals are so imperative to master, then why are they typically the most neglected elements within our lives instead of the most carefully managed? Why don't we make these practices a daily habit? Simple: It's easier to ignore them and spare ourselves the effort. Just because something is "basic" doesn't mean that it's easy to do, which is precisely why we often say things like, "I know that I should do such-and-such, *but* _____." Why the "but"? Why fill in the blank with some lame rationalization about why we can't seem to get our act together? Is there anything more important than self-mastery?

To master yourself, master the basics by making them your primary focus. Be diligent. Prioritize. Simplify your life. Don't complicate things. Stay steady and dedicate at least ten minutes a day to the practice of meditation. In the beginning, if you are at all like me, you will find it incredibly difficult to quiet your mind. I know that early on I would start the process and immediately gravitate to thinking, *This is ridiculous; what's the point? I know who I am. Let's get on to something important. I have a lot to do today.* But I realized there wasn't anything I could possibly have going on that was more important, so I consciously recommitted to the process.

If you practice meditation, I believe it will pay bigger dividends than time spent doing almost anything else; it is an investment that pays compound interest. Tremendous transformative power is in this simple exercise for those willing to dedicate themselves to it. It helps us tap into the ever powerful now, a key concept we will look at more thoroughly in the next chapter. Meditation will positively affect every area of your life, helping you acquire invaluable self-knowledge. Once you truly know who you are, what you were designed to do will to come to light.

Purpose Built

"I like to imagine that the world is one big machine. You know, machines never have any extra parts. They have the exact number and types of parts they need. So I figure if the entire world is a big machine, I have to be here for some reason, too.
Maybe that's why a broken machine always makes me a little sad, because it isn't able to do what it was meant to do . . .
Maybe it's the same with people," Hugo continued. "If you lose your purpose . . . it's like you're broken."
From Brian Selznick's *The Invention of Hugo Cabret*

Have you ever put on an undershirt or T-shirt backward during the early morning hours while it's dark and you're still a bit groggy? I bet it didn't feel right. It's awkwardly tight where it should be loose and loose where it should be tight. Wearing a T-shirt backward is a bit like doing something other than what you were designed to do: It won't feel right to you. It takes an awful lot of energy to convince yourself that you're doing what you should and to maintain appearances and pretenses as you daily toil at something contrary to your natural design. Maybe you're great at wearing a mask, quite convincing in your unfitting role, but people are pretty smart and will generally know something's a bit off. You'll never have true peace until you do what you were designed to do.

In my case, I didn't really start to home in on my design until I was in my late twenties, despite actively searching for it since I was about eleven years old. One reason it took me this long is because I looked to other people and things to tell me what I should be, what it was "good" to be. Another reason—and this is key—is that I didn't consider myself particularly gifted in my area of strength. That may sound odd, but it is a more common belief than you might think.

For years I had casually helped friends train and understand their dogs better in order to strengthen the dog-human bond. It was something I just kind of did without giving it much thought, and I certainly didn't consider making a career out of it, because it was easy for me to do, and it didn't strike me as a special skill. Plus, we're always told to "work hard," which seems to ingrain the notion that work is a struggle. In some respects it is, but I have found that living according to one's design is in many ways effortless. People who do what they were designed to do flourish in their work; those who do what they were not designed to do struggle. People who do what they were designed to do find flow, creativity, and satisfaction; those who do what they were not designed to do find stop-and-go frustration.

You may find, as I did, that your area of talent lies right out in the open. To other people, your gift is quite obvious, because it's something that doesn't come naturally to them. To you, though, it doesn't even register because it's not something that you've had to work especially hard at. That's the reason it's called a *gift*. You didn't have to put the gift on the inside; it was already there. You didn't have to work hard for fifty years to develop a knack for it. Don't get me wrong. You can become very skilled in areas you're not especially gifted, but when you are gifted in some way and you add skills on top of that gift, you'll soar above the crowd.

To discover your design, start by answering these basic questions:

- What do other people find difficult to do that are relatively simple for me?

_____

_____

.at captured my imagination as a kid? What were my ɔbbies and interests?

_____

_____

- What do I naturally do well with very little conscious effort?

_____

_____

- Are there any patterns to professional or vocational suggestions given to me over the years by close friends and family?

_____

_____

- What kind of work or activities do I tell other people "I love"?

_____

_____

- What things require my energy but simultaneously energize my spirit?

_____

_____

- What skills do I possess that allow me to add value to people in a unique and special way?

_____

_____

- What activities bring me into balance, capture my attention, and help me stay fully engaged in the present moment?

_____

_____

- What do I *have* to do? In other words, what would I do even if I didn't get paid for it?

_____

_____

In answering these questions, you'll begin to develop a list with clues about your design.

Next, review the list and consider your natural aptitude and giftedness for each of the items you wrote down. For instance, you may find that you enjoy cycling. It may even be a long-time hobby of yours. In fact, maybe you are entertaining the idea of racing competitively. Obviously you wouldn't want to rashly assume that you should drop everything and embark on a new career as a professional cyclist. Keep your day job. One of the most important things to consider with all of the items on your list is your inborn ability or talent for them. If you want to be a world-class cyclist, you'd better have world-class genetics to go along with your passion for the sport. There's a difference between gutting it out to become marginally competent at something and having God-given talent that allows you to naturally separate from the pack. Sure, you can stubbornly pursue something merely because you enjoy it, but in the end, you'd be giving your best to something you can't be the best at. I'm not talking about outshining others; I'm cautioning you not to squander your gifts and deny the world what you have to offer. Instead, actively pursue and refine your *greatest* strengths.

I firmly believe that you have a unique design, which is an intricate combination of talents, many of which lie dormant until awakened. Questions attract answers, so ask yourself about your greatest areas of gifting and then cultivate them. Bringing those design qualities out will inevitably inspire people around you to find their own gifts and talents. If your unique gift isn't developed and shared with the world, it's lost. No one else in history can make up for it.

One way to determine your level of natural talent in a certain area is to connect with others who are experts in it. Observe them. Find out how they think. Ask questions about what it took for them to get where they are today. Does it require special training or education? If so, how much? Can this talent be developed and monetized? Why do they continue to do it? This is all about exploring opportunities and not settling for anything less than the perfect fit that satisfies you at the deepest level and serves other people at the highest level. Why is this important? Identify the great people in your life who have had a tremendous influence on you. Maybe a teacher steered you in a different direction than you were headed and it literally saved your life. Or perhaps (as was the case with me) your spouse encouraged you to explore your underdeveloped talents and you found satisfaction through discovering your very design. There's no price tag you can put on how certain people encourage us in dark times and inspire us to stretch and become more. The more you think about it, I believe you'll find that these influential people are almost always folks who have also found *their* callings and are living them out.

If you've been fortunate enough to have other people do this for you, pay it forward and do the same for someone else. People are watching you, and even when you're not aware of it, living according to your design will touch them in a way nothing else can approach. Think about this: Have you ever been tremendously inspired by people who hate their jobs and are not living their callings? I doubt it.

As you uncover unique talents within yourself, you'll want to develop those skills. Keep in mind that when somebody is fully functioning in her design, she doesn't have a single gift. She has many. Gifts are combined within individuals in a special way that gives their lives a unique flavor. When you discover your gifts, nurture them. Stretch toward your potential by investing the time necessary to further develop and creatively combine them, and make this discipline a mainstay of your daily routine.

We all have obligations and a million other things we can use as excuses for not pursuing what we were meant to do. Instead of putting the pursuit of your purpose on the backburner until things are "a little less crazy" (i.e. a day that will never come), use those struggles to strengthen your resolve to cultivate and refine your talents. Set aside time, schedule it in your calendar, and make it happen. Find mentors who can encourage your gifts and guide you in developing them. Obviously, you'll need to find someone who is already accomplished in your areas of strength. It may take some time to find mentors, but don't give up the search. One or more will come your way. You'll find that doors always seem to open when you're eagerly pursuing your purpose. Just be patient and stay vigilant for opportunity.

Make sure to invest time reading books, even if it's only five minutes a day, on the subjects related to your gifts. Attend seminars, listen to audio programs, and watch videos. Recognize that your combination of gifts is one in a million—gifts that are eagerly awaiting your resolve to diligently nurture them.

Anything truly great takes time to mature into the fullness of its design. Think in terms of possibilities and use what you have to work with. If you get hung up thinking about all the resources you don't have and the seeming impossibilities, you'll stall and never get to where you want to go. That was the case for me. If at any time during my journey I would have gotten lost in the overwhelming odds against me, I never would have known the joy I found in aligning my life with my design. Finding meaning and developing purpose is a lengthy discovery process. So be grateful: Focus on what you have and take one step at a time toward your grand architecture. If you have only fifteen minutes this week to study something pertaining to your gifts, invest those fifteen minutes wisely in the pursuit of defining your purpose.

Oftentimes we value other people's skills but not our own. We watch movies and are moved. We admire people who are masters at their trade. It's wonderful to be inspired by others; however, that inspiration shouldn't move us to look on enviously, wishing we had another person's gifts. Rather, we should be inspired to discover our own genius and flesh it out. No one can do what only you can do, and no one will put greater value on you than you put on yourself. So make yourself a person of value by investing in *you*. It's a bold way to live your life and the finest way to serve other people. Don't rob the world—or yourself—of your gifts and abilities, for that is a great tragedy. Being true to oneself by living according to one's design has always been the greatest triumph a person can experience. As Marianne Williamson wrote, "It is our light not our darkness that most frightens us."[1] Acknowledging our potential for greatness and pursuing it unapologetically is the ultimate act of courage.

Putting It All Together

We have identified that all things in nature have a design, a purpose. Your dog has certain inborn needs that are consistent across members of her species. Your dog also has needs stemming from her unique temperament, breed(s), inborn energy level, and various drives. Through experimenting with different activities for your dog, you'll begin to see her come into her own and experience a new level of contentment as you discover the perfect combination of outlets for her. This is complimented by providing her with ongoing education through training.

Only stability can create stability. Therefore you must
. . . 'n your life if you want to help your dog experience it
your dog's most constant companion, you have a
pportunity to enrich her life every day. By developing

balance and creating positive change and peace within yourself, these qualities are sure to spill over into her life also. Develop steady equilibrium in your life, and you'll not only reap the many personal benefits it affords, you'll also help sustain peace in hers and strike a bond that most people only dream of having with their dogs.

With respect to functioning according to your design, we discussed the pitfalls of comparisons. We found that other people and mere labels can never tell you who you are. Your list of accomplishments and failures, as well as what you often identify with (professions, interests, opinions, etc.), all fall far short of pinpointing your essence. Become a seeker of self-knowledge and work to establish a direct connection with your authentic identity; understand that your physical and outer world is a manifestation of your intangible inner world, so engage in meditation daily, tap into a higher power and level of consciousness, and align with your true nature, which is central to who you are but is so often drowned out by the world in which you live.

Finally, you began to explore your purpose and appreciate the value of investing in and developing yourself according to your unique design characteristics. Through asking key questions about different aspects of your highly individual architecture, answers about certain talents, gifts, and latent potential began to rise to the surface. Recognizing the value of your talents has moved you to invest in bringing them out, and you know that developing each gift to its fullest potential is an ongoing process—not something you should rush to finish.

Is your life is aligned with your purpose? Are you daily functioning according to your highest design specifications? Are you investing in yourself and bringing out your greatness? Do you know who you are? Knowing your *identity* grounds you; knowing your *design* gives you wings to rise to greater heights. Only when you are at ease with yourself can you experience lasting happiness. Finding mentors and resources can help you grow over time and transcend limitations by continually adding value to yourself, your dog, and other people.

Practical Application Exercises Related to Design

For Your Dog:

1. Make a list of the amount of time your dog spends in various activities during an average week. Include walks and the kinds of activities you share, in addition to time spent just hanging out together. Look over your list to see if there is an appropriate balance between those activities. Is your dog getting enough exercise? Does she have plenty of outlets? Are you investing adequate time in her training? Is she expected to work hard for the attention you give her, or does she have free rein to do whatever she wants and then receive excessive amounts of affection? Be honest through this assessment and make specific adjustments wherever necessary to strike an appropriate balance. Anytime you notice that things seem out of whack with her, perform this exercise again and fine-tune your approach.

2. Research your dog's breed(s) more thoroughly to gain insight into additional activities that more closely mirror specific needs she has. List five possible activities below, and take steps to get involved with at least one this week:

   _____

   _____

   _____

   _____

   _____

3. Become a keen observer of ways in which your dog's behavior patterns reflect both stability and instability in

your life. What tendencies do you observe in your dog that you find distasteful (standoffishness, insecurity, pushiness, etc.)? Are any of these possible reflections of your personal tendencies? Keep in mind that dogs often respond with the same energy and state of mind their people are projecting, mirroring their very way of being.

For You:

1. Set aside ten minutes to sit quietly without distractions. Reflect upon the concept you have of your identity. Where does it come from? If someone asked you to tell about yourself, what would you say? Now, recognize and peel away from your concept of self any labels (particularly disempowering ones), comparisons, and other external sources you thought of. You might be surprised by how many outside influences you've been allowing to define you.

2. Dedicate ten minutes every single day this week to the practice of meditation. Block out the time in your calendar. If you find value in this practice (and I believe you will after a week of consistent use), make an ongoing commitment to continue. Employed properly, this technique will allow the world around you and any mental chatter to fade. Out of the silence, your identity will begin to emerge. Get to know that feeling, because it is your essence and your power source.

3. Dedicate a minimum of fifteen minutes every day for the next week to defining and developing your purpose. You can spend this time reading, researching, or working in your areas of talent and gifting. As the

saying goes: Do not despise small beginnings. Small steps in the right direction are significant in both dog training and in realizing higher levels of personal potential. They really do add up and compound over time—it's how great things are ultimately accomplished.

Chapter Two

What's Wrong with Y'all?

Have you ever been driving and realized you had no recollection of the previous five minutes . . . or five miles? Were you amazed that you had arrived somewhere without dedicating any real attention to the road or the driving process? We've all had this experience many times, and while in certain situations it's beneficial to go on autopilot so we can focus our efforts on more complex tasks, it can also have the negative side effect of numbing our awareness. We live in a task-oriented society. Many of us enjoy checking items off our to-do lists; it gives us a sense of accomplishment. The problem with this is that it causes us to undervalue the process and *how* we are doing things.

Imagine being at a party where everyone is having a good time and getting along. Then one of your friends gets upset during a normal conversation, makes a nasty comment, and storms out of the room. On the surface he was socially engaged and smiling but overreacted to something someone said or did. In all likelihood, he wasn't really responding to the situation at hand. This person probably had a number of underlying factors and frustrations that remained unaddressed for quite some time which made an emotional blowup the inevitable result. Running on autopilot prevented him from being in tune with his emotional well-being and dealing with it constructively. Because he was not thoughtful and proactive, he became irrational and reactive.

We often get so lost in our routines that we lose touch with the many important subtleties of life. The "big" events in our lives are typically what we feel are most worthy of our attention and effort, but haven't you found that it's the little things adding up that affect you the most? The typical person will go through his day with such speed and inattention that he doesn't notice his body has been giving him signals for the last six hours to eat, and now his blood sugar is lower than a pregnant ant, and he's feeling irritable. Staying alert and perceptive of important details requires that we train ourselves to be more consciously engaged in our daily experiences.

I often witness this same problem when doing private training for clients. In addressing behavioral concerns they have about their dogs, I have discovered that the answers almost always lie in the subtleties. There's typically either a breakdown of basic fundamentals related to how they live with their dogs (i.e. the person is high-strung so his dog is immersed in a stressful living situation), or they are not aware of signals their dogs are giving them in an effort to communicate how they feel.

For instance, a dog might be nervous about children, but the owners aren't watching for details of their dog's behavior, like a hunched back or eyes held open so wide that the whites are showing as the dog meticulously keeps careful distance from the child. They only notice there's a problem when the dog (feeling he has no other options) growls and snaps because the child has cornered him. The dog normally is reprimanded for his "aggressive" behavior, when, in fact, he has done everything he can to avoid the situation. To make matters worse, the dog, who is afraid of children already, is now being punished in the presence of the child, and his fear is being reinforced. On the other hand, an observant owner recognizes the early signals of discomfort in his dog and can instruct the child to ignore him. He has made a crate available for the dog to go into anytime he's feeling overwhelmed and needs some space.

We can find the solution to many of our dogs' issues if we learn to pay greater attention to the little things. All big problems start as small, barely perceptible problems. The longer they go unnoticed and unaddressed, the more entrenched they become and the harder they are to fix.

In this chapter, we will examine how to master the art of scrupulous observation. This skill saves us precious time and energy, while minimizing our frustrations. No more pulling out our hair, wondering, *What the heck is wrong with my dog and why is he acting like this?*

What's Your Dog's Problem?

Countless owners have told me what their dogs' problems are, yet I can also count on two hands the number of times they actually knew what their dogs' problems were, and most of those people were only able to do so because they'd already been to a trainer who helped them figure it out. This saddens me somewhat because we pride ourselves on knowing our dogs better than anyone else. And while we may know them better in certain respects, when truly knowing "where it hurts" for our dogs, many of us miss the mark entirely.

Why does this happen? There are a variety of reasons, but two very conspicuous culprits block our understanding of our dogs' real issues the most: lack of awareness and jumping to conclusions. The previous chapter touched on jumping to conclusions in our discussion on labeling and how it is part of our normal human conditioning to slap a title on something as quickly as possible. We hate the unknown, and giving something a name makes us feel more at ease. We call our dogs aggressive, temperamental, bossy, fearful, or stubborn. By associating a label with their behavior, we breathe a momentary sigh of relief and, in a way, resign ourselves to the fate of an owner with a "such-and-such" kind of dog.

Labels, however, aren't categories that dogs fit neatly into, and they certainly lack the descriptive depth we can obtain through objective observation. Unless we take the time to slow down, step back, and thoughtfully examine our dogs' issues, our ability to provide fitting solutions is ineffectual.

Recently a client and I were working with his dog in open space off-leash. In speaking with my client and observing his energy and overall presence, it became quite clear to me that he was constantly anticipating what his dog would do next. On the surface he seemed relatively relaxed, but he was quite nervous, embarrassed, and frustrated. His dog had amassed a history of "aggressive" incidents toward both people and dogs. The owner kept telling me he knew what his dog was going to do next, mistakenly assuming he had an understanding of his dog's problems. He had tunnel vision and was blinded by memories of his dog's past episodes of inappropriate behavior. He was essentially living in a constant state of fear and anxiety when he was with his dog.

In reality, this gentleman was unconsciously cueing his dog to be on the lookout anytime they encountered other people and dogs. He had developed a system with his dog to help him be better when approaching others, but the message his dog kept receiving was *Get ready for battle—here they come*. Remember, it's not the message we're trying to convey that counts but the message that is *received*.

I observed this routine the owner had concocted of stuffing his dog's face full of treats whenever other people approached with their dogs. Unfortunately, my client's dog was being fed those delicious treats and being told "good boy" while his mind was in a stalking mode and he was targeting on the approaching, and unsuspecting, group of hikers ahead. The result? His dog's habit of being in stalking mode was constantly being reinforced.

I discussed with my client a different way of approaching these outings with his dog from a psychological standpoint. I asked him to consciously interrupt his thoughts if they drifted toward memories of past incidents with his dog while on walks. Similarly, if his mind started to anticipate what was going to happen next, he needed to consciously stop himself. "It will amaze you what you'll start to notice if you stop your mental chitchat and just watch what's actually happening," I said. "Take a step back and pretend you're watching each scene like you'd watch a movie. Observe without judging, and pay close attention to the entire picture, because you've been missing a lot of it." Once he did this, he was able to see what was really going on with his dog. We were subsequently able to dissect each situation, identify patterns in his dog's behavior, and develop a comprehensive training plan to address the real issues.

I have a question for you: What's your dog's problem? Your first response might be, "He jumps up on people." On the surface, jumping up is the problem. Now I'm going to challenge you to dig in a little deeper. Let's assume for the moment that jumping up isn't the problem. For one thing, if your dog has pent-up frustration and energy due to a lack of mental and physical outlets, jumping up is a natural consequence.

Because this book is designed to provide a systematic approach to Transformational training, if you haven't taken a full week to institute the principles from the previous chapter into your life, I challenge you to stop, go back to chapter one, and do all of the exercises. Make sure you've done the simple daily practices for both you and your dog and given it all time to sink in. Once completed, you can confidently say that your dog has his basic needs fully met, that he's being provided with sufficient exercise and other stimulating activities.

With this foundation, we can eliminate lack of outlets as the culprit for his obnoxious behavior and evaluate its cause more thoroughly. I would propose that the issue isn't starting the moment a guest comes into your house; it more likely began long before that. Perhaps when you get ready for company you are cleaning frantically or maybe just excited to see your friends. Both of these scenarios will affect your dog's energy as well. Or you could be transferring nervous energy to your dog because the people coming to visit aren't exactly your favorite folks. Another possibility is that your dog's energy ramps up the moment he hears a car pull into the driveway. The trigger might be the sound itself. If you're not aware of this because you've decided the problem is jumping up, you can miss entire portions of the behavioral sequence and, furthermore, an opportunity to stop the jumping before it ever begins.

In elevating your awareness, step back. Making a specific shift in how you direct your attention in the moment will make all the difference. The kind of shift I mean is sometimes referred to as adopting the perspective of the Observer. This can be accomplished by placing your attention on (not in) the constant stream of flowing thoughts and emotions, judgments and opinions. In your normal day-to-day routine you'll generally find yourself being carried along in this stream, either accepting whatever comes along or fighting against the current. Usually it's a mixture of both. Neither of these options is particularly empowering. So let's explore a different option: making a conscious decision to swim to the shore and step out of the stream altogether.

From the stream bank, you can watch what's happening. You're not trying to stop the thought stream, just detach yourself from it in such a way that you can understand it better. You're effectively observing not only situations as they unfold but also your thoughts, feelings, and emotions in real-time. Again, the goal isn't to "do" anything. The goal is to witness the situation and yourself in such a way that you begin to objectively identify what's happening in both the external and internal worlds. In so doing, you'll find it far easier to notice a situation's dynamics and subtleties.

Pure awareness, which is naturally rooted in the now, is devoid of all thought and interpretation (although it observes thought and interpretation) and is connected to the real you, or, more specifically, your essence. You are not your mind. You are not your thoughts. Let this sink in: The real you is that elevated realm of your consciousness that is *aware* of your mind. On acknowledge and honor the Observer's existence, you can enlist this mighty force at any time. Previously untapped potential is now available to you whenever you consciously choose to shift to a higher level perspective.

The deepest, most authentic human experience lies at the level of the spirit. Whereas the mind functions in a past-present mode, the spirit, as well as the Observer, is ever present. It may help to think of the Observer as the connecting entity, or the bridge, between the mind and spirit. Since it is seldom utilized in our society, we live a majority of our lives feeling tired, empty, and devoid of joy because our mind-body-spirit continuum is broken. Most people are completely oblivious to this reality, or they try to understand it in a purely intellectual way, all the while substituting pleasure in one form or another for the personal peace and lasting joy they already have within them but seldom enter into. Transformational revelations are actualized on a plane that transcends intellectual understanding, so most folks are operating at a disadvantage from the get-go, unable to operate from a place of true power or summon higher levels of creativity.

So let's revisit the scenario of your dog jumping on people and see how this works. Your first directive is *not* to address the situation any different from what you have in the past. Don't get tunnel vision. The first step is to consciously direct your attention to observing the situation by stepping onto the stream's shore and into the shoes of the Observer. You may notice for the first time that your dog is already beginning to show early signs of hyperactivity by pacing the living room when he hears people walking up the steps to your front door. You might further observe that you begin to feel slightly nervous at this point, anticipating that your dog will rush the door and spin excitedly in circles when the doorbell rings. By the time the guest rings the doorbell, your dog has gotten himself quite worked up. He bounds to the door and then glances at you before reorienting to the door and barking excitedly.

Instead of approaching the front door calmly, you yell to your guests, "Just a second," and notice that your physical motions are a bit rushed and herky-jerky, which seems to escalate your dog's hyperactive state. Right before you open the door, you grab him by the collar, pull him back, and hold him behind you. The last thought you have before you open the door is, *Oh my God, here we go again. This dog is totally crazy right now.*

Once the door is open, you drop your dog's collar to give your guests a hug, and the floodgates crash open. Your dog is excited beyond control. You feel embarrassed as you helplessly watch your company weather the storm and play down their annoyance with your four-legged pogo stick. You start yelling, *"No,* Fido! Get down!" in a not-so-calm way, but he doesn't seem to hear you. In fact, he is not acknowledging your presence, which adds to your mounting frustration.

Adopting the perspective of the Observer is absolutely necessary in identifying the reality of the situation and separates it from your personal thoughts, emotions, hang-ups, and your ego. Problems with our dogs often seem insurmountable when viewed as a whole. If we watch each scenario and break it down into its component parts, however, things begin to make more sense and feel less overwhelming. Great training and behavior modification work with your dog begins with a more in-tune awareness, which leads to accurate and objective observation of the real problem. Then it can all be broken down into manageable steps you can work on.

Keep in mind also that attaching general labels to your dog, like stubborn, defiant, and too-smart-for-his-own-good, is not helpful in the behavior modification process. Categorizing your dog results in tunnel vision and causes you to filter out of your conscious awareness any information that isn't consistent with the label you've chosen. This can cause you to subconsciously omit important details during the observation process. Let go of you preconceived notions about your dog and be descriptive about his *behavior*. For instance, rather than labeling your dog as stubborn because he darts around you to greet guests and ignores your pleas for his attention, make an objective description instead. It's far more useful to describe the situation point by point. Instead of calling him stubborn, which implies you can do nothing to change the behavior, you can say that his high level of excitement around guests is not being effectively redirected by your verbal reprimands, and you need to search for alternative strategies that put you back in control of the situation.

Keep in mind that *Transformational Dog Training* identifies powerful universal principles—like greater personal awareness— you can put into practice in any situation you and your dog encounter. It's about creating greater sophistication through simplicity and utilizing powerful models to address situations with greater ease and effectiveness. An exhaustive amount of "how-to" material is available on dog training techniques. And though it's great to be diligent and study those resources, it's all too easy to get confused with the seemingly conflicting advice. I highly recommend enlisting the help of a professional with years of experience who is familiar with a variety of tools and techniques. This person will be able to skillfully combine them into a perfect fit for your dog's present needs. Finding the right person to help will prevent unnecessary frustration and save you time and money in the long run. Having another set of eyes on the situation helps identify things that you have been missing, as well as new things you can incorporate into what you are already doing.

Don't Skew the Pooch

When scientists design an experiment, they eliminate any extraneous variables that might skew the results and lead to inaccurate conclusions. Scientists refer to these much-loathed "confounding variables." A well-designed experiment ariable(s) being studied and eliminates as many others The fewer variables within a given experiment, the simpler it is to draw salient conclusions about cause-and-effect relationships of the variables being measured.

In my experience working with people to help isolate and solve their dogs' problems, more often than not, people tend to be their dogs' greatest confounding variables. That doesn't mean that they don't love their dogs and do their best to help them. It just means that they are unaware of the impact they have on their dogs' psyches and behaviors. This is exactly why I often work with "problem" dogs at my center first without their people around. It gives me an opportunity to get to know the dogs and assess who they are in the absence of their owners. Then I like to observe the dogs in the homes with their people, and it's amazing how both issues and solutions begin to present themselves immediately. The good news is that while people can be the greatest impediment to their dogs' progress, they can also be the most powerful catalyst for positive change. We can be our dogs' greatest allies and assets.

The first and most important step in becoming our dogs' greatest allies is to create balance within ourselves. This is not necessarily the most popular theory, and plenty of folks want to keep the two separate. They want dog training to be addressed independently of their personal lives. To me, though, the two are inseparable. If dogs are an integral part of our families and we have tight-knit bonds with them, how can we possibly create arbitrary divisions between such interrelated aspects of our lives? The answer is that we can't, because everything is connected. We can pretend one doesn't affect the other, but it doesn't change reality. The reality is that things like marital bliss—or strife—will absolutely affect our dogs, just like it affects our children.

So I have to ask: Do you have personal stability and harmony? Is your energy and way of being worthy of being emulated by your dog? One of the greatest tools we have for expanding our personal awareness is observation of our dogs' behavior. Dogs have often been likened to personal mirrors because they are so honest in reflecting our internal states back to us. I cannot tell you how many times I've watched a "nervous" and "neurotic" dog practicing behaviors like whining and spinning—an outward expression and reflection of the owner's internal angst and tension—and the owner looks at me completely puzzled by the behavior, unaware that it's a reflection of him! If that owner can open up and recognize the real problem, he can begin to change himself from the inside out, and his dog's behavior will transform instantaneously. I have seen this time after time after time. But where does such a transformation in our dogs begin? With us, our dogs' people. Our dogs' behaviors are, in many cases, merely an outward representation of our internal states.

It's understandable that people generally don't like exploring this area, because it requires honest self-examination. It can be disconcerting to look at our dogs and admit that we have played a large role in creating their instability. I know; I have been there. And unlike people, dogs don't have the ability to deny how they're feeling. So when their owners are unstable, it is automatically reflected in their behavior patterns. This is especially obvious in dogs that are sensitive and not naturally stable themselves. They have less of a buffer against the environment they are subject to. We must become greater advocates for our dogs by not labeling them as "problem dogs" if, in fact, they are merely responding to *our* problems and energy or lack of inspired leadership.

Dogs are so pack oriented and dialed in to the well-being of family members that they are naturally affected by changes within the family (good and bad). Just think about the effect it would have on a naturally shy and anxious dog to be living with a large family chock full of exuberant children whose friends are constantly coming and going. Add to the mix parents who are high-powered corporate executives with hectic schedules keeping them perpetually stressed out. Is there any way for the dog in this 'n to relax and thrive in such an environment? No. There's no amount of training that can help him live in peace. The only way for a shy and sensitive dog to experience stability in this scenario is if his people are willing to make personal changes. Otherwise, the dog should be given the opportunity to live with a family that has a lifestyle more suited to supporting him. It's only when our lives, our energy, and our way of being are all in harmony that we can experience peace and share it with our dogs.

Breaking the Pattern

Once we become acutely aware of how we may have unknowingly contributed to our dogs' issues, we recognize the importance of removing ourselves from the picture by becoming more neutral. In this way we can isolate which of our dogs' issues are theirs alone.

If we return to our front door example, we observed the following sequence:

A. Fido showed low-level hyperactivity by pacing the living room floor at the sound of people walking up the steps outside.

B. At the sound of the doorbell or knocking, he raced to the door.

C. He glanced back at you from the front door.

D. He turned back to the door and barked excitedly.

E. Having his collar held as you opened the door seemed to escalate the intensity of his barking and hyperactive energy.

F. You released his collar, and your dog proceeded to bark, spin in circles, and jump on your guests. At this level of excitement, your dog in no way acknowledged your directions or attempts at redirecting his behavior.

By witnessing several consecutive instances of this sequence playing out when guests come over, you have identified the predictable pattern outlined above. Now you want to develop a training plan to fix the behavior and help Fido stay calm when you have people over, so you developed strategies to address the behavior. Below is an example of what your plan might look like:

A. *Fido showed low-level hyperactivity by pacing the living room floor at the sound of people walking up the steps outside.*

Therefore, I will recruit family members to leave the house and come back a few minutes later, and I will instruct them to pace up and down the steps outside without ringing the doorbell or knocking. When Fido perks his ears forward and then paces the floor, in a relaxed manner I'm going to walk over to him and use his collar to guide him to his dog bed. I will patiently wait with him until he relaxes and lies down. If he tries to sneak around me, I will repeat the process until he gives up the idea of pacing and relaxes on his bed instead. Once this is accomplished, I will present Fido with his favorite rawhide to chew on as a reward for staying calm. I will repeat this process twice daily for a few days and monitor Fido's progress.

B. *At the sound of the doorbell or knocking, he raced to the door.*

After Fido has mastered step one, he will probably start to go to his dog bed at the sound of people outside automatically. I will have my family help me by coming up the steps and knocking on the door. This time I will withhold his rawhide until the knocking starts. If Fido stays on his bed for even a split second instead of rushing the door, I'll tell him "Good boy!" and present him with his rawhide as quickly and calmly as possible. If he leaps off of his bed instead, I'll tell him "Uh-uh" and gently guide him back to his bed once again. I will repeat this process several times each day with Fido until he is consistently staying on his bed, despite hearing knocking or the ringing doorbell.

C. *He glanced at me from the front door.*
The first two exercises will preclude this as a possibility, because he won't be at the front door.

D. *He turned back to the door and barked excitedly.*
I'll allow Fido to bark a maximum of three times to let me know someone is outside; I'll even tell him "Good boy!" But if he keeps barking and starts to get worked up, I'll calmly tell him, "That's enough," and remove his rawhide if he doesn't quiet down right away. When he's mastered this exercise as well, I'll move on to the next step of gradually making my way to the front door while keeping an eye on Fido and consistently repositioning him on his bed each time he gets up to approach the front door. I'll practice this several times a day for at least a couple days until he's a pro and doesn't move off his bed, even when the door is opened and I greet the people outside. I will also have prepped my "guests" (family members in the beginning of Fido's training, because he seems a little less exuberant with them than guests he hasn't met before) to ignore Fido and pretend they can't see him when they enter. I will explain that he'll be able

to stay relaxed easier if they aren't offering him eye contact and using his name.

E. *Having his collar held as the door opened seemed to escalate the intensity of his barking and hyperactive energy.*

The earlier exercises will preclude this as a possibility, because Fido won't be at the front door.

F. *I released his collar, and Fido proceeded to bark, spin in circles, and jump on my guests. At this level of excitement, Fido in no way acknowledged my directions or attempts at redirecting his behavior.*

Once again, the earlier exercises will preclude this as a possibility. Instead, my final step is to allow Fido to stay on his bed for several minutes after my guests are inside and he is completely relaxed. I can then calmly tell him, "Okay, come say hello," and invite him over to greet my guests. He'll likely be much more appropriate, since he won't be all hyped up, but if he forgets himself and jumps or greets my guests inappropriately, I'll calmly tell him, "Uh-uh," and guide him back to his bed. Once he calms down completely, I'll invite him back over to try again.

Obviously, this is only an illustration of one possible way to work your dog through the situation, and the plan assumes a few things. For one, your dog would clearly need to be highly motivated by his rawhide and not guard it from you. It also assumes that your dog's underlying issue is overexcitement with guests (as opposed to territorial issues, fear, etc.). More important than the specific techniques outlined, because there are many alternative ways to train your dog to succeed in this type of situation, is having an understanding of how to create awareness of what's really happening in a given situation by stepping into the role of Observer, identifying patterns in your dog's behavior, and then breaking it all down into manageable steps to fix the problem. Through this process you'll learn how to interrupt the old habits your dog has developed and provide him with a rewarding but nonnegotiable alternative set of behaviors to practice. Teaching your dog new habits that are incompatible with old, undesirable ones is one of the best ways to eliminate problem behaviors.

Fight or Flight

We all have heard of the fight-or-flight response. This is typically used to describe an animal's reaction to stressful situations. For example, your dog might be confronted by another dog at the dog park. In that moment he will react in one of two ways: He will either run away from the situation (flight), or he will engage the other dog in conflict (fight).

The problem with this model is that it oversimplifies animal, and specifically dog, behavior. The fight-or-flight response is generally associated with the sympathetic nervous system, which is responsible for adrenalized responses and is tied to the dog's hindbrain—the portion of the brain that is reflexive in nature. When engaged, little or no conscious thought is taking place and the dog will start to "freak out" or panic. Once he enters this state, no beneficial cerebral activity or learning takes place. He's merely reacting. This is an oversimplified explanation of a complex process, but you get the gist.

The point is that other options are available to a dog beyond a panicked or reactive response. While the sympathetic nervous system is absolutely essential for survival purposes in that it is designed to get animals out of dangerous situations quickly, it is certainly not a healthy state for a dog to live in consistently. Adrenalized states are for the short-term and they consume a tremendous amount of energy. A dog that doesn't have well-developed and sophisticated coping mechanisms will over-engage his sympathetic nervous system and consequently live in an anxious state a majority of the time.

An alternative to this is to employ the complementary system, namely the parasympathetic nervous system. This branch of the nervous system is associated with rest, digestion, and non-adrenalized responses. When a dog is in this state, he's moved out of his hindbrain (the non-thinking portion) and into his "front brain" and is now in a position to thoughtfully process situations. The parasympathetic nervous system gives dogs the ability to relax and weigh their available options. When this system is engaged, a dog is no longer caught up in panic mode, and instead of reacting to situations he is *responding*. Your dog should spend the *vast* majority of his time operating from the front brain.

We all know about the ill effects that prolonged stress has on people; conversely, we are aware of the soothing effect and health benefits associated with adequate rest and a balanced lifestyle. The same goes for our dogs, and we can teach them how to engage more sophisticated mental processing. When a dog is well versed in the use of his front brain, he has an array of options available if confronted by another dog at a dog park. Instead of automatically shifting to his hindbrain fight-or-flight response, he can maintain a calm state and make a more thoughtful determination about the best way to address the situation. For example, instead of running away, your dog can choose to skillfully diffuse the situation through conveying calming signals to the other dog; he can use his body language to tell the other dog "I don't wish to engage in conflict. I'm not a threat." At this point the other dog is likely to oblige yours, thus leading to a peaceful resolution. A number of constructive options are available to any dog that is savvy enough to recognize this fact and use it to his advantage.

Therefore, as a dog owner, your job is to nurture front thinking. Encourage your dog to be thoughtful and not re becoming reactive in stressful situations. To do this you must first become more aware of how your dog responds to stress. Is his first response panic and reactivity when he encounters stressful scenarios? Or has he been doing everything he can to use subtle language cues to tell other dogs and people that he is uncomfortable? If you're like me, when you become purposefully aware of your dog's behavior, you'll probably find that he normally makes many attempts to diffuse stressful situations and resorts to a fight-or-flight response only when all else has failed him. If you notice this type of a pattern in your dog, you can once again develop a systematic plan for strengthening appropriate responses and reducing the occurrence of undesirable choices.

As a trainer I often am asked, "How do I fix my dog's aggressive outbursts toward other dogs?" Such people are usually desperately searching for some kind of magical quick-fix technique, and they want someone else to provide a solution to their dogs' behavior issues that is minimally intrusive on their personal time and attention. There's no real sense of wanting to know how they can grow in their personal awareness to help their dogs; they just want it over and done with. Each of us must realize that we have within *ourselves* every essential tool necessary for addressing our dogs' behavior problems. That isn't to say that we won't need guidance from experienced professionals on the finer points of dog training, but we sometimes squander the best opportunities to learn and grow as people by not investing time and attention in our dogs' education. We miss the chance to create understanding and deepen our bond with them. Instead, grab hold of those opportunities. Be thankful for them. Use them to your advantage. Let them help you grow and develop your awareness and deepen your relationship.

You can do a number of things to encourage front-brain thinking in your dog. One is to model a healthy lifestyle. You can't give something you don't have. If you are totally out of balance, how can you possibly help create it in your dog? Always remember that your dog will give you clues about the state you are presently in. Dogs are very sensitive to their people, which is why you will often see nervous dogs owned by nervous people, and fearful and insecure dogs owned by people who exhibit those same characteristics. Granted, dogs do make their own decisions and can have issues not related to their people, but I have found that most of the issues my dogs have seem to disappear when I am relaxed and stable. So I work to make sure I am in balance—I encourage you to do the same—so that I don't share instability with my dogs or, worse yet, create it.

Second, map out a plan for encouraging your dog when he is in the right state of mind. This will look similar to the exercise we discussed earlier with Fido being over exuberant at the front door. First, you'll want to step back and observe the particular scenarios in which your dog shifts between his front brain and hindbrain. Become more aware of the subtleties of these situations by expanding your awareness. In the beginning, you might find yourself getting frustrated and thinking, *This looks the same as it always has. My dog absolutely panics when other dogs approach him at the dog park.* If you stay diligent and observe the situation with detached objectivity, however, you might start to pick up on some details you didn't initially see. Perhaps when other dogs approach yours, prior to his tucking tail and running away in a panic, you notice him sniffing the air (trying to pick up on the other dog's scent). Then you observe that he follows the air sniffing with slow, exaggerated eye blinks. He also tends to gently lift up one of his front paws and turn his head as the other dog approaches.

With this observation, you realize that all of these actions your dog is practicing (air sniffing, eye blinks, paw lift, head turn) are actually front-brain activities designed to communicate to other dogs that he's feeling uncomfortable. You see that he practices appropriate dialogue when dogs come to say hello, but the real problem is that he doesn't practice the behaviors quite long enough to give approaching dogs time to respond to his cues. Now you can develop a plan to verbally encourage your dog anytime he's giving calming signals to oncoming dogs and resolve not to play into things by chasing him down and petting him for comfort when he goes into escape mode and runs away.

As you implement this plan over the next couple weeks at the dog park, you notice that your encouragement and praise is causing your dog to linger in his front brain for progressively longer periods of time—he's holding it together better and giving the other dogs more time to respond to his communication. As a result, approaching dogs are recognizing his discomfort and letting him be. Encouraged by your progress, you continue working your plan until one day you're struck by the realization that your dog hasn't panicked in weeks. Even better, he has started to show curiosity toward other dogs and has developed enough confidence to occasionally initiate greetings on his own. You still encourage him periodically, but you phase out some of the praise because he's doing things on his own now.

All of this progress has motivated you to supplement your work at the dog park with some additional modalities to help nurture and encourage front-brain activity in your dog: You've employed the services of a canine massage therapist once a week; you feed him only when he is calm and not pacing anxiously or begging for his food; and you put a couple drops of lavender essential oil on his collar every morning to further support his relaxation. Once again, greater awareness has provided you with insight about your dog's behavior, which has allowed you to support him more thoroughly. His life has been enriched in many ways, not the least of which is his newfound ability to spend more of his days in a peaceful state.

What's Your Problem?

If you are depressed you are living in the past. If you are anxious you are living in the future.
If you are at peace you are living in the present.

Lao Tzu

One of the greatest gifts we can receive from our dogs is the power that comes from living in the present. They can teach us how to master being in the moment if we'll allow them to. Think about it: Dogs are not regretful, judgmental, harsh, or critical. Every morning and each time we come home they meet us with unmistakable joy. Dogs are genuinely happy, and that happiness is contagious. Dogs are great therapy for humans for many reasons, one of which is their ability to instinctively meet our most immediate needs. Have you ever had a bad day at work and on your lunch break avoided interacting with people, but then spotted a dog happily trotting along with his owner and it brought an instant smile to your face? That carefree spirit drew you in, and next thing you knew, you were petting the dog and chatting with the owner as if he were an old friend.

Our dogs are masters at this kind of thing. If we aren't feeling well, they aren't consumed with worries, personal agendas, or preoccupied with questions about how they're going to coordinate their young ones' activities later that week; they are entirely aware of how we're feeling in that moment and comfort us by nuzzling our hands or just sitting next to us calmly. They meet the needs of the moment with precision because all of their attention is completely dedicated to it.

An important distinction exists between humans and dogs with respect to the essence of their psychological issues. While humans have complex emotions, memories, unconscious hang-ups, hidden agendas, histories, and egos, dogs have memories that are more basic and association-based. In other words, people's psychological challenges are characterized by convoluted and deeply embedded emotions and memories all knitted together by a pervasive, invisible strand of self-importance. By contrast, dogs' psychological challenges are simpler in nature, characterized by associations with varying degrees of strength.

A person will relive a traumatic situation countless times in his mind, asking, *Why did this happen? Was it my fault? Is there something I should have done differently to avoid the situation? Why did that person wound me so deeply after we've known each other all this time? Did I unconsciously want this to happen? Do I tend to self-destruct whenever I get into a serious relationship?* Throughout this questioning process, emotions like guilt, regret, shame, and sorrow are gushing like a punctured artery, bleeding out and leaving multilayers of emotional scars that must eventually be removed. It can be a monumental task to rehabilitate people when one considers the depth and complexity of our psychological and emotional makeup.

The beauty of working with dogs is that despite having their fair share of challenges, they aren't entangled by the personal hang-ups we so easily get caught up in, and, most important, they don't indulge the insidious practice of self-importance. They *can* experience discomfort relative to certain stimuli in their environments, but due to their lack of negative "imaginings" about those stimuli, they can form new meanings and associations much more quickly than people can.

For example, let's suppose that your dog had a powerful negative experience in his past, where a previous ill-tempered owner got fed up with him on several occasions and struck him with a stick. You've noticed that your dog reacts anytime he sees a person holding a stick-like object; he shirks away even though no one is threatening him. You also know that your dog loves tennis balls and playing fetch more than anything in the world. You decide you'd like to help your dog have a better association with people holding sticks, brooms, etc. (remember: dogs think more in terms of associations, not convoluted and complex memories the way people do), so you start down the path toward changing your dog's perception. Previously, the equation might have looked something like this in your dog's mind:

Person with stick = danger/fear

But you'd like your dog's new association to look more like this:

Person with stick = cheerful anticipation of rewards

Using a Chuckit to associate people and sticks with a fun game of fetch.

In thinking back, you realize that your dog has never acted fearful when you play fetch using a Chuckit tennis ball launcher, and since it is similar to a stick, you start there. Then you transition to raising the Chuckit in the air, but without the tennis ball cupped inside. Instead, as soon as your dog displays his characteristic eagerness to fetch, you throw the ball from your other hand. Once you have this down, you start to integrate other "sticks" into the routine in place of holding up the Chuckit. Over time, your dog begins to associate the raising of a stick in your hand with the beginning of a game of fetch—his favorite thing in the world.

Once you've conditioned him in this manner with all different sorts of sticks and stick-like objects, have some friends go through the same sequence with your dog so he begins to see that anytime a person holds up a stick, a game of fetch is sure to follow. If you've done your work correctly, your dog that was once terrified by this kind of situation now chomps at the bit in eagerness whenever he encounters a similar one. What used to be associated with imminent danger is now associated with his favorite activity.

This is just one example of how you might approach modifying your dog's perception of such a situation. The point is to realize that you need to de-emotionalize the situation and stop ruminating over how terrible your dog's past trauma must have been. He doesn't need a therapist to talk with him about his feelings. He needs a confident leader to step in and show him a new way of understanding his world. Help him develop a new association, and you will help him feel confident and relaxed where he used to gravitate to fear and panic.

What does this have to do with you and me? Everything.

It can teach us is to recognize and acknowledge when we're in a situation that triggers negative emotions in us. We need to first become aware of such a response and then follow that up by redirecting our attention into the present. In so doing, we will find that what's going on during any given moment when we experience negative emotions is often a completely neutral situation that we've assigned a very specific meaning to, and thus any power that situations wield over us emotionally is power we have given to them—power that can be reclaimed.

Instead of living mindfully in the present, most of us spend our lives hung up in one of two powerless worlds: the past or the future. Living in the past either leaves us in an indefinite holding pattern with feelings of guilt and regret, or it makes us nostalgic, wishing we could return to our romanticized vision of the good old days. Living in the future is either marked by feelings of worry and fear of the unknown, or it keeps us mentally bound to escapism, where we fantasize about getting to a magical place in life where we've somehow "arrived" and moved beyond the stressors of life.

Neither of these options can ever lead us to a place of peace. Certainly, some folks almost thrive on being out of balance. They'll tell you all about their problems and are dying for a sympathetic ear but have no real desire to move past them. Playing the role of the victim is satisfying to them at some level. They may say that they want to change, but their actions consistently belie that assertion, and over time they experience very little, if any, positive change. Because you are investing time and energy in studying and applying this material, you must genuinely want to make positive changes and experience greater balance in your life, and the next step toward that end is learning to be present.

Being Present

And in the end, it's not the years in your life that count. It's the life in your years.

Abraham Lincoln

Stop reading right now and take the next two minutes to imagine what your tomorrow would be like if your mind was no longer able to drift into, or linger in, the past or future. For that one day your mind could experience only the present moment. How would that change the way you go through your day? This thought experiment will also lend you valuable perspective as to how your dog's brain functions: in the now.

Does performing this thought experiment create angst? Does your mind immediately resist and wonder, *How on earth is that supposed to work? This doesn't make any sense.* If so, you are certainly not alone. Human nature will have us all grasping for control; but none of us can control the future or the past, so why do we insist on spending so much time in a mental rut trying to do just that? Although we can live only in the moment, our minds are seldom in sync with it. Consider this: You and I have control over our thoughts and actions right now. Let that truth sink in. A single, thoroughly evaluated thought, after all, can change the way we see things forever. We cannot control the outcome of any situation. We can control how we think and act but not the outcome of those thoughts and actions. If this is true (and let's assume for now that it is), it actually has the power to dissipate a lot of completely unnecessary tension and pressure that is present in our lives.

Can you focus on the moment? Can you act in the present? Absolutely. Then why all the tension we live with each day? The stress is caused by runaway thoughts about the past and future as well as the associated and complex "what if" scenarios we run through in our minds as we deceive ourselves into thinking we have control over the future. The purpose of thinking about the past and future is only to gain perspective and apply knowledge to our present situation. We run into trouble when we confuse gaining perspective and making wise decisions with having some sort of control. Remember: We can control only the purity of our actions and intention in the moment.

What we do has consequences and inevitably influences outcomes, but we get tripped up anytime we shift our focus from quality, present-moment actions to worrying about their results. A given situation has far too many uncontrollable variables for any human being to force a specific result. Present action, however, has incredible power and is completely within our control. Internalizing this powerful paradigm and establishing it as one of our core values can radically alter the quality of our lives.

Those who are devoted to reducing their stress levels and experiencing perpetual joy must dedicate themselves to mastering this principle and let go of identifying with the past. It is near and dear to my heart because by nature and the way I was raised, inclined to be very intellectually driven. I can't tell you the num of times I've had mentors say to me, "Stop thinking and just do it." It's taken years of concerted (and ongoing) effort to keep myself in the present. I have found it very difficult to stay focused on the now without getting sidetracked by overthinking, but as I've grown and become more adept at this skill, it has had a profound effect on my life.

So what's so great about the "now"? For one thing, it increases our awareness, which, as we've already seen, is of paramount importance to Transformational training. Like eating food too fast and not really tasting any of it, thinking rather than being causes us to miss the magic of the moment, which passes much too quickly. People often describe traumatic events as taking place in slow motion. When crazy things happen, our sense of time can be altered, making an event that took place in five seconds seem like it took more like fifteen or twenty. It's like watching a movie in slow motion while simultaneously processing information and thinking at an accelerated pace. This is also related to the reason I believe time seems to pass so slowly when we are children but passes progressively faster as we age. Children are more intuitive in nature; adults are more intellectual. Children are curious and they encounter new experiences and learn every day; adults are usually running on autopilot. We're so task driven that we tend to overlook new information. This can have a detrimental effect on our development as we age, but we can also resolve to gain the discipline necessary to change over to a present-moment orientation and savor every moment we are given.

Right now as you're reading this, you are filtering out of your conscious awareness an extraordinary amount of information. While there's nothing wrong with this, per se, and the ability to focus is an indispensable cognitive ability, it can also lead us to develop tunnel vision and thereby miss out on the richness of

. Here's a question: How much of your life are ıcing?

ᵉ to stop reading and close your eyes. How become to the sounds in your environment? ...ɪs can you smell? Open your eyes. Instead of looking directly ahead, diffuse your vision to take in the maximum amount of information from your entire visual field. How does that change the quality of your experience? Now direct your attention inward. How are you breathing? Is it shallow, or are you belly breathing? What sensations can you feel in your body? Once you get a general feeling, direct your attention to individual muscle groups or specific areas of your body. How does that change your present experience?

If you've seen James Cameron's 2009 movie *Avatar*, you'll recall that scientists had developed a procedure for mapping a person's brain into a genetically engineered alien body. People could then explore the planet Pandora while operating within the body of a creature native to it. Imagine yourself in a similar setting here on Earth, having the same brain you do now but being connected to and operating within a completely different body on an entirely different continent than any you've visited.

Imagine moving through your new environment (a city, a jungle, a desert, etc.) in your new body. How much more aware would you become of the sounds around you? How much more would you drink in every sight and smell? How much more in tune would you be with your body and how things feel to the touch as you move around and explore your surroundings? You can intentionally heighten your awareness in day-to-day situations, and this is one example of a conceptual model you can use to do so.

After going through this exercise, you may find yourself surprised by how much information is available to you every moment. Step outside and take a quick walk around your block while keeping your attention focused solely in the now. Dedicating ten minutes to experiencing and sensing everything you can will provide a unique experience. You may even be surprised by how much you enjoy the exercise. It might amaze you that you have lived years without taking the time to fully appreciate your surroundings. The trick is to keep conscious thought to a minimum so that you can absorb as much information as possible.

We feel more alive when we inhabit our bodies and raise our awareness.

Without present-moment awareness there can be no enlightened or enduring change. If we desire such change, it always begins by cultivating a "now" focused mind, because we can rise above the status quo and what we've resigned ourselves to only when we illuminate it. We need the light of our attention daily shining on our unconscious habits so that we can truly know ourselves. The best map in the world is no good at all without a label that says "You Are Here." So if we desire to improve our lives and move in a new direction, we need an instrument that shows us where we currently are, not just where we want to go.

Make being present a priority for the next week. To help you, keep something in front of you that reminds you of your intention to do this. It can be a new bracelet, a watch worn on the opposite wrist, or even a small, colored sticker in your car or on your desk at work. The specific reminder isn't important; only that you know what it means and keep it in front of you for the next seven days. Never forget that the ever-important now is a gift—that's why it's called the *present*. By staying in it, you will learn much about your personal tendencies and become conscious of the emotions and behaviors that different situations and thought processes trigger.

In his book *The Power of Now*, Eckhart Tolle gives a compelling account of the importance of being present. He explains that the now is the only thing that's real and the only thing you can lose. Not to embrace this truth leads to certain unhappiness. He also tells us that identification with the mind is our most formidable barrier to connectedness with our deeper essence, or "Being":

> What is the greatest obstacle to experiencing this reality? Identification with your mind, which causes thought to become compulsive. Not to be able to stop thinking is a dreadful affliction, but we don't realize this because almost everybody is suffering from it, so it is considered normal . . . The mind is a superb instrument if used rightly. Used wrongly, however, it becomes very destructive. To put it more accurately, it is not so much that you use your mind wrongly—you usually don't use it at all. It uses you. This is the disease. You believe that you are your mind. This is the delusion. The instrument has taken you over.[1]

He also explains that emotions are "the body's reaction to your mind—or you might say, a reflection of your mind in the body" and that we are bound to have them control us as long as we are identified with our minds instead of operating from a higher perspective.

I wonder how many of the diseases we human beings suffer from are a result of living in our minds. We are disconnected from our spirits—that coveted higher ground—and our bodies when we are not present. The spirit is timeless and the body is rooted in the moment. When we are in our minds, we are in a past-future orientation. There is nothing wrong with this, *assuming* that we live in the now with only occasional visits to the past for reflection and the future for planning. But most of us spend a vast majority of our time disconnected from the reality and power that is contained in the present. We wish things were different. We ruminate over what might have been and worry about things we can't control. We are preoccupied by what we need to do next and what will happen tomorrow. Whenever we engage in these behaviors, we experience an internal disconnect, we lose our joy, and we become increasingly ineffective. But when we form and stay true to an intention to remain anchored in the moment, we are on the path to renewing our energy and our strength, and we can experience peace that pervades our entire beings.

Tolle lends great insight about the negative impact mind identification has on our pets and the lessons we can learn from simply observing animals in their natural state:

> The only animals that may occasionally experience something akin to negativity or show signs of neurotic behavior are those that live in close contact with humans and so link into the human mind and its insanity. Watch any plant or animal and let it teach you acceptance of what is, surrender to the Now. Let it teach you Being. Let it teach you integrity – which means to be one, to be yourself, to be real. Let it teach you how to live and how to die, and how not to make living and dying into a problem.[2]

Whenever you want out of situations, when you desperately desire to break free, it is actually the *mind* you want freedom from: from its anxieties, compulsions, fears, the cares of this world—from entrapment in the ego's schemes. You were never meant to live in your mind. Doing so grants external situations the authority to control and intimidate you. Choose to practice living in the now. Be the Observer. Stay connected to your essence. Engage in thought to strategize and plan when needed, but return to the present straightaway. When you leave your mind behind, apprehension is transfigured and serenity emerges.

Not-Doing

We are creatures of habit. As much as we like to think of ourselves as having free will, we might consider how much free will we really have. As Charles Noble observed, "First we make our habits and then our habits make *us*" (emphasis mine). Think about it: How many things do you do each day that aren't entrenched behavior patterns? I believe you'll be surprised at what you learn when you perform the being-present exercise this week and start to recognize the regularity of impulsive—and compulsive—behaviors that take over without "consulting" you first.

All significant change starts with shaking things up. First, we become aware of our habits and realize that although they are comfortable and familiar, they are not always helpful. Then, once we are aware of our habits, we can move on to interrupting patterns in our lives that enslave us. This process is much like pulling up the anchor on a ship. No longer tied down, we can move out of harbor and explore the fullness of the possibilities that surround us. There's much more available to you than what you're currently experiencing. On the surface, your day-to-day circumstances may appear to be the same, but don't let that keep you from seeing the vastness of what's within your grasp once you raise the anchors in your life.

Step one is awareness. Step two is practicing what is referred to in Eastern literature as "not-doing," which is just what the name implies. When you're confronted with a familiar situation, instead of responding in the habitual way, consciously interrupt yourself and do nothing. By not-doing you begin the process of destabilizing old habits and impulsive knee-jerk reactions. The second step of not-doing is intentionally inserting a non-habitual response. In the beginning, your focus will simply be to interrupt the pattern and insert *any* new behavior. With continued repetitions you'll become more deliberate in selecting and integrating a new set of empowering actions until you have formed an entirely new set of responses to old, familiar situations.

For example, let's say you have become aware that when you are walking your dog and someone else is approaching with his, you tighten your grip on the leash, become nervous, and walk to the opposite side of the street. All the while you picture in your mind past instances of your dog barking and lunging at approaching dogs; your attention is focused solely on getting out of the situation quickly and with as little embarrassment as possible.

The next time you are out with your dog and a similar situation presents itself, mentally step back from the experience as the Observer and become aware of your mind's tendency to gravitate toward negative replays of past encounters. Form an intention to bring your focus back to the present moment and remind yourself to practice not-doing. Insert a definitive pause in your mental loop by telling yourself to *wait*. This pause is characterized by non-action, which is your key to interrupting the pattern. Next, substitute some new behaviors for the habitual ones: instead of tightening your grip on the leash, you consciously loosen your grip; and rather than walking to the opposite side of the street, move closer to the approaching dog and person while maintaining a safe distance. As your mind tries to bend y attention toward replaying negative past experiences and brings up worrisome what-if questions, gently guide it back to the present moment and stay there, fully aware of exactly what's taking place each and every second of the experience.

You may observe that loosening your physical and mental grip on the leash (and the past) and moving closer to the so-called "problem" created a vastly different experience. Perhaps your dog began to pull forward initially, but then turned his head and made eye contact with you, so you said, "Good boy." He turned back around, and you were able to pass the approaching dog and owner while you and your dog maintained a relaxed posture and energy. You are surprised to find that all the things you used to do in similar situations to prevent outbursts from your dog may have been contributing to, or even creating, them. This new knowledge can be combined with information from subsequent outings until you fine-tune your strategy and develop more empowering habits and obtain better results.

Not-doing is an essential psychological strategy that can be used to modify undesirable proclivities, with the exception of certain entrained behaviors (addictions in particular) that require raising one's level of consciousness, which is beyond the scope of this chapter. Indeed, the vast majority of habits we harbor can be changed if we master the art of not-doing, and simple, habitual actions that aren't necessarily detrimental make great candidates for practicing and becoming more proficient at it. A simple way to begin breaking away from ordinary is to take a different route to work in the morning—try it the next time you are headed in. This will naturally cause some discomfort because your perfunctory routine is being disrupted, and human nature is such that we cling to what we know. Since your routine commute puts you on auto-pilot, it will require a concerted, conscious effort to remind yourself not to turn where you ordinarily would.

As you do this exercise, pay attention to how much mental resistance you encounter. If you stay self-aware throughout the process, you will probably find that you experience a lot of mental push-back to this relatively nonthreatening variation in your morning routine. But this exercise holds plenty of upside potential. Getting creative in mapping out your commute can have you traveling through areas of town you have never seen before and noticing businesses, establishments, and parks you didn't know were there but would like to visit. You might take some wrong turns and encounter detours. This is all part of purposely changing your routine and shaking things up.

Whatever you might find, settle into the moment and give yourself to the experience. The core purpose is to embolden your will to engage life and thereby gain a novel perspective, and to avoid stagnation by promoting progress. People who travel to different countries often come home "changed" because their previous fixed and static perspective has shifted and become more dynamic. We think the way we do because of our individual points-of-view and life experiences. We add depth to our knowledge when we move to a different place and see things from an alternate vantage point. For example, a hiker and a pilot would describe the same mountain terrain very differently, according to each one's position in relation to it. Both perspectives would be completely valid, even though they would vary significantly from each other. It stands to reason, then, that a person who views anything from multiple angles will have a more comprehensive grasp of its nature. Mastering the practice of not-doing makes it possible to see more, extend our experiential reach, and move beyond old habitual patterns of thought and action.

Our minds can be tremendously convincing when telling us all the reasons we don't need to change. Some habits are good, but I believe that all of them should be questioned, because "good" is the enemy of "great." Driven daily by our ingrained habits, we are robbed of possibilities, but we can change that scenario anytime we are willing to subject ourselves to temporary discomfort by practicing not-doing.

Some people might ask, "Why bother?" That's a good question, and I think a lot of people are satisfied with their lives, the way things are, what they know, and with continuing to get more of what they already have. For the rest of us who are restless for adventure, though, we cannot settle for that. We need to make a habit of disrupting our habits because we are warriors and we *need* to see what else is out there. We need to learn and grow and feel alive. We aren't content to be what Deepak Chopra calls a "prisoner of past conditioning," and we feel the pull to experience life beyond the walls we've built and others have built for us. We want—we need—to break out. We understand that courage is the price of progress, and intentionally challenging our habits is the cornerstone.

Stay with It

> *Dogs cannot act different than how they feel.*
> Sarah Wilson

The principle that whatever is in the well comes up in the bucket is true; who you are and the nature of your being will eventually be revealed. This is especially evident in the tone of people's energy and speech. The way you feel when you're with someone and the recurring themes in what he says tells you a lot about where he's at in life. You don't need to know anything about his past or personal history. Just listen with an open and curious mind and you'll recognize patterns in his energy, speech, and actions. Let me repeat what I said earlier: People have the ability to temporarily mask their emotions and feelings, but dogs do not have the luxury—or curse, as the case may be—of denial, and therefore express exactly what they're feeling in the moment.

You can take two primary paths to change negative thoughts, emotions, and actions. The first starts with a change in the way you *act* in a given situation until you begin to think and feel differently about it. Consistently putting on a genuine smile and walking taller at work will engender feelings of confidence and affect the way people interact with you and the results you see. Conversely, if you shuffle and slouch and look down at the ground while walking, you will find it nearly impossible to feel confident and at ease. There is also the ever important energetic component to how you project yourself: your presence, if you will. For further study on this important subject, I recommend the book *Leadership Embodiment* by Wendy Palmer and Janet Crawford.

The second path starts with a change in the way you *think and feel* about a given situation, which causes your actions to change as a natural byproduct. Both paths lead to a place of greater peace where positive thoughts, feelings, and actions reign. So which approach should you use? Either one is perfectly viable, because what we ultimately care about is the power to change the way we think, feel, and act.

But let's briefly discuss changing the way we think and feel through a process I call "retracing." In a nutshell, retracing is backtracking through emotional footprints to understand the origins of our negative thoughts and emotions. The premise is simple and postulates that we often don't know where we're coming from with respect to how we're feeling. This is certainly an odd concept at first glance, so an example will help us understand. Let's say you consistently experience intense negative emotions whenever you encounter a certain coworker, especially when you are together in group settings. You may be thinking, *I know exactly why I'm upset with him,* and then spout off a laundry list of things he did "to" you to make you feel the way you do whenever you're around him. But if you momentarily set aside your assumptions and dig a little deeper, you will start to see that you are upset because that particular person is striking a nerve within *you.* Why is that?

Instead of lashing out at your coworker or letting toxic anger boil in your veins whenever you see or think about him, probe to understand why he provokes such an intense reaction. Perhaps you note that his manner of speech is similar to that of your older sibling who has a knack for making condescending remarks every time you are together. As you dig even deeper, you consciously begin to recollect similar scenarios that date farther back . . . even into your younger years. You can recall several humiliating incidents involving this sibling when he ridiculed you in front friends who eventually stopped hanging out with you as a result. Through the process of retracing, you are able to identify a number of past situations related to your sibling that trigger the same negative emotional state you experience whenever you see your coworker.

Going through this process takes a great deal of time, as it requires us to flesh out the roots of major emotional hang-ups we struggle with daily so that they can finally be uprooted and overcome. Retracing is an emotionally demanding process, because you will most certainly recall events that you have not thought about in a very long time, whether through unconscious avoidance or because they were simply forgotten. I encourage you to be very thorough and take your time. Stay with it, because the payoff is greater self-awareness. We may hesitate to go through this painful process because of our natural defensiveness and reluctance to revisit old wounds, but let me assure you that the outcome is quite liberating. Once fully explored, experienced, and understood, these issues can finally be released. Avoidance may be tempting but will cost you your emotional freedom. Retracing can buy it back.

So why does this process work? After we identify that our negative emotions are an assemblage of specific life events, something interesting happens: We find compassion for *ourselves*. We realize that we have reasons for feeling the way we do and that our seemingly insurmountable emotions are nothing more than a composite of experiences our minds have linked together. If left unchecked, they grow into strongholds, but they can also be dismantled. Each experience is like a playing card with a picture of the memory, and we discover that we've allowed ourselves to be intimidated and surrendered massive amounts of our power to emotions when they're merely a house of cards!

Retracing changes our perspective, allowing us to deconstruct emotions one piece at a time by understanding where they come from and what they're made of. Emotions stem from a multitude of experiences that have been associated, or grouped, together in our minds and assigned a meaning. That meaning creates the emotion we feel. Negative emotions build up like toxins in our minds, bodies, and spirits due to the interconnected nature of our beings. Each of us must squarely face these issues, because if we don't deal with them, they will most certainly deal with us.

At this point it might be tempting to call the process of retracing "psychobabble" or skim over it without putting it into practice so we can get on to something more interesting. However we might frame this tendency, it ultimately boils down to defensiveness and avoidance. It's like when we have something important to do and procrastinate until we just can't put it off anymore and finally take care of it. Haven't you generally found that the thing you put off for so long wasn't nearly as big a deal as you had made it out to be? In fact, the act of continuing to avoid it contributed to the feeling that it would be an unpleasant thing to do, but once it was done there was a tremendous sense of relief. That's the way it is with retracing. The price is personal fortitude, an inquisitive mind, and a whole lot of patience, but the liberation is priceless. Each time you practice retracing, you chisel away layers of unconscious conditioning that affect the way you think, feel, and act. When you understand the root of the issues, their fruit (anger, impatience, fear, anxiety, etc.) come into proper perspective and become less overwhelming to deal with. Retracing makes conquering old, undesirable habits of thought and action a qualitative and actionable objective, which is necessary for the journey ahead. You simply can't travel very far—or fast—while dragging around a bunch of baggage.

If you're a movie buff like me you may have seen the 1997 film *Good Will Hunting*. It's a fantastic film that explores the impact of retracing in a relatable, entertaining, and moving fashion. It illustrates how the practice of seeking out the root of negative emotions can loosen the chains of the past that continually sabotage our present efforts. Breaking those chains allows us to move forward unencumbered, but we must have the courage to face the past if we ever hope to be free from it.

In Chapter four we will look deeper into the workings of the mind and examine ways in which we process and code experiences, as well as how we can change the quality of our memories and the meanings we assign to them. For now, utilize the awareness exercise this week and note instances when negative emotions surface. Then set aside a block of time and use retracing to gain perspective and insight, and to destabilize them.

Putting It All Together

The greatest impediment to creating lasting change in your dog's life and in yours is a lack of awareness. The good news is that expanding your awareness is the greatest tool you possess in identifying both the true nature of your challenges as well as the array of resources you can utilize to move forward.

It takes a tremendous amount of intentionality to become more conscious and observe how situations unfold. Instead of falling into the old habit of rushing to put a label on issues your dog has, become a seeker of knowledge by stepping back, becoming the Observer, and accurately identifying his behavior patterns. Let go of any past assumptions and tune out mental chatter so you can watch situations unfold, unobstructed by mental filters such as beliefs, expectations, fear, anxiety, prejudices, and preconceptions. Whenever you identify patterns of behavior that prove to be detrimental or undesirable, create a plan to interrupt them (the equivalent of helping your dog practice not-doing) and systematically teach him alternative and constructive behaviors so that healthy behavior patterns are developed instead.

In an effort to isolate the source of your dog's issues, become aware of your own behaviors, states of mind, and ways in which you influence his behavior. Sometimes you think your dog has a problem, when he's simply responding to you and the energy you project. Once you change yourself, many of your dog's problems may show marked improvement or disappear altogether.

In the quest to examine, evaluate, and change or refine your habits, become proficient in the art of not-doing. Identify patterns you wish to change, and instead of habitually reacting, remind yourself to *wait* and consciously insert alternative behaviors. By not-doing, you'll reclaim your power to choose, and then fine-tune your actions until you have developed more empowering routines.

Finally, recognize and acknowledge the need to squarely face any deeply entrenched negative sentiments you experience by retracing their history and origin. As your mind lumps experiences together, powerful associations and emotions build like storm clouds. They loom ominously, blocking the light and depleting your strength. Understanding the nature of your negative feelings diminishes their power and makes the task of dismantling them less daunting, imposing, and open-ended. As you chip away at negative emotions, you free up vast reservoirs of energy that can now be channeled into other tasks. This is an essential step in casting off limitations and can propel you forward into a bright, opportunity-laden future.

Practical Application Exercises Related to Awareness

For Your Dog:

1. For the next two days, practice total silence as you interact with your dog. This is an invaluable and enlightening exercise. Most of us are unaware of how much we over-rely on verbalization to communicate with our dogs, and how unnecessary it is. One of the greatest benefits to this exercise will be expanding your awareness of subtle communication strategies your dog uses that you have missed. Watch his body language cues. Sense his energy and demeanor. A little effort in this area will undoubtedly expand your nonverbal repertoire, and the most natural and sophisticated communication with dogs is always done silently. Note how this exercise changes the quality of your interactions.

2. Pick a familiar activity to do with your dog, and as you move through the experience with him, consciously expand your awareness. Remove yourself from the equation as much as possible and pick up on each subtle detail related to your dog's responses within the situation. For example, take your dog to your dog-friendly store and observe how he interacts with the environment. With each new stimulus he encounters (people, dogs, objects, doorways, etc.), observe the following: his tail carriage; overall posture and demeanor; the amount of tension he holds in his body; how and when he uses his nose; when his pupils dilate and constrict; the positioning of his ears; and other

ways he responds to his surroundings. See how many things you can identify that you never noticed before.

3. Identify a challenge point for your dog and help him develop an alternative response (this can be any behavior, but it's best to start with something basic). Let's say your dog jumps onto your bed uninvited first thing in the morning. You've isolated the trigger for the behavior: your alarm clock buzzer. So the following morning, have a dog biscuit sitting on your nightstand next to your alarm, and as soon as it goes off, toss the biscuit onto his dog bed before he can leap onto yours. Monitor how he responds and make adjustments to your routine until you've shaped to your liking the way he behaves when your alarm goes off; namely, staying on his dog bed.

For You:

1. Make a list of habit patterns identified through practicing the personal awareness exercise, and select a basic one from the list to focus on for the next week.

2. Take the habit you selected and write out its specific sequence. For example, if you have a habit of biting your nails while you watch television at night, your sequence might look something like this:

I watch television at night . . . the commercials come on . . . I bite my nails.

This is the basic pattern that you identify. Your next step is to practice not-doing and then substitute a different behavior. Your new sequence might look like this:

> I watch television at night . . . the commercials come on . . . I catch myself raising my hand toward my mouth and tell myself to *wait* . . . I reach for a glass of water instead.

Remember to use these steps in this order:

1. Identify the pattern (Awareness)
2. Interrupt the sequence (Not-Doing)
3. Insert a new action (Change)

Personal change always begins with awareness and is preceded by not-doing. It might be helpful to remember the change formula by the acronym ANDC (sounds like the word "antsy"): Awareness, Not-Doing, and Change.

3. Things aren't always as they seem, so the next time you experience an intense, negative emotion, take note. When you get home or have time by yourself later in the day, utilize retracing to recall as many situations from your past related to that specific emotional state. One memory leads to another, which leads to others in a chain-like fashion. Dissect the emotion by sifting through the composite of memories it is comprised of. Gain as much perspective as possible about the root(s) of the issue and realize that it is possible to honor emotions without becoming their prisoner.

   Retracing is a practice you will use throughout your life to gain insight and to dismantle toxic emotions, and you must be willing to occasionally revisit the past so you can move into the future unencumbered.

Chapter Three

Intuition, Fear, and Freedom

Fears are the greatest hindrance to realizing our potential and helping our dogs experience the fullness of their abilities. Fear originates from one of two places: intuition or ignorance. Fearful reservations based upon intuition are healthy, and we should not ignore them. Fears based on ignorance can hold us prisoner, and we cannot afford to live with them. It is only through developing a sophisticated understanding of our fears that we can gain freedom.

Think back to a time when you almost did something or went somewhere, but you felt a subtle and quiet uneasiness that ultimately led you to decide against the action. Was it a good decision in retrospect? Chances are it was, and the way things turned out confirmed it. Haven't you also experienced the same uneasiness but ignored the urgings of that quiet inner voice? Things probably didn't go so well. *Intuition knows what you don't know that you know*, and overlooking it is a risky, and sometimes deadly, choice.

Now think back to some scenarios that generated anxiety and had your mind and heart racing; the kind that produced trepidation and affected your breathing at the thought of doing something. Did you investigate the situation and realize that once you had gathered more information about it there was nothing to fear after all? In these instances, fear is intellectually based and hinges on "unknown" factors that require further exploration to diminish, eliminate, or perhaps validate our concerns.

Your Dog's Greatest Assets

Not everything that counts can be counted and not everything that can be counted counts.

Albert Einstein

Picture yourself enjoying a relaxing walk with your dog on a gorgeous summer evening. The hot sun has dipped beneath the horizon and the cool breeze is a much welcomed guest. The sweet aroma of freshly cut grass and the heady scent of flowers in full bloom drift on the breeze. Just enough light is left so you can see and greet your neighbors as they pass. You think, *This is perfect. I could keep walking like this for hours.*

Your dog's sudden growling, subsequent barking, and explosive lunging at an approaching figure startles you out of this perfect world. You tell your dog no, but she doesn't seem to hear you. You tell her no again, and in a last-ditch effort you move to the other side of the street while apologizing to the gentleman she's viciously barking at. He smiles politely, reassures you that "It's no problem at all," and continues on his way.

Once your dog finally pulls it together you continue your walk—a little rattled, embarrassed, and frustrated. You didn't like the feeling of her catching you so off guard. Neither did you appreciate how she ignored your directions to cease her tirade. You think back over the day to identify little changes in routine or anything out of the ordinary that might have caused her to be "a little off," but you tire of this when nothing comes to mind. You return home, eventually turn your attention to other things, and hope you'll never see that side of her again.

Two days later you are jolted back to the memory of that night when you recognize the picture of a man on the news who was arrested for assaulting several women. He has a noticeably tall, thin build and well-defined facial characteristics that unmistakably identify him as the man you encountered the other night. The sudden weight of fear sinks into your chest and you realize for the first time that your dog was trying to protect you against a legitimate threat. You ask yourself what would have happened if she hadn't been with you and made such a scene as the man approached. You are, for the first time, acutely aware of the frightening reality of the situation you were in and feel a deep sense of gratitude for the wisdom your dog demonstrated that evening.

Intuition and Instinct

I make a distinction between intuition and instinct because I believe intuition to be a more fitting term for our subject matter. Whereas instinct implies a fixed action pattern or response of a species to certain conditions in the environment, intuition captures the essence of an intangible internal guidance system. Dictionary.com defines *instinct* as "an inborn pattern of activity or tendency to action common to a given biological species," while it defines *intuition* as "direct perception of truth, fact, etc., independent of any reasoning process; immediate apprehension." Intuition, then, is a far more reliable guidance system, unencumbered by pre-determined and reactive ways of thinking and feeling. It isn't constrained by past experiences, anticipation of the future, or traditional thinking.

Intuition verses intellectualism is quite possibly the greatest difference in how dogs and humans think. Dogs have a wonderful habit of trusting their gut. Their survival requires a good sense of, and reliance on, their feelings about situations. Particularly if they are feral (the closer they are to having to survive in "the real world"), they will be more inclined toward fully developed intuitive capacities. This is not intended to downplay the value of human intellectual abilities; it's to showcase an area in which dogs have a decided advantage over people.

In people, intuition is the culminating result of integrated intellectual, spiritual, and physical abilities. It is intimately connected to the subconscious mind (which we will examine in the next chapter), the body (which we will discuss in Chapter five), and the spirit (which has been mentioned already and we will be briefly revisit in Chapter six). It is what can give a person special knowledge about a situation she has never encountered before, and it is what helps dogs adapt and why they can make great decisions despite their inability to intellectualize and consciously select the "best" option available to them. Without all the mental clutter and second-guessing, they are free to trust their gut without being subject to analysis paralysis.

Whenever I am working with a dog at my center and looking to gain insight about her true nature, instead of focusing on watching her directly, I observe how other dogs interact with her. I know my pack well, and a balanced group of dogs can tell me much more about a dog than I can ascertain through watching her directly. Also, my pack members are unencumbered by the constraints of overthinking and prejudice that I am subject to. All of their attention is available to respond to the dog before them, as well as the energy and presence she exudes. Their intuitive assessment of one another is far more accurate than a human's intellectual approach. If I bring a new dog into my pack and they all keep their distance from her, it tells me there's something about her we can't trust yet. If they readily approach her in a relaxed and cheerful manner, I know that her energy is inviting and amiable. If they keep a little distance from her and only slowly approach with an air of curiosity, she is probably friendly enough but may be a tad overwhelmed and projecting energy that tells them *I am kind by nature but need a little space right now until I feel more comfortable.*

These are just a few examples of ways our dogs can tell us about other dogs we encounter. Keep in mind that I am looking to *balanced* and socially savvy dogs for feedback. If a dog is unstable, she can still tell me about another dog, but the information is less reliable and I might get a misread. There's a greater chance that the information will be skewed because of the dog's own imbalances. That's why I'll always put more stock into what a dog with social wisdom shows me about another dog than one who is a little out of whack herself.

Dogs can most certainly read another dog's energy and visual communication (body language, postures, facial tension, etc.) faster and more accurately than a person can. For one, a dog's olfactory system is far more advanced than a human's. It's estimated that the typical human has about 5 million scent receptors, while dogs have in the neighborhood of 220 million. The olfactory bulb in a dog's brain accounts for over 30 percent of her total brain volume, while it accounts for only about 1 percent of total brain volume in a human.[1] The sophistication of dogs' scenting abilities has a drastic impact on the way dogs experience the world around them.

One time I was working one of my dogs in a group class, and we were directing our dogs to go lie down on some mats we had spread throughout the room. My dog had advanced obedience experience and was very reliable with commands. On this night, however, she sauntered over to the mat I pointed to, sniffed it, and refused to lie down on it. Needless to say, I was puzzled. We had done this exercise a million times before. Later in the class, though, it occurred to me that another dog had been lying on the mat before our class began. This particular dog was unquestionably dog aggressive. Remember earlier when I mentioned how rare true aggression is in dogs? Well, this dog was the real deal, and when I later directed my dog to lie down on the same mat, she could smell something about the other dog's body chemistry that was way out of alignment. She wanted nothing to do with that scent or the dog on the other end of it—even without having met her before or seeing her aggress toward another dog.

Response-Ability

Responsibility is such an important aspect of transformational training that we must have a clear picture of what it encompasses, especially regarding our role as dog owners. The bottom line is that responsibility is the capacity to address a situation in a thoughtful and level-headed manner. It is the *ability* to *respond* (not react) to what happens around us.

The first order of business is to find the balance between not exposing our dogs to situations they cannot possibly navigate successfully while not holding them back by babying them and not allowing them to make decisions on their own. This requires discernment based on trial and error as well as good old-fashioned—you guessed it—intuition. Aimee Sadler (whom I mentioned in the Acknowledgements) has a mantra that I adopted and have always kept in mind with regard to training. She would always say: "Dogs are responsible for their actions and behavior. We [owners] are responsible for reinforcement. We allow the dogs to make choices and we give them information about those choices." From a legal standpoint, you may be responsible for your dog's actions and behavior, but from a training standpoint, your dog is 100 percent responsible for them. You are 100 percent responsible for the reinforcement: i.e. supporting your dog based on where she's at and providing her with feedback about her decisions.

From a practical point of view, if your dog knows how to sit and stay at home and in most other places but is not so reliable at the park with squirrels darting about, this places responsibility on you to first put her in a situation where she has a good chance of success; and once that is in place, hold her accountable for the decisions she makes. It's a process, so you will have to be patient and systematic in approaching the goal of having her hold a sit-stay at the park. This might mean having her practicing sit-stays on the way there. Maybe she demonstrates compliance until you get to the park entrance, where she develops a "hearing problem." Working her on the threshold of her current limitations is a perfect training opportunity, so take advantage of it.

Here's where most people cross their fingers and hope that things go well as they march blindly forward into the fray, but you've recognized by now that hope is not a strategy. Instead, you choose an active role and stick to your plan to let your dog make her own choices while you provide her with feedback. At this point you might see that her ears and eyes are directed toward the center of the park where the squirrel colony, her arch nemesis, has been teasing her daily as they frolic about in the trees. Hearing her low-level anxious whining, you sense she still considers you at least somewhat relevant, because she is occasionally nudging your hand with her nose.

So you set up shop at the entryway leading from the parking lot into the park. You ask her for a sit. At first she ignores the command, but as soon as she notices you aren't moving any closer to the park, she makes eye contact with you and finally sits down. You then ask her to stay in that position, which she does for about three seconds before standing back up and whining. You use your leash to gently guide her back into a sitting position. This time she holds the stay for a bit, so you tell her "Good girl" and offer her a treat. You release her from the stay, move away, and then re-approach the entrance.

You arrive back at the entrance gate and ask her for a sit. This time she complies almost immediately. She is encouraged by a couple of pets, and then asked to stay once again. She holds the stay and earns a couple of treats. After a couple more repetitions, you release her and take five steps into the park and repeat the process, gradually working closer to her ultimate challenge spot. This goes fairly smoothly, but when you get about twenty feet away from the trees with squirrels zipping about, everything breaks down. Your dog is consistently making poor choices. So you backtrack about ten feet. This distance is far enough away from the problem that she is able to comply, which gives you more opportunities to reinforce with treats and praise instead of applying pressure with the leash or your hand on her butt to get her to sit. Once she's gathered herself, you retry the closer distance with greater success.

After a couple of days of revisiting the park and working her, she starts making quality decisions, even at very short distances from the squirrels. Also, she has begun to relax and let go of the anxious whining she used to do. She is focused on performing her task of holding a sit. She seems more happy and dialed in, so on the third day at the park after she's held her sit-stay for a minute at the base of the trees while offering an alert but relaxed state of mind, you decide to unclip her leash and release her from the stay—the ultimate reward for her work is freedom. She is delighted and explores the area, keeping an ever-vigilant watch for squirrels and playfully chasing them, but with a much lower intensity than when you started a few days earlier. You've helped her do her job well and given her the freedom she's earned. As a side benefit, she is periodically checking in with you as she explores, which she would *never* have done before, and she is even willing to come back to you when you call her. Because she is so responsive when you call her to come back, you reach into your pocket, pull out her cherished tennis ball, and throw it for her. She chases it to her heart's delight. Life is good.

Training your dog in a thoughtful and systematic way puts you in charge. Placing her in a situation appropriate for her current skill and attention level and then allowing her to make decisions positions her for success without preventing her from failing. Success and failure are both important. In my life I have learned just as much, and probably more, from my failures as I have from my successes. My failures have taught me valuable lessons. So while I always make the best effort to set myself up for success, I also understand that failure is a part of the success process and appreciate that my failures can teach me how to make better choices the next time around. The words *failure* and *success* are merely labels we assign to the concept of feedback. When we perform tasks, the outcome provides us with feedback about the choices we made during the process. Training your dog is no different. Your work together will give you feedback in the form of results. You can then adjust your approach in the future to modify the outcome.

Once you accept that you are responsible for reinforcement and that your dog is responsible for her actions and behavior, you can let go of trying to control everything (which is not only unrealistic but produces stress in you, and your dog will certainly pick up on that and be negatively influenced). It really doesn't matter if your dog's next decision is a good one or a bad one. Either choice presents you with an opportunity to supply her with information. You'll communicate to her either "I want more of that behavior" or "I want less of that behavior." Once you dive in and embrace this type of work, it becomes fun. It should feel like a dance. You're leading, your dog is following, and as the dance unfolds, you are always there to support her and provide real-time feedback.

This is where intuition really starts to kick in (*if* you listen to it and allow it a place in your training), and you'll feel things begin to connect. There's a flow to it and it starts to feel more like an art than a science. While there is plenty of science involved in training animals, it also has to become an art if it's to be as effective as possible. Some of the most effective dog trainers have far less technical knowledge than their colleagues but consistently outperform them in terms of producing positive results for their clients.

Think about it this way: The information is certainly available for you to learn all about the physics of surfing. You can stuff your brain full of every scientific fact possible, but that doesn't mean you could actually surf. Even if you were an über-genius with all the technical expertise in the world, it wouldn't keep you from getting crushed by the deep blue. There's a knowledge that comes with doing something that can never be gleaned from a book or from simply understanding it intellectually: the feel of the water and the pulsing ocean beneath you; the rumbling of the perfect wave as it approaches; the way the sunlight dances on the water; the way you direct your thoughts and use your body to coordinate each movement, making constant adjustments based on the ever changing conditions of the moment. You must combine all of your knowledge, experience, coordination, and especially your intuition to make it all culminate in an impeccable performance.

If you are addressing a particularly difficult training situation or issue with your dog, you will appreciate the added benefit of having a professional come alongside you to provide additional guidance. She can lend experience and perspective on appropriate methods and timing, as well as contribute wisdom about how to best meet your dog's particular needs. Having the right expert with you will reduce the time it takes to accomplish your goals. It will also help you and your dog develop proper habits from the outset, thus avoiding the costly mistake of acquiring bad ones and having to undo them later on.

Some of the most challenging dogs I've ever worked with were that way *because* their owners did a lot of training with them. Surprising, right? But I have learned that if training is not precisely tailored to the dog and her needs, or if it's not executed well, it builds immunity to training and teaches her to ignore people. Enlisting the help of an expert can help you avoid this problem.

Freedom

Freedom, as we saw in our earlier example with your dog at the park, is the ultimate reward. One of the most critical factors in raising a well-adjusted dog has to do with the timing of giving her freedom. Most dogs that develop problem behaviors had far too much freedom given to them way too fast when they were young.

Freedom is only adequately valued and respected when it is matched with a commensurate level of demonstrated responsibility. Freedom and responsibility are intimately linked and should be proportional to each other. In practical terms, this means that as your dog matures (not ages—the aging process is separate from the maturing process), she demonstrates that she can handle responsibility. Once she has proven that she has moved from a level 1 in responsibility to a level 2, her level of freedom should move from level 1 to level 2.

For example, giving your dog free rein of the house should be a thoughtful and managed process. In the beginning, she might be in her crate or even a small area like the laundry room when you leave the house. When she has exhibited consistent good manners in that space over a period of time, you can give her a slightly larger space. The process is repeated until she eventually has access to the entire house when you're away. She might even have a doggie door leading out into the backyard as well. Not only does this pair the right level of responsibility with the right level of freedom, but it gives you a controlled, phased rollout without the finger crossing that accompanies the all-too-common "let's see what happens" approach. In this way you can limit destructive behaviors and avoid lamenting the evisceration of your favorite decorative pillows.

It can also keep your dog from being put in an uncomfortable position. For instance, your dog might tolerate being left alone in a large area and will do so because it's her normal routine, but what if she's uncomfortable in that situation? Many people with good intentions try to see things from their dog's perspective but make the mistake of thinking about it like a human. This is when you start to say things to yourself like, "I would never keep my dog in a crate; that's so cruel. I would hate to be locked up in a tiny space. It would be so confining and lonely."

When we make decisions for our dogs, it is best to keep in mind that they have an entirely different psychological makeup. As a human moving into a new house, I would prefer to have a large, open-concept home with plenty of light, fresh air, and space to move about. My dog, on the other hand, might want the complete opposite. Being a denning animal, my dog might feel overwhelmed and fidgety in a big open room; however, in a small, dimly lit, enclosed space she might feel cozy and right at home. It might give her a tremendous sense of comfort, ease her loneliness, and allow her to stay relaxed while I'm away. In preparing your dog to experience higher levels of freedom, keep in mind that the important thing is what freedom means to her. To you, freedom might mean having run of the house; to her, it might mean being free from the overwhelming feelings that come along with being left alone in a huge, empty home.

Work

For the strength of the pack is the wolf, and the strength of the wolf is the pack.

Rudyard Kipling

In the first chapter we touched on the subject of dogs working, but it is worth revisiting here. While there is much debate about how and when dogs descended from wolves and even the extent to which they share certain behavioral traits, there is no doubt that they are related, even if it's a distant relation. Each dog's DNA carries deep within it the roots of her wolf ancestors. So while we must keep in mind that significant differences exist between domesticated dogs and wolves, it is valuable to our understanding of our dogs if we know about their origins.

Wolves spend an unbelievable amount of time working each day—in the neighborhood of eight hours of walking as they search for food and manage their territories. Traveling thirty miles a day is normal. Working hard for a living is hardwired into their system. They also spend plenty of time resting from their work and playing, but the primary focus is on work because it is how they find food and survive. In short, wolves work hard and play hard.

Wolves are also a very social, pack-oriented species. They have sophisticated communication systems that generally allow them to peacefully coexist. It's far more desirable to seek a peaceful resolution to conflicts than to risk injury or even death through physical confrontation. A wolf in the wild that needs stitches and a blood transfusion can't exactly call the local vet to see if she can be worked into the schedule. Wolves have a strong sense of self-preservation and don't tend to play hokey pokey with their lives. They have a deep reverence for the value of social and pack structure, which allows them to spread out responsibility among members of the pack according to individual strengths. They work hard together and pool their resources because they know they can survive and thrive only within a well-functioning family unit.

Wolves thrive within healthy and close-knit social structures.

What are the salient takeaway points for us as dog owners? Work is important; the security of living in a healthy, stable, and structured social group is important; regular feeding, rest, and play is important. Most dogs, especially in America, wake up in the morning and are met with praise and food and toys without ever engaging in any kind of real work. Their mere existence is rewarded in a way that oddly resembles worship. We don't do this with our human kids (unless they are very young), so why do we do it with our dogs?

I believe that a majority of people who profess to want a dog don't actually want a dog; rather, they want a mobile, tail-wagging plush toy. They think they want a dog (usually for companionship's sake), but they give little if any consideration to what that dog needs in order to thrive as she was meant to. Shouldn't we as dog owners uphold honoring our dogs' nature as our first priority? I have observed in my profession that work is the most common missing ingredient in companion dogs' lives. You may have heard phrases like "dogs need jobs" and "nothing in life is free." Both are useful mantras we can use as owners to remind ourselves always to be promoting balance by properly prioritizing our dogs' daily routines.

A couple of years ago, I attended a Buck Brannaman clinic. Buck is a master natural horseman who does inspiring work rehabilitating horses. Nicholas Evans named Buck as the primary inspiration behind his book *The Horse Whisperer*, which was later made into a movie. The documentary *Buck*, which chronicles Brannaman's life and work, is a fascinating film that won a slew of awards as well.

Sitting in Buck's clinic and listening to him talk about the value of hard work, I wrote down something he said that I considered simple yet profoundly important: "Play is a privilege earned through hard work." He went on to explain that work gives horses purpose, much as it does people. He talked about how a majority of kids coming out of high school are lazy, feel entitled, and have a crummy attitude about going out and getting a job to support themselves. Buck continued by saying something to the effect that "I've been accustomed to working hard since I was eleven years old. So when someone said, 'You need to go out and get a job,' I was like 'Great! Bring it on! I've been working hard for as long as I can remember.'"

The wonderful thing about teaching your dog the value of hard work is she's already pre-programmed for it. It's inside her already, just waiting, yearning to be drawn out. When she's just a young puppy, her hard work may consist of more basic things like following you on short walks, accepting handling by people, waiting patiently before she's given her food, and playing games that teach her how to use her mouth appropriately. Similar to children, as your pup grows older, she needs to shoulder more responsibility. Gradually, the walks become longer and you might incorporate specific tasks, like obedience work. Ask her to work harder and longer as she matures, and always make sure to balance the work with play, affection, and other rewards *at the end* of her workday.

In addition to basic activities, you'll want to explore some specific working tasks that are challenging and fun for her. This can be anything from agility to search-and-rescue work. A dog that earns what she gets has a sense of confidence that can only come from working hard to earn her keep. Work is not something to be dreaded or avoided; it's something to be cherished and highly valued, and you are the one who has the opportunity to share that wonderful gift with her.

Scaredy Dog

So what if your dog has access to the things she needs in life, enjoys her training, knows how to work, enjoys her earned freedoms, but is occasionally plagued by fear? Fears and phobias markedly affect the lives of many of our dogs, and while the intricacy of their causes and treatments are well beyond the scope of this chapter, we will touch on some key tenets to aid our understanding of how they can be resolved.

Well-established fears and phobias are usually remedied by using one of the following modalities: systematic desensitization or flooding. They are both useful techniques designed to eliminate debilitating fear responses. Systematic desensitization is a stepped process of exposing a dog to a feared stimulus until her panic subsides. As the name implies, this process is methodical, beginning with low levels of exposure and building up over time to more intense encounters with the feared stimulus.

For a dog prone to panicking when she hears gunshots, you might begin by exposing her to gunfire-type sounds, like playing movies with shootout scenes or hunting shows at very low volume during the day. Initially the sound would need to be turned down so low that it is hard for her to even hear it, which would prevent any concern from developing. The next day, you might have the same sounds playing on the TV but at one volume level higher. Proceed like this, increasing the volume level each day by one or two notches over the course of a couple weeks until the volume is on high and your dog exhibits no signs of stress or fear toward the noises whatsoever.

Once she's comfortable with that, have a family member fire a cap gun out in the backyard (at a good distance so that the volume of the gun firing is very low) while your dog hangs out with you inside the house. Over the course of several days or even weeks, gradually move your dog closer to the backyard until she's in closer proximity as the gun is going off.

After this process is complete, begin to expose her to actual gunfire sounds at a great distance (and thus at low volume). As before, *gradually* expose her to the gunfire at closer distances. If you do this properly, she will remain reasonably comfortable throughout the process. She will experience low levels of stress spread out over a long period of time (unlike flooding, which induces high levels of stress but is over with very quickly). Through proper use of systematic desensitization, you could cure her debilitating phobia, or at least reduce it to a mild level of fear.

It is critical to ensure that the process is not rushed, that it's always done in baby steps. In short, it begins with a very mild form of the triggering stimulus presented at levels below the threshold of her fearful response, and eventually builds to the actual stimulus itself, thus desensitizing her over time. The effectiveness of the systematic desensitization process can also be enhanced by pairing the feared stimulus with things she already has a positive association with like dog treats, playing tug, etc.

Flooding is another very useful technique in the treatment of phobias. It has the same aim as systematic desensitization: to reduce the dog's overreaction to a stimulus. In flooding, the dog is presented with the stimulus that induces panic, but unlike systematic desensitization, which exposes her to the stimulus in many gradual steps, flooding jumps to full exposure of it. The dog being treated is exposed to the panic-triggering stimulus in its full-blown state and comes out the other side far more relaxed when she realizes the world didn't end. She will have confronted her worst fear and realized that it wasn't such a big deal after all. Flooding can cure a phobia very quickly and in some cases within a single session.

For a dog that panics (becomes excessively defensive and snarly) whenever she sees new dogs on leash, flooding might involve exposing her to an overwhelming number of dogs by taking her to a local dog-friendly event at the park (breed exhibit, dog product fair, etc.), where she cannot run away because dogs are being walked by their owners everywhere around her. She might initially panic, but by staying with the triggering stimulus, her brain would be so overloaded that it might be forced to let go of her old panic response and find a new, more adaptive one. By giving the brain too much to handle at one time (essentially a form of circuit overload), it resets and finds an adaptive new meaning.

It is important to note that flooding is a particularly risky technique because, while it is intended to desensitize a dog to a stimulus, if something goes wrong in the process, it can actually further sensitize her to it. Flooding properly and safely requires a tremendous amount of skill and expertise. For these reasons, using a powerful tool like flooding should be performed only with the help of an experienced professional.

Some training professionals are opposed to the use of flooding because it subjects a dog to acute stress. While this is an understandable stance to take, it might be helpful to think of it in a different light. If you have to remove a Band-Aid that's stuck to your skin, would you rather pull it off fast or slow? Flooding would be the equivalent of removing it quickly, while systematic desensitization would be the slow approach. Pulling it off quickly produces a sensation that is momentarily intense but is over quickly. Pulling it off slow hurts less in the moment but is sustained over a longer period of time.

Your Greatest Assets

We but mirror the world. All the tendencies present in the outer world are to be found in the world of our body. If we could change ourselves, the tendencies in the world would also change. As a man changes his own nature, so does the attitude of the world change towards him. This is the divine mystery supreme. A wonderful thing it is and the source of our happiness. We need not wait to see what others do.

Mahatma Gandhi

The two greatest assets we possess as humans that allow us to create positive change in ourselves and the world around us are our imaginations and intentionality. The responsibility lies with each of us as individuals to first recognize that all real change begins on the inside and has a ripple effect on everything we influence, especially our dogs. In a sense, we create our outer worlds based upon our ability to harness our creative faculties, and then translate our inner imaginings into tangible, outward effects. Intentionality, a purposeful dedication of one's attention and resources to create a desired tangible result, is the bridge between ideas and outward effects, between the unseen and the seen. After all, every man-made creation was at one time nothing more than an idea in somebody's mind. Take a minute-long break from your reading to examine your surroundings and the myriad man-made creations around you right now. Now consider that each of those things was at one time only an idea in someone's mind, and none of it existed outwardly. The human mind has extensive creative aptitude, and when we are aware of the way we combine our imaginations with intentionality to guide the creation of our worlds, we can thoughtfully direct our efforts and be more conscious about what we are developing.

Worry is an example of the misuse of creative faculties. For example, a person imagines a negative scenario and dedicates her attention to the imagined, albeit undesirable, outcome. Sure enough, the very thing she feared comes to pass. I have often seen the powerful negative effects worry can have in the context of pack work: someone walks into my behavior center with a balanced group of dogs, and the next thing I know, the dogs are "bickering" with one another. Noticing this, I'll often ask the person what she was thinking about when she first came into the area. The reply is often something like, "I was kind of afraid and kept wondering what would happen if a fight broke out."

Conversely, I have witnessed other people enter the same scenario, but instead of the dogs breaking into conflict, the pack stayed calm and stable. When I'd ask that person what she was thinking about, I'd hear something like, "I kept thinking about how well the dogs were getting along and how peaceful it felt." Both of these examples illustrate the power of imagination and intentionality. While one person used these abilities to manifest her own worst-case scenario, the other person produced peace.

These qualities give us the power to change our outer worlds by the conduct of our inner worlds. We can construct a mental picture and form an intention of a desired result and then go on to make it a reality. Our dogs are limited in their creativity in the sense that they don't possess the robust intellectual capabilities to apply intentionality in the same way we can. Instead, they utilize intuition and the knowledge gained from past experiences to make decisions in the present.

While dogs have a leg up on us in terms of their natural tendency to approach life more intuitively, we have a leg up in the intellectual department. Despite the fact that we are often tripped up by our intellect, we must absolutely harness it if we are to maximize our potential. The way we direct and apply our intellectual abilities will determine, to a large extent, the results we get. We must learn *how*, and just as important *when*, to use our minds, striving to strike a proper balance between our intuitive and intellectual selves.

Can Fear Be Managed?

The answer to this question is emphatically no. Fear cannot be managed. It is a reality of the human condition. What can be managed is the way you use your mind and direct your attention. The difference between top performers in any field and those who always seem to barely make it through lies in the way they utilize their own faculties; namely, their minds and what they choose to focus their attention on.

How do you respond to situations that produce fear? Do you avoid them? Do you run from them? Do you try to distract yourself? Do you face them head-on? The first thing to realize is that everyone is subject to the same feelings. I am often asked how I work with aggressive dogs without being afraid. That someone would even ask the question tells me they don't understand that I'm just like they are. Fear creeps up in my mind about the work I do with dogs. The difference lies in the way I think about it. First, I don't think of it as a negative thing. Fear can keep us grounded and remind us of the reality of dangerous situations. It would be a problem to have no aversion to danger, and calamity would swiftly befall us because of the carelessness with which we would engage dangerous situations.

Fear in proper perspective becomes our helper. It helps us make good, self-preservation decisions. The key is to know what we're dealing with. The source of our angst is the first thing that needs to be identified, so with that first prickle of fear, we should ask, "Where is this coming from?" We need to learn to decipher between those subtle, uneasy feelings that can be attributed to intuition and those that are brought on by our imaginations. If we determine a fear to be intuitive in nature, we should always listen to it and disengage from the situation.

Let's say you take your dog to the dog park one day. As you are driving there, you feel a sudden uneasiness about it, a feeling that you shouldn't go. Maybe you make it all the way to the park, even approach the fence and scan the area. Everything looks normal, the dogs inside seem friendly enough, and your pup is wagging her tail. Logically, everything seems perfectly in order, but something feels off, so you decide to walk your dog instead of entering the park. That's a good decision. It's also one most people won't make because they're so used to analyzing and trying to make sense of things, they don't know how to listen to their gut.

Each of us has felt our intuition kick in at various junctures in our lives. I would guess that your experience has been similar to mine: Every time I ignored that quiet voice inside, I ended up regretting it later; and every time I listened to it, things worked out pretty well. The difficult thing about trusting intuition is that logic will always raise objections to it. It is easy to let our intellectual side win that battle and launch us into situations that we have no business being in. We can talk ourselves right out of wise, intuitive decisions by examining them in the light of "reason." In his brilliant book, *The Gift of Fear*, Gavin de Becker shares the following insight:

> Intuition is always learning, and though it may occasionally send a signal that turns out to be less than urgent, everything it communicates to you is meaningful. Unlike worry, it will not waste your time. Intuition might send any of several messengers to get your attention, and because they differ according to urgency, it is good to know the ranking. The intuitive signal of the highest order, the one with greatest urgency, is fear; accordingly, it should always be listened to... The next level is apprehension, then suspicion, then hesitation, doubt, gut feelings, hunches and curiosity.[2]

Ego is the other adversary intuition faces. It is always grasping for the selfish. If the ego had a slogan it would be "Lookin' out for number one" (although, ironically, it isn't ever looking out for your best interests because it seeks only to strengthen itself). It is the agent of human pride and is conniving and surprisingly subtle most of the time. Our scheming egos would have us believe that it's okay to do certain things to preserve our sense of self-importance. It's what drives us to keep up with the Joneses and do things to impress people that we don't even like, despite the detrimental effects such things have on our lives.

I had a very wise man once give me the following sage advice: "Always check your motives." When I began examining my motives driving certain things I said, I noticed that my ego had many cleaver disguises: "It isn't fair" (translation: I feel slighted and I am entitled to this); "Who does she think she is?" (translation: I am superior to some people and inferior to others; I don't like feeling inferior); "I'm not sure I want to be in charge of that" (translation: I'm afraid I might fail, be exposed, and look silly in front of others). Abraham Lincoln said something during his presidency that was so telling of his character and underscores the significance of staying true to ourselves and not getting derailed by our egos: "I desire so to conduct the affairs of this administration that if at the end, when I come to lay down the reins of power, I have lost every other friend on earth, I shall at least have one friend left, and that friend shall be down inside of me."

You will know you're growing in your awareness when you start to realize that your ego is at war with your highest potential and your true self, sabotaging it at every turn. It will cause you to disregard well-founded intuitive feedback and get you into negative situations with other people. Don't get caught in this trap. The ego is the root of almost every argument we have with those we love. It seeks to strengthen itself through the preservation and bolstering of pride with no regard for others or even our own well-being because it values self-importance over love and truth.

The weapons we have against the ego are twofold: 1) awareness, which causes us to be vigilant and identify when the ego is grasping for control; and 2) understanding who we are and being at total peace with ourselves, which keeps us grounded so we don't need external achievements to validate us. When we have these two weapons locked in place, we can ward off the onslaughts of the ego and listen to our gut. Once we develop trust in ourselves and our intuitive natures, we can say no to things like skiing that last run with our friends when intuition says "don't" but our intellectual justifications carry on about how we still feel fine and our internal dialogue is screaming, *If you don't do this run, you're going to look like a flake! Just do it!*

So then, what if you are experiencing anxiety and have ruled out your intuition as the cause? The path you will take to address this kind of fear leads in another direction altogether. Intellectual fear *cannot* always be trusted. You must put it through investigative lines of questioning. Test the soundness of such reservations through objective examination by clarifying your concerns, separating them from your emotions, and making well-informed choices based on concrete information about the inherent risks within a given situation.

You may be wondering how to differentiate between intellectual and intuitive fear. Intellectual fear will be thought driven. In other words, as you approach a situation and fear presents itself, you will experience a cacophony of internal dialogue and mental chatter. This is typically accompanied by fearful recollections/imagined scenarios. This process escalates your trepidation and feels much different than the inklings of intuition.

Let me give a couple examples to illustrate the difference. The very day I was writing about trusting intuitive fears, I had a feeling (not any kind of logical thought sequence) that I shouldn't put my personal dogs out with the pack at my center that day. As most of us do, I let my mind talk me into putting them out anyway, rationalizing that my dogs needed to go out to potty (although I could have just as easily walked them outside to a grassy area on leash) and that it didn't make any sense not to put them out. After all, it was a beautiful day and the other dogs that were present were good buddies with my dogs. As is the case anytime intuition is ignored, it didn't work out so well. I let my dogs out with the pack and within a couple minutes, a bee stung my youngest dog on her paw. Although it was intellectually a good idea to put my dogs out with the pack, in reality it was a poor decision, per my intuition and the ensuing negative outcome.

Intuitive fear starts as a subtle urging, and most often no obvious external evidence supports it. Intellectual fear, on the other hand, might look something like this: You go to a friend's house, and after you greet her at the door and exchange pleasantries, you step into her living room and see a huge dog you've never met before sitting on a dog bed next to her couch. Your friend explains that she's pet sitting for a coworker and calls the dog over to say hi. The pure size of the dog, coupled with her resemblance to a dog of a family friend that bit you as a kid makes you very nervous. You say hello to the dog to be polite, but you are scared the whole time and avoid the dog as much as possible after that.

Throughout your entire visit you are preoccupied by your fear that the dog might become aggressive. You are distracted as you talk to your friend, because you keep picturing the incident you experienced as a child. Your mind is consumed by thoughts about how much of a behemoth the dog is, and you keep wondering what would happen if she attacked you. This type of fear is intellectual and involves a lot of mental murmuring. It also tends to escalate your mind to higher levels of anxiety because your negative imagination spirals out of control and reinforces the fear.

In a case like this, when you identify intellectual fear, have a curious attitude and ask yourself some questions. Observe your internal dialogue—all the reasons your mind tells you to be afraid—and consider whether or not the fear is justified. Sometimes this is easier to do after an incident, when you have more time to evaluate the experience. In this example, some of your internal dialogue might have revolved around the fact that the dog looked like the one that bit you as a kid. Is that a valid reason to be concerned? No. While it's understandable that such a scenario would trigger a fearful response in you, you determine that it's not a justified concern; the way a dog looks doesn't have anything to do with her actual behavior.

One of your other thoughts about the dog is related to her size. Again, you identify that this is completely unrelated to whether a dog is aggressive or not and is therefore not useful in assessing the safety of the situation. Your mind then jumps in with an objection about the breed of the dog. You quickly identify that this thought is not helpful either. You remind yourself that there are no aggressive or friendly breeds, only aggressive or friendly individual dogs. Right before the dog came over to visit you, you also created a mental image of her rushing you aggressively; you pre-played a possible negative scenario that elevated your angst about her. You pictured the hair up on the back of her neck and imagined her flashing her teeth at you while she snarled menacingly. In retrospect, all of your internal dialogue and visualizing created a purely fictional scenario—and fear.

In a situation like this, the first thing to do is consult your intuition and stay open to any signals it might give you along the way. Remember, your intuition can advise you about unsafe situations even if everything looks fine on the surface. As far as utilizing your intellect, first activate your awareness of what's happening in the situation right now. Imagining what *could* happen only diverts your attention away from the reality of the situation that is unfolding. You need every bit of your mental energy available to you to assess the situation. So whenever you notice negative internal dialogue and visualizations activating in your mind, consciously stop yourself by not-doing and bring your attention back to the present by engaging your senses. Because the body can function only in the now, which is exactly where your mind needs to be to gather information, it is where you must send your attention whenever you encounter fear.

Breathing is the most essential tool you possess in accomplishing this, because it is the great bridge between the mind and the body. Both your conscious and subconscious mind can control your breathing. It can be voluntarily or involuntarily controlled, so by bringing it back under conscious control, you are bringing attention to the present.

Focus on what you can *see* by using your eyes to capture every possible detail in your field of view. Notice any scents. Have a general awareness of your body and how you *feel*, and engage your kinesthetic senses, such as touch. Pay attention to internal processes, like your heart rate. What about your muscles? Are any areas of your body particularly tense? Notice the way you move and position your body. Is your posture upright and open, or slumped and concave? Employing your senses in this manner makes more of your attention immediately available to you, and thus makes you more effective at gauging, and engaging, the present situation.

Don't let your thoughts run away with your attention. Your insecurities and worries can tell you nothing about whether you should listen to a particular fear, but your God-given senses can tell you everything you need to know if you utilize them properly. They will keep you from missing important details and help you stay safe. Your mantra for bringing attention to the moment should be: Breathe-See-Feel, Breathe-See-Feel, Breathe-See-Feel . . . This is useful in *any* situation when you begin to feel helplessly caught up and swept away by the mental sludge of fear, worry, insecurity, doubt, and anxiety.

Once you've gathered as much objective information as possible about a scenario, you can pull it all together and make a decision about whether or not to trust an intellectual fear. The act of stepping back and observing a situation for what it is and then systematically evaluating it will oftentimes diffuse intellectual fears completely. Generally, we are fearful because of the unknown—not because of a legitimate concern. And if we find there's nothing to fear, we should move forward unreservedly with the single-minded purpose of passionately applying our skills, time, and attention to the task at hand.

Having a detailed mental game plan and strategy for dealing with fear and the demands of the present gives you a decided psychological advantage, so use these tools every day, especially when the stakes are high! Athletes experiencing the rigorous demands and inevitable stressors of vigorous physical activity can benefit from this kind of mental construct, as can business people, parents, performing artists—anyone willing to recognize its value and utilize it. Professional athletes, in particular, are forced to develop psychological stamina and resiliency because their livelihoods are dependent upon it, and the very best athletes are those who are most precise in how they apply their physical and mental resources, especially during competition.

Thoughtful and thorough evaluation of situations we face is integral to determining if our intellectual fears are justified.

This requires deliberate, focused attention and seamless integration of their minds and bodies. The athlete who chokes has not mastered her own mind, while the athlete who stands atop the podium has learned to process her stress and fears by applying her attention with precision.

Can Stress and Panic Be Managed?

Stress, like fear, cannot be managed; it just is. Stress is a fact of life. You deal with it by setting up your life in a way that is balanced. Just like with fear, bringing your attention to the present moment and keeping it there is essential to dealing with stress effectively.

Panic, as you may have guessed, is not manageable either. It is a "reflexive" reaction that is closely related to the sympathetic nervous system, which activates fight-or-flight responses. It is highly undesirable (unlike fear and stress, which are both adaptive responses) because it is essentially fear run amok. Once you are in a state of panic, your rational abilities go out the window. If this state had a welcome sign, it might read: WELCOME TO PANIC: WHERE PANDEMONIUM RULES AND THERE'S NO ROOM FOR COMMON SENSE. POPULATION: 1.

Panic is the cousin of another purely reactionary state: rage. Panic and rage are two *very* stupid, inbred relatives that both fell off the ugly tree and hit every branch on the way down. Rage is anger out of control, while panic is fear out of control. And just as a person in a rage can no longer access her rational thought centers until the anger subsides, a person in panic mode is no longer in control of her mind, either. So we have two issues with respect to panic we should explore: How to avoid it, and how to overcome it.

The answer to avoiding panic lies in becoming aware of what scenarios provoke a panicked response. Once you are aware of what is triggering the panic, you can simply avoid the trigger. Obviously, this does not solve the problem but is the most prudent option in many cases, because continued rehearsal of panicked responses can make you more susceptible to future instances of it.

As an example, let's say in college you went skydiving for fun and had a full-blown panic attack. In the future, you can bypass the trigger by simply avoiding skydiving; after all, there's no need to press the issue. However, if your lifelong dream is to be a paratrooper, you will need to overcome that panic to realize your dream. Whether to avoid or overcome panic is a matter of identifying if it will hold you back from pursuing your purpose or interfere with your life. If you decide that it is holding you back from what you value, you will need to create a plan for overcoming it.

Please note: Should you choose to address panic, whether in yourself or in your dog, you should immediately enlist the help of a professional. Because panic is such an intensely powerful state of mind, any mistakes in the treatment process can have severe consequences. Paying the price for professional help is far less than paying the price of lifelong psychological trauma. In some cases, traditional or alternative medicine may also be necessary components in the treatment process. For people, this might require team-tackling the problem by enlisting both a therapist and a psychiatrist, or a psychologist and an acupuncturist . . . the possibilities are endless. The key is to find the right combination based on the individual. If it is your dog needs to overcome panic, working in collaboration with your veterinarian and dog behavior professional is a wise option.

Treating Panic

A crucial step toward overcoming panic is leading a balanced life. When you are in balance, you're less susceptible to expressing severe psychological responses. It's why people aren't as vulnerable to losing their temper if they are spiritually, physically, and psychologically stable. Having balance provides good psychological immunity. Once that psychological "immune system" becomes compromised, however, you will have less protection against the adversaries of emotional health. So make sure to set yourself up for success by establishing and maintaining balance. *Then* you can move on to treating panic via some form of systematic desensitization or flooding.

Let's take an example of a person who goes to see a therapist to treat her phobia of spiders, and the therapist decides to use systematic desensitization to treat her. During the first sessions, the therapist could show the patient cartoon drawings of spiders from children's books, or simply ask her to picture a small cartoon spider in her mind. Later sessions might include having the patient look at real spiders from across the room, eventually moving to the point of having the patient relax on a chair while a spider is placed on a table right next to her. If the patient is desensitized to spiders in a thoughtful and gradual way and the therapist can help her maintain relative relaxation (through progressive muscle relaxation techniques, for example), her phobia is likely to disappear, or at least its intensity reduced so that spiders elicit only a mild level of anxiety.

Treating panic with flooding could be performed, for example, with an individual who panics when she encounters butterflies. To help her past this, a skilled and experienced professional could take her to a butterfly exhibit as the setting for her treatment. If the patient trusts her therapist and is willing to walk into the room with hundreds of butterflies, the therapist can take her through the experience and expose her to her greatest fear, helping her face it instead of running away or avoiding it, until she moves through the panic response and ultimately experiences calm in the midst of the storm. Flooding can be especially helpful in situations where systematic desensitization has produced no positive results, progress has plateaued, or the fear seems to be strengthening over time.

Intuition for People

There is no logical way to the discovery of these elemental laws. There is only the way of intuition, which is helped by a feeling for the order lying behind the appearance.

Albert Einstein

Cease trying to work everything out with your minds. It will get you nowhere. Live by intuition and inspiration and let your whole life be revelation.

Eileen Caddy

Over the course of your career, you may recall a time when someone outside your line of work gave you feedback about a problem you had been struggling to solve, and her suggestion made complete sense, something you had never considered. She was able to do it so effortlessly because she was not limited by the constraints of traditional and intellectually based thinking. She found a simple, common-sense, and intuitive solution. It proves that even if you are an expert in a subject, over-intellectualizing stifles progress and keeps you from finding answers that are readily available if you would only tap into your intuition. Men are particularly guilty of this. We won't do something if it doesn't make any sense to us. What drives this notion is a belief system that says if something isn't backed by flawless logic, it couldn't possibly have any substantive value. Haven't you found, though, that the greatest breakthroughs and blessings in life do not follow a logical road map?

For a long time, professionally working with dogs made absolutely no logical sense to me, which is why I dismissed the idea for so long. If it wasn't for my wife's encouragement and intuition about pursuing it, I would be working hard in some other line of work, stressed out, unfulfilled, and squandering my greatest gifts. I'd have a corporate gig, probably with great pay and benefits and still be helping out some folks with their dogs on the side for free; all of which "makes more sense" but doesn't quite measure up in the soul department. It's such a blessing to have my work aligned with my purpose. It is very satisfying.

If you figure that most of us spend the first eighteen to twenty-two years (or more) of our lives in educational institutions where intellectual capacity is highly esteemed and allows us to reach the upper echelons, is it any wonder we've lost touch with our intuitive side? Interestingly enough, people considered masters in their respective fields are all highly intuitive, while their intellectual aptitudes vary widely. IQ level isn't the limiting factor everyone seems to think it is for those who want to pursue excellence.

Statistically, successful people are all over the board in terms of their intelligence. From legendary sports figures to top artists and business moguls, *intuition* is the great separator of people, guiding masterful performances and birthing new creations and creative solutions. It allows people to lead lives of significance and separates those who display an almost superhuman knack for creating out-of-this-world results from those with high levels of skill who never seem to get ahead. Don't get me wrong; skill plays an important role and it must be present, but applying our know-how without the guidance of our intuition never produces world-class results.

Great men and women may not be consciously aware of it, but they are consistently functioning in the intuitive realm, and watching them work leaves the rest of us scratching our heads, asking, "How did they do that?" It guides the great artist's hand that seems to be directed by an invisible force; the parent who effortlessly comforts an inconsolable child; and the coach who brings out the absolute best in her athletes. Intuition in action inspires people. It is the magical force that connects and focuses every bit of our talent and ability at the right time at the right place for the right purpose. It transcends logic, which is why it can be so difficult for people who use it well to explain exactly *how* they did something. While some people think of intuition as being an innately psychological/subconscious process, others identify it as a physical or even spiritual one. I believe it to be a synthesis of all three. Regardless of the mechanisms behind it, however, intuition is the most reliable tool we have to help us make good decisions and experience peak performances.

Intuition is a feeling we have about a thing or situation as opposed to a rational thought process. Yet we find that it is anything but far-fetched and fanciful when we simply examine the fruit it bears. It is always urging us, silently, subtly, and steadfastly, to make superb decisions. Over two thousand years ago, Jesus pointed out "A good tree can't produce bad fruit, and a bad tree can't produce good fruit" (Luke 6:43), so here's the acid test: If to this point you've depended on your intellect and it's gotten you to exactly where you want to be in life, continue to rely on it exclusively. If, however, you have fallen prey to constant struggles in life despite your hard work and best efforts, be open to the idea of change. It isn't your job to go out and find intuition; it is simply to learn to hear its call and to trust it. And if your intuition consistently produces good fruit, thereby demonstrating it is a reliable guide, wouldn't it be wise to listen? Betting on your intuition, even when logic contradicts it, will require faith on your part, obliging you to act accordingly despite the lack of tangible "proof" we humans always want to see before we believe in something. The reality is that the proof comes *after* we act on intuition.

One morning several weeks ago I woke up, brushed my teeth, and prepared for the day. I was proud of myself for getting all my clothes set out the night before so I didn't have to wander around in the dark, stubbing toes as I searched for them. As I was getting dressed, I had this feeling that I didn't need to wear my long johns or wool socks. *That's really odd*, I thought. I checked the outside temperature. It was a scorching nine degrees below zero. I was skeptical at this point, almost annoyed, as I put on my cotton socks and jeans. How could I possibly *not* need long johns and warm wool socks on such a day as this? I soon got my answer when my beautiful wife left for work, only to walk right back through the front door a few minutes later. Her car wouldn't start. We went out front, got the jumper cables and . . . her car hood was frozen shut. Awesome. That particular day she had some important deadlines and had to be at work, so she ended up taking my Jeep and I stayed home—in my cotton socks and jeans.

Like anything else, intuition must be intentionally developed. Any time we have that courtly gut feeling about something and disregard it, we deny intuition its rightful place in our lives and weaken it. But every time we trust the subtle urging of intuition and act on it, we validate its place in our lives and nurture that all-important side of ourselves. We need both sides, intellectual and intuitive, working in tandem. Nearly all of us have an intellectual bent, so we must invest extra time and devote special attention to growing trust and reliance on our intuition in order to strike a balance.

Intuition flows and is effortless. It happens when you stop thinking. It's in the space between your thoughts. It is a feeling and not a thought at all, free of preconceptions, personal agendas, and logic. It is your purest and wisest advisor. Have reverence for it. It sees a way, even when you feel lost and uncertain. It will guide you to a place of peace and give you rest, but you must follow its lead and learn to trust in it.

Response-Ability for People

You can't moan and lead at the same time.
John Maxwell

What began as an experiment in a Dutch town has caught on in recent years, and an increasing number of locales throughout Europe have adopted it. It has resulted in significant increases in traffic safety, creating remarkable reductions in collisions, pedestrian deaths, and other traffic-related incidents. With all of the mind-blowing technological advances, it was bound to happen sooner or later, right? Can you guess what measures created such a powerful effect? The answer may surprise you. The experiment involved the removal of nearly all traffic signs, lights, speed limits, and lane markers.

Hans Monderman, the Dutch engineer who pioneered the approach, explained that it leads to greater awareness of surroundings by forcing motorists to take personal responsibility for their safety, instead of relying on road signs to somehow do it for them. Isn't it interesting that removing the so-called "traffic safety" measures actually resulted in far greater public safety on the roads? Once the safeguards were pulled off the street, the drivers, bikers, and pedestrians became acutely aware of the need to pay attention and protect their own well-being.

Taking responsibility for your personal safety is the best measure you can take to avoid calamity. If another motorist isn't following the rules of the road, it is still your responsibility to be aware of situations as they unfold around you. Just because there's a road sign doesn't mean other people will always see it or obey it. And if you are driving one day and make a left turn at an intersection because you have the right-of-way (assuming that you are in the clear) and someone plows into the side of your car and kills you, you may not have been at "fault" legally, but you're still dead, which is a very inconvenient and avoidable circumstance.

We are living in a day when people will do almost anything to shirk responsibility. Just look at the rising tide of lawsuits. People lose their jobs and sue their former employers; or trip on their neighbor's driveway, break their hip, and then sue their neighbor because their property is "dangerous." A disturbing trend is running rampant in our society: of moving away from personal responsibility toward casting blame on other people, situations, family background, companies, politicians, the government, ad infinitum. . . . It's critically important to recognize that assigning blame renders you powerless as you gradually relinquish more and more control of your life to other people and circumstances. It's a surrender of your influence and a nasty habit to get into.

Someone who does not embrace personal responsibility often demonstrates what Donald Trump and Robert Kiyosaki refer to as an "entitlement mentality." In their book *Why We Want You to Be Rich*, they discuss the growing tendency for people to believe they are somehow entitled to be taken care of by someone or something else, that life should be fair, and that society owes them something. It is a destructive mental attitude becoming increasingly prevalent in our culture that renders people powerless—angry and indignant for sure, but powerless. We are wise not to trade power for an entitlement mentality. The following quote from their book is specific to the subject of finances, but the concept holds true and has important implications across many areas of life.

> The best way to solve the problem of bad financial results is to change our thoughts—to start thinking like rich people rather than poor and middle-class people. That means losing the entitlement mentality—whether you are a military officer, government worker, school teacher, employee or just poor. If we do not stop expecting the government to take care of us, we will continue to have the same results—a bankrupt nation filled with well-educated but financially needy people.[3]

I've met successful people from all walks of life, and they are tremendously diverse in terms of their personal histories and how they do things. They can be young or old or from one place or another. Some are high energy and others are surprisingly laid-back. It's difficult, if not downright impossible, to say that they all share a common trait or characteristic, but I have noticed one thing that *none* of them have: the mentality of a victim. Some of them have endured tremendous hardships and suffered misfortunes that are difficult for me to comprehend. They may have gone through seasons of questioning why something happened or why someone did them wrong. At the end of the day, however, they are surprisingly resilient and can recognize when they are playing the blame game and snap themselves out of it. They change perspective early and see setbacks as something that happens *for* them instead of *to* them.

Despite the unfairness of any situation, the most successful people possess the ability to rise again, examine how they can take greater responsibility for their lives, and move forward. My choir director in high school, Ron Revier, is a man I greatly admire and consider extremely successful and resilient while significantly impacting the lives of his students and community. He commented on the subject of responsibility to me once when he said, "There are so many things that are out of our control in this life; that's why it's so important to take hold of everything within our control and to do it with excellence." I thought about that for a long time. That really stuck with me. It shifted my thinking and helped me relish the opportunity to take greater responsibility for my life.

Going back to a traffic example, I may not be able to control how other people drive, but I have a surprising amount of control (if I accept responsibility) over many other factors. I can turn down my music so I have greater access to any auditory cues in the environment; I can control the temperature in the car so I am not distracted by being uncomfortably cold or hot; I can control how I use my eyes to be aware of cars, people, and general details of the road conditions; and I can control how I direct my attention so it is focused on the task of driving. I could go on and on, but you get the idea. A great many things are within our control, and each of us has been guilty at one time or another of giving up control and expecting someone else to shoulder the burden. We may have even done this unconsciously over a long period of time, but if we want to maximize our influence over our own lives, we must seize the opportunity to reclaim that responsibility.

Let's look at another example. If an employee gets passed up for a promotion she was next in line for, she will naturally be disappointed for a time, but to linger in self-pity would be a mistake. For a warrior to go down the path of blaming her disappointments on her coworker who "sabotaged" her, or her boss who never appreciates how hard she works, or office politics would only displace responsibility, giving away her power— something a warrior can never afford to do. Instead, she would recognize that she doesn't have control over the decisions other people make and the actions they take. If her coworker sabotaged her, that is her coworker's problem. To be angry and linger in unforgiveness would only drain her energy and the influence she has in the situation. Better not to take it personally and choose to forgive. She knows that power cannot be taken away, only *given* away, and she is not about to give it to her coworker by allowing bitterness to take hold of her. If her boss doesn't appreciate how hard she works, and office politics has been standing in her way, to say that it's other people's fault she didn't get the promotion, even if it's true, is a helpless position. A warrior would never back herself into a corner like that.

What should she do instead of bemoaning the unfairness of the situation? She has several viable possibilities and can choose any number of them to take responsibility and reclaim power, as long as they consist of two things: 1) looking inward and 2) identifying ways she can change her approach. She would want to isolate exactly what her coworker did that qualifies as "sabotage" and then go about identifying ways she may have contributed to the issue. Perhaps she overheard the person speaking poorly about her to someone in management. She can't control what was said, and she can't control if management believed what was said. The next time it occurs, however, she could choose to speak up and confront the situation instead of staying quiet and seething with anger.

Another possibility would be to seek out every possible opportunity in the future to express genuine praise for her coworkers. She can do this in meetings where she can share credit for projects that are running smoothly, at lunch with other people from the office, or in private meetings with members of management. This way she is becoming the change that she would like to see in the office. She is setting the example for others to follow and could result in some unintended positive repercussions. Suppose the very person who bad-mouthed her found out about the nice things being said about her to others. Being "killed with kindness," she might change her mind and even be instrumental in helping her get a promotion in the future.

Will making these changes in any way ensure that no one sabotages her again? Nope. It just ensures that she's assuming her responsibility for the situation and making a positive change in her own life. And in her time spent reflecting, let's say she identified numerous other courses of action she can take to position herself better for future promotions. One includes dressing the part, wearing clothing more suited to the position she wants rather than the one she currently has. She also discovers management training courses being offered at the local community college. Finances are tight so she approaches her boss about the possibility of tuition reimbursement, explaining that she is more than willing to take an online course on her own time that will boost her productivity and effectiveness at work if he can help her pay for it through the company. She has also become proactive about being a greater contributor at work through volunteering to help with multiple projects and initiatives that are central to the mission of the company.

She has endless ways of taking greater responsibility for her career. The obvious question at this point becomes "What if she does all these things and gets passed up for the next promotion, too?" It doesn't matter. The issue is one of taking responsibility for what she can control, not maintaining an outcome. Besides, making herself a better employee is something she will carry with her, a benefit that will make her more valuable to any company she works for in the future. It will expand her skills and perhaps position her to ultimately accept a better job at a different company, something she never would have gotten had she not been willing to make changes. The moral of the story is that by adopting a personal responsibility mentality instead of an entitlement mentality, when a person experiences a setback, she naturally reflects on ways she can learn from the situation and always comes through it a stronger, more powerful person.

When working with your dog, this means recognizing what you can control and what you cannot. You cannot control the things your dog chooses to do; you have to decide to let go of that. You *can* control the way you eat (so you are well-nourished), the way you think (so you are well-adjusted), and the choices you make about your attitude and energy so you can be a stable leader for your dog. You can also choose to become a better teacher.

I like to tell clients I am working with to "always be reinforcing." The truth is we are reinforcing our dogs at all times regardless of whether or not we are doing it on purpose. When your dog comes up to you for the fifth time in ten minutes and jams her nose under your arm to demand that you pet her and you unconsciously begin to scratch her head, you are inadvertently reinforcing that pushy "pet me *now*" behavior. So "always be reinforcing" is a good reminder to be responsible for and intentional about your reinforcement throughout the day.

People normally want concise answers and a cut-and-dried, three-step plan to follow, whether they are planning their financial futures or settling on a training protocol for their dogs. Then they can just follow it and if the plan doesn't work, they have something or someone else to blame. We should seek expert advice and get guidance, but then we must take ultimate responsibility for our decisions, for our actions, and for being flexible along the way and changing our approach as necessary. The most significant strides we make in life often occur when we cast off old limits, think outside the box, and move forward, fully responsible and resolute with purpose and a curious mind open to exploring new possibilities that cross our paths.

A Final Word about Fear

For God has not given us a spirit of fear, but of power and of love and of a sound mind.

2 Timothy 1:7 (NKJV)

Before we close out this chapter, the subject of fear warrants additional mention due to its notorious ability to seize us in its clutches and immobilize us, robbing us of the fullness of what our lives can ultimately become. In one form or another, fear will *always* stand between a warrior and her destiny. It will stand between her and those things that would bring her the greatest joy.

It is of utmost importance that we recognize that our ability to deal with fear will determine how far we can go in life—whether we rise above obstacles and see our dreams come to pass, or relinquish our dreams and settle for mediocrity. Fear is the gatekeeper and faith is the key to your unlocking our potential, but personal courage and the will to act and step through the door is an individual choice. The fears we face, the faith we activate, and the doors we step through: this is what defines our character.

I often think about my most beloved activities, things I enjoy today that at one time triggered significant fear in me. I used to have a fear of pit bulls as a kid because of stigmas propagated by other people as well as misrepresentation in the media. Now I have three of them and absolutely love them. I used to be deathly afraid of heights but decided I wasn't going to let fear control my life and took up rock climbing, which I enjoy wholeheartedly now. Ever since I was a kid, I would panic in the water if I went swimming; I feared competition and having lots of people watching me. Now I swim competitively and can't imagine not having access to a pool and a team. These things serve as constant reminders to me to press forward and explore my fears and address them with courage, because I know they can hold me back if I allow them to. I'm sure that right now you can think of similar examples in your own life where you powered through to overcome an unnecessary, burdensome fear, and it's made all the difference.

Become a master at dealing with fear and you will take the limits off your life. This is an essential skill and ongoing process in the life of every warrior. Put into practice the knowledge you have gleaned from this chapter. The skill of precisely applying your attention in fearful situations can be learned, so endeavor to develop and refine this indispensable ability. Start with engaging low-level fears and slowly build up to stronger ones as you become more proficient in the art. You will be glad you did, and you'll be well on your way to integrating and balancing the three elements referenced by the quote at the top of this section: the mind ("sound mind"), body ("power"), and spirit ("love"): the subjects of the next three chapters.

Putting It All Together

In examining life with your dog, appreciate your differences and how you can combine them to complement each other. You can support your dog toward her greatest potential by employing your intellectual capacities to plan out reinforcement strategies, and your dog then supports you by reminding you to eliminate worry from your life, focus on the present, and trust your intuition.

Through the continual development of your personal observational skills, you'll start to see things with greater clarity. Your dog is responsible for the choices she makes, and you are responsible for providing her with feedback about those choices. Your dog is no longer given carte blanche access to food and toys and freedom but rather earns such things by working and clearly demonstrating that she can handle higher levels of responsibility. Use your imagination to develop creative solutions and visualize positive outcomes for your dog in her areas of need and then step out with intentionality and work to bring those things to pass.

Having personal discipline in how you direct your mind and thoughts provides numerous practical and positive benefits. You can differentiate between fear that is born from intuition and fear that is of the mind itself. Always trust intuitive fear and withdraw when it tells you to, but be skeptical of intellectual fear and question it with a curious mind. Digging deeper into your intellectual fears involves gathering the maximum amount of objective evidence about a situation and then isolating legitimate risks and fears from imagined ones. If you determine a fear to be imagined, choose to disregard it and move forward.

Weigh the evidence of any intellectual fears you have determined to be justified against your personal knowledge, experience, and applicable skills that would help you proceed through the challenge. If you can accept the consequences inherent with taking a particular risk and you also possess adequate skills to meet the challenge, move forward without hesitation, confronting the situation head-on and applying every ounce of your attention to it. If you find, instead, that the consequences of pursuing a particular course of action are truly dangerous and unacceptable, consciously withdraw.

Also withdraw if you determine that the consequences are acceptable but you lack the necessary skills to navigate the situation with any degree of success. Then take responsibility for cultivating the necessary skills and resources to meet the challenge and revisit it when they are more developed. If the consequences of a course of action are acceptable but you are ambiguous about whether or not you possess the necessary skills to meet the challenge, poke around the edges a little bit. This allows you to do some further investigation into the situation while staying on the periphery and not placing yourself too far into a risky situation. In other words, commit only to exploring the outer edges of the challenge, such that you can withdraw immediately if additional investigation provides new evidence that justifies the fear. On the other hand, you may find it to be an appropriate challenge to pursue after all; you just didn't have enough information on the front-end to make that determination.

Whatever decisions you make, take responsibility for them. Recognize when you are tempted to play the blame game and be aware when your mind seeks responsibility escape routes. Instead of trying to limit personal responsibility, seek to expand its scope so that you can maximize your personal influence over your world. Be honest with yourself about those factors that are outside your realm of control. Be vigilant and avoid getting sucked into the trap of trying to control anything in your life that you can't, because it diverts valuable attention away from areas where you do have influence. If you have an opportunity to take control of something, seize that opportunity. Also, recognize when you cannot bring something within the scope of your control, and let it go. Focus on what you are responsible for so you don't have time to entertain worry. Become masterful at directing your attention toward those things that help you maximize influence over your life.

Practical Application Exercises Related to Intuition, Fear, and Freedom

For Your Dog:

1. Spend thirty minutes with your dog in the morning or evening at home. Without changing the way you normally interact, spend the first fifteen minutes making meticulous mental notes about how you naturally reinforce her for choices she makes. For example, are you missing opportunities to reward her when she's being well-behaved (like waiting patiently on her bed while you talk on the phone)? Does she exhibit certain behaviors you need to discourage, such as hovering around your feet while you are cooking, or barking in the backyard at the children playing next door? Have you been petting her to "calm her down" when she growls at something she doesn't like, instead of waiting until she relaxes to give her affection? Do you give her a treat when she sits or lies down on command to encourage her?
Spend the last fifteen minutes being highly intentional about your reinforcement. Make any necessary adjustments to the feedback you have been giving her. Note any differences in her responses and resolve to be more conscientious about your reinforcement for the rest of the week.

2. Take a full day if possible, but not less than a half day, to work with your dog. You'll need to dedicate a short block of time the night before so you can sit down and lay out a schedule for the following day. The idea is to plan very specific working tasks you will assign to your dog. While taking into account her current physical and psychological conditioning levels, create a challenging yet realistic day of

work that will require a concerted effort on your dog's part to complete. You will also need to be careful to provide her with sufficient rest, relaxation, and rewards to compensate her for her efforts. Make sure to be thoughtful in planning your day, and pick activities appropriate for you and your dog. Below is an example of what your "work" day might look like.

7:00–9:30 AM Focused hiking on mountain trail
9:30–10:00 AM Food, water, and relaxation time
10:00–11:00 AM Drive home
11:00–12:00 PM Lunch and nap time
12:00–12:30 PM Drive to local lake
12:30–1:30 PM Bring out her favorite floating toy, show it to her, and let her smell it. Have her wait in the car while you hide the toy in some brush a distance away. Return to the car and guide her to track the toy's scent until she is able to find it. When she does, throw the toy out into the water and let her retrieve it. Repeat routine three times.
1:30–2:00 PM Snack and relaxation time
2:00–3:00 PM Easy walk around the lake (or neighborhood), interspersed with lots of obedience exercises (sit, down, stay, come, etc.) and a couple opportunities to fetch her toy from the water
3:00–3:30 PM Drive back home
3:30–5:00 PM Nap and relax quietly in her crate
5:30–7:00 PM Go to the dog park and allow her to socialize
7:00–7:30 PM Drive home
7:30–8:00 PM Practice obedience exercises at home
8:00 PM Feeding, water, and relaxation time

Take note of your dog's ability or inability to stay on task (psychological stamina) and perform the work (physical conditioning). Also be very aware of how requiring hard work prior to supplying rewards and freedom affects your dog's demeanor, energy, and attitude. How would you rate her level of fulfillment today versus days when she is asked to do very little but given a lot?

3. When you are out and about with your dog this week, observe how she responds to other people and dogs. Is she normally quite comfortable but shows signs of distrust or nervousness around select individuals? What might her behavior be telling you about the people and dogs she feels comfortable with when compared to her behavior around others that make her feel insecure? Can you identify moments when she appears to be engaging her intuition rather than relying on what her brain is telling her? Work to identify every intuitive decision she makes. This skill takes time and patience to develop. It can be difficult to distinguish between moments of angst or joy that are triggered by specific stimuli from similar responses that are intuitive in nature.

For You:

1. Consider an area of your life that has caused a high level of frustration because things feel out of your control (a situation at work, a strained relationship, the way your dog behaves when your kids' friends are over, etc.). Choose a situation you will encounter in the week to come and are willing to dedicate some attention to. Write that situation at the very top of a piece of paper. Now, draw a line down the center of the page from top to bottom. On the left side at the top, write the word *Uncontrollables*. On the right side, write the word *Controllables*.

   Identify the specific elements within the situation that are out of your control and write them down on the left side of the paper. Next, make as extensive a list as possible of things you can control on the right-hand side of the paper. When you are finished, look over your list and resolve to let go of trying to control the Uncontrollables, and for emphasis rip off and throw away the left half of the page. Come back to the remaining list and apply all of your focus to the items listed under the Controllables.

Keep this list in front of you for the week. You will probably be surprised by how many things you actually can control and may even find yourself overwhelmed by the task. Pick one or two specific items from your Controllables list to focus on for a day or two, and then add one or two more items each day for the rest of the week. You will be so busy working on what you can control that what you can't control will become nothing more than background noise. This process will help you reclaim power in an area that once made you feel helplessly frustrated.

2. Make a point this week to lean heavily on your natural intuition, listening to its urgings. Choose to nurture this part of yourself and allow it to outweigh the influence of your internal intellectual dialogue. See if, as a result of this practice, you begin to "receive" intuitive messages with greater frequency. Remember, intuition comes in the form of a feeling as opposed to a thought.

One way to tap into your intuitive abilities is to silently ask yourself questions. If you have a scheduling conflict with two important events and are having a hard time in deciding which to attend, silently ask yourself about both events: *Should I go to event #1?* and then be still and notice what internal sensations you experience in response to the question. Next, ask *Should I go to event #2?* and then with a quiet mind, observe what sensations you feel that are associated with that question. If you do this a couple of times, you will notice a difference in the feelings you encounter when asking about one versus the other. This will be independent of intellectual reasoning or personal preference. You will have greater peace about attending one or the other. The last thing to do is let go and trust what your intuition has revealed to you.

3. Make a list of two or three things that elicit mild fearfulness in your life that you would like to move past. Make sure you have clearly identified them as intellectual rather than intuitive fears. Now select one item from the list to start with. Systematically evaluate the variables within the situation. Do as much research as necessary so that you maximize the amount of information available to you to make an intelligent decision about whether to proceed.
If in the information gathering process you realize there is nothing to justify the fear, move forward. If you find that the potential consequences of the situation are acceptable to you and you also have sufficient resources to apply to it, move forward. If the potential consequences are unacceptable or overly risky, withdraw. If you determine that the consequences are acceptable but you lack the necessary skills to effectively address the situation, temporarily withdraw and embark on an intentional personal growth plan to develop the skills you need. Only after you have sufficient resources to apply to the situation should you move forward. If you find the consequences to be acceptable, but you are not sure whether or not you possess sufficient skills and resources to take on the challenge, commit to exploring the situation further. This means moving forward and engaging the task a little at a time so as to mitigate inappropriate risk taking while maximizing the opportunity to overcome the fear. This allows you to expand your knowledge of the situation until you have enough

information to decide whether moving forward or withdrawing is the best choice.

Any time you move forward, do it with all of your might and without looking back. Any time you withdraw, do so unapologetically and completely. No matter which decision you make, make it absolute and don't second-guess yourself. And if you have decided to proceed, if at any time during the process of moving into the situation you feel fear trying to creep back into your mind, redirect your attention toward the task at hand and into your body by repeating the mantra: Breathe-See-Feel.

Chapter Four

A Mind-Boggling Mechanism

According to Hans Moravec of Carnegie Mellon University, the human brain is capable of performing in the neighborhood of 100 trillion calculations per second. Pause for effect. To put that in perspective, consider that the number of seconds that pass during the life of a person who lives to be seventy-five is only about 2.4 billion, and it takes 1,000 billion to make up a trillion. So, it would take close to 32,000 years for a trillion seconds to pass. And that's only 1 trillion seconds! A hundred trillion would equate to the number of seconds in about 3.2 million years.

The previous paragraph took me about forty minutes to complete due to my relative ineptness in working with large numbers, and my lack of super-precise calculations will probably have some engineers, accountants, and mathematicians writhing in mental agony. When my wife (who was a math major in college and continues to be the brains of the operation) read this chapter, she literally set up a spreadsheet and ran through the calculations just to check my numbers; she couldn't help herself. I wonder what it's like to live in a high IQ brain . . . Nonetheless, the example above shows that the raw power of the human brain and its sophistication is, ironically, beyond our minds' comprehension, especially when we ponder how the brain renders conscious thought and seamlessly integrates with our bodies' systems to regulate movement and other processes.

In college I majored in psychology and especially enjoyed coursework that focused on neuroscience. Learning about the neurological system and brain chemistry was (and still is) absolutely fascinating to me. What I find equally fascinating is studying how best to use our own personal supercomputers to accomplish what we desire in life. What a shame it would be to let such a marvelous tool that can do 100 trillion calculations per second go to waste! Yet many people fail to harness the power of their minds and instead live a life of constant physical, financial, and personal struggle. John Maxwell, in his book *Put Your Dream to the Test*, contends that "The greatest gap between successful and unsuccessful people is the thinking gap" and the way they use their minds.[1] The mind makes an excellent slave but a terrible master. The limiting factor of the human brain lies not in its design or capacity but in how it is directed and used by the individual operating it.

In an effort to keep things simple and straightforward, I have purposely avoided getting bogged down by in-depth research analysis and unnecessary scientific jargon. My purpose is to provide simple, practical, and effective information that has a scientific basis but in a format that anyone can put to use right away. Use the principles in this chapter daily and watch the effect they have on your life. I believe it will be profound.

The information in this chapter is based on my personal experience with the most salient mental tactics, specifically from the standpoint of dog training and behavioral rehabilitation. Of course, the principles stretch across the boundaries of species and subject, so we will explore the broader implications and application of the principles in creating personal transformation as well. I have taken the best information gleaned from studying the mental practices of the most effective people in various fields and laid it out in an understandable and usable form.

The human mind shares much in common with a canine's, and there are many differences as well. In this chapter we will look at principles of reinforcement, specifically within the context of training your dog. Understanding the principles of learning makes effective teaching possible and will shorten the time it takes to train new behaviors. We must not only have a foundational understanding of the precepts of dog training but also be able to communicate well with our dogs so they grasp the information we *intend* to pass along. Make no mistake, we are always training our dogs. The question is *what* are we teaching them?

The art and science of dog training and rehabilitation relies on people finding how to best motivate and support their dogs so they can learn the lessons being taught to them. This is accomplished with a training approach that combines thoughtfulness and intuition to efficiently deliver information in a way that minimizes that which is lost in translation. Learning is defined as a change in behavior, so the best teaching can be, in large part, determined by examining the resultant changes it produces in those being instructed—in this case, our dogs.

So let me ask, how is your dog doing in these areas? Rank him on a scale of 1 to 10:

- obedience in the home
- obedience outside of the home
- manners (keeping all four paws on the ground when greeting people; waiting patiently for food; staying off furniture, etc.)
- general disposition (peaceful and content or anxious and hyperactive)

When we're not sure where to start, it's best to gain clarity about where we stand. After you've completed this short exercise, I believe the areas you need to work on next will jump right off the page at you.

How to Train Your Dog's Brain

I have always thought the actions of men the best interpreters of their thoughts.

John Locke

Because we are specifically exploring the realm of the mind in this chapter, we are going to home in on the principles of conditioning. We will not be discussing states of mind as much as we have in the other chapters. Instead, we will look at training as it pertains to the reinforcement of observable behaviors. This is by no means an exhaustive guide, but it is a practical one. I present some of the most powerful and enduring concepts and techniques of animal training that have been used for thousands of years.

Two of the most often asked questions I get from clients are "What are your training methods?" and "What is your training philosophy?" These are both great questions and they can elicit valuable discussions. I believe that, generally, people are expecting to hear that I believe in training a certain way or that I think a certain style is best. This is understandable because it is typical of the answers they are used to getting if they have spoken with other trainers. When someone tells me about problems they're having with their dog and then asks, "How are you going to train him?" my answer is, "I have no idea." I then sit back, relax, and enjoy the look of befuddlement on their faces before I continue.

I tell my clients that every dog is different and so is every situation. A lot of variables must be considered when developing a training plan for a dog. I absolutely do *not* believe there is a "right" way to train dogs. I also don't subscribe to the idea that training tools are inherently humane or inhumane; it just doesn't make any sense. Any tool can be used to help a dog or hurt him—it all depends on the skill level and intent of the user. I *do* believe that it is important to recognize your dog's unique needs and to fairly and skillfully apply the most fitting training tools and principles to meet his needs. There is no one-size-fits-all teaching style, as anyone with children can attest to. Children require a unique mixture of tools, teaching methods, and support to help them grow. As they continue to age and develop, these needs will change, and so must the way we teach and relate to them. And so it is with our dogs. We limit our ability to help them when we decide that they need to fit within the dictates of a particular training methodology.

For example, during a training appointment, I have a variety techniques at my disposal, including ones I create in the moment as I decipher new, more fitting ways to communicate information. I also have a box of training tools in my car, full of everything from clickers, tennis balls, tug toys, treats, and nylon collars to choke chains, no-pull harnesses, regular harnesses, head halters, prong collars, martingale collars, retractable leashes, long lines, electronic (remote) collars, doggie backpacks, muzzles, and more.

When I work with people, I always adjust my approach and find a way to speak their "learning language" so they can understand how to help their dogs; how to live with them in such a way that they promote peace and balance. No two appointments are ever alike. Some people learn best by encouragement; some by admonishment. Some need to believe in themselves more; some need to have a wake-up call and realize they are their dog's biggest problem. Some are visual learners and need to have someone *show* them how to do something; some are auditory learners, so they need someone to *tell* them how to do it. Some are kinesthetic learners and need to do a thing themselves so they can *feel* how it is to be done, and there are countless combinations of these learning styles, requiring me to concoct a unique mixture according to the individual's needs. To me, it's a fascinating riddle to solve: How can I combine all of the ingredients in the best way possible so the person I'm teaching is empowered and equipped to make the necessary changes and have a better quality of life?

Classical Conditioning

Classical conditioning is a fancy term for a basic concept of how animals and humans form associations. In dog training, it is essentially the art of associating a previously neutral stimulus (i.e. the words *good boy*) with a specific reaction in your dog (i.e. tail-wagging happiness). This is usually accomplished by repeated pairings of the neutral stimulus of "good boy" with pets and praise. Over a period of time, saying "good boy" becomes a predictor of the praise to follow and therefore elicits a happy response in your dog. Eventually, even in the absence of actual praise, your dog will exhibit the same behavior each time he hears those wonderful words uttered.

The thing to recognize is that the sound "good boy" is given meaning only when it has been consistently followed by praise over a period of time. Dogs do not understand English: I promise. The phrase "good boy" is initially a completely neutral stimulus. In the same way, shouting "bad dog" (which I don't encourage) followed by stern looks and banishing your dog from the scene of a crime eventually conditions him to cower anytime he hears the phrase. Words that would have initially fallen on deaf ears now produce a visceral response in him. Classical conditioning allows dogs to form associations that help them survive by adapting to their world.

Another example is a dog that hears the garage door open on a weekday afternoon and feels a rush of excitement. Having experienced many-a-time the sound of the garage door followed by the arrival of his people, the stimulus of the sound alone eventually produces joyous anticipation. A more extreme example on the flip side would be a dog that experienced a powerful negative stimulus, such as a rattlesnake bite. The pain he felt, the shock of the sensation, and the near death experience could leave a lasting impression from a single encounter with a snake. That same dog would, in the future, likely display extreme fear and run away at the sight of a rattlesnake or the mere sound its tail, which previously had no particular connotation for him.

One specific form of classical conditioning used frequently in training is called "counterconditioning." It involves changing an entrenched response in an animal by modifying an existing association. If your dog reacts to the sight of bicycles by shirking and hiding (i.e. bicycles = terrifying metal monsters), you could potentially countercondition his response by pairing the sight of bicycles with his favorite treats instead. If every time your dog sees bicycles in the future you toss a handful of yummy hotdog pieces on the ground, he will likely form a new association (i.e. bicycles = favorite treats falling from the sky). This new association would require some time to take root but could be very useful in helping him overcome his fearful reaction. While in the past, he feared bicycles and tried to avoid them, he might now enjoy seeing them and maybe even go out of his way to find them.

Operant Conditioning

While classical conditioning is more specific to basic stimuli and the forming of simple associations, operant conditioning is concerned with consequences of actions. Classical conditioning deals more with reflexive (non-thinking) responses to stimuli, whereas operant conditioning deals with responsive (thoughtful, decision-based) learning. In classical conditioning, the dog's actions within a situation have no bearing on the presentation of the new stimulus. In our bicycle example, you dropped treats for your dog whenever he saw a bicycle, regardless of his response. We did not require him to sit or do any specific behavior to earn the treats. We were interested only in providing an alternative perspective (bicycles = a meteor shower of cookies).

By contrast, in operant conditioning a dog's actions and behavior are significant in that they determine whether the dog receives a reward or correction. If you ask your dog to come to you and he obliges, you give him a cookie, pet him, and give him some praise to encourage the good decision. But say you ask him to come to you and he runs out the front door instead and leaps in the air, body slams your grandmother, and knocks her down, spilling the bag of groceries she was carrying. You might want to catch him in the act, tell him "uh-uh," and remove the privilege of being a part of the social situation by putting him in the backyard for a couple minutes (it would also be prudent at some point to make sure your grandmother is okay and help her get back to her feet).

Four core components comprise operant conditioning, often referred to as the "four quadrants of operant conditioning": positive reinforcement, negative reinforcement, positive punishment, and negative punishment. In learning these concepts it is often helpful to see them in the following format:

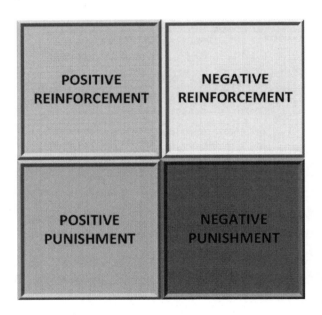

One very important point to keep in mind when learning the four quadrants is that the terminology used here has different meanings when used in common conversation. Normally these words have emotional significance. We naturally associate the terms *positive* and *reinforcement* with good things, while *negative* and *punishment* are bad things. These particular connotations must be set aside to minimize confusion, as they are irrelevant to the scientific designations. Below are the basic translations for these concepts in learning theory terms:

Positive = applying or giving something
Negative = removing or taking something away
Reinforcement = a consequence that *increases* the likelihood of a behavior recurring in the future
Punishment = a consequence that *decreases* the likelihood of a behavior recurring in the future

It may be helpful to think of the words *positive* and *negative* in mathematical terms, with positive meaning adding something (+) and negative meaning subtracting something (–). We will briefly delve into each of these quadrants to explore their meanings and applications as they pertain to training our dogs. We will look at how each of these principles can be applied to a simple behavior such as training a dog to sit.

POSITIVE REINFORCEMENT

Positive = applying or giving something
Reinforcement = a consequence that *increases* the likelihood of a behavior recurring in the future

When you combine these definitions, the concept as a whole becomes quite clear. Positive reinforcement involves giving or applying something after your dog offers a particular behavior in order to promote the recurrence of that behavior. When you ask your dog to sit and he does so, you give him a treat, which is considered positive reinforcement because you are giving or applying something (positive) that will encourage him to practice this behavior in the future (reinforcement).

When your dog approaches you with that adorable puppy-dog look in his eyes and you pet him, you are encouraging repeat performances in the future through positive reinforcement. You are also employing positive reinforcement if your dog jumps up and you start petting him. If you withhold your attention and manage to teach your dog to not jump on you, it can still be challenging to teach your dog to not jump up on other people, because most folks will pet him while he's jumping (positive reinforcement) and say things like "I don't mind. I *love* dogs!" This is where differential reinforcement (using positive reinforcement to teach and encourage an alternative/incompatible behavior like sitting for pets when other people approach) comes in very handy.

Positive reinforcement training often utilizes "clicker training," in which a simple handheld plastic device with a button is pressed when a dog correctly performs a behavior. The button makes a clicking sound and the dog is offered a reward (usually food) right afterward. The sound of the clicker starts to become synonymous in the dog's mind with anticipation of the treats to follow. It is a powerful tool to capture wanted behaviors the moment they occur. Practically any sound can be used as a "marker" noise to pinpoint a desired behavior. Marine-mammal trainers often use whistles when they work with dolphins. Other types of animals, such as dogs, can be trained with whistles also but are more commonly trained using voice feedback. In my training, I generally use a verbal marker of "yes" to capture a behavior I want to reward. Using auditory markers followed by rewards, such as food, is called "mark and reward" training.

Note that it normally isn't feasible to physically reward a dog the exact instant he does something right. If you ask your dog to lie down from far across the room and he does so, you can't physically deliver a treat to his mouth to reward him the moment he lies down, and yet animals live and think and learn in the moment, so how do you capture the coveted moment when he offered the behavior you wanted? You use some type of a marker the instant he performs it properly. If he has an association with the sound of a clicker or the word *yes*, which tells his brain that food is coming, you have, in effect, instantly rewarded him. Psychologically, he has been given his reward in a timely manner; the physical reward of food to follow is a foregone conclusion. This is a central concept and tenet within training and one you'll want to familiarize yourself with.

It might be useful to ponder a more exciting example: winning the lottery. How would you feel the moment you looked at your ticket and realized you'd hit the jackpot? Wouldn't that be magical? That's how your dog feels the instant you use a marker (assuming he's associated it with a powerful reward). Depositing your winnings into your bank account is your reward. This is what happens when your dog has the treat in his mouth. What's most important is the timing of telling your dog he's won the lottery. It feeds his brain. The ensuing treat feeds his body.

When your boss watches you perform a task well and encourages you for doing a great job, he is using positive reinforcement. When your kid whines and you give him what he wants to get him to pipe down, you have used positive reinforcement to encourage whining. When you do something thoughtful for your spouse and he shows appreciation, he is employing positive reinforcement and increasing the chance that you will continue to do thoughtful acts in the future. We are using reinforcement with one another every day of our lives. If we are intentional about our reinforcement, we can increase the quality of our communication and draw out the best in ourselves and in each other.

Positive reinforcement is the quadrant of choice when working to establish new behaviors. Whenever you are teaching your dog a brand-new task, he will need to be given lots of encouragement and rewards along the way. Why? Think of your first day at a new company: it's exciting . . . and stressful! There's pressure to make a good impression on your new boss and coworkers, to learn lots of information quickly, and to perform your job duties well. Being in unfamiliar territory is stressful. And so it is with our dogs. Even well-trained dogs experience stress when trying to discern a new task they have no experience with. This is why it is so important to give rewards as they make incremental progress. Once your dog has learned a task thoroughly, you no longer need to provide positive reinforcement so frequently, just as your mom no longer needs to tell you how proud she is of you for using the "big-boy" potty. After a job is learned, you (hopefully) move on to new or more sophisticated tasks and the cycle begins again.

Negative Reinforcement

Negative = removing or taking something away
Reinforcement = a consequence that *increases* the likelihood of a behavior recurring in the future

Negative reinforcement involves the removal of something to increase the likelihood that a certain behavior will happen again in the future. When you put your dog in a sit-stay and he holds it for a few seconds but then stands up, slowly walk toward him. With your moving closer, he is likely to feel your social/body pressure and sit back down. As soon as his bottom is back on the floor, step away from him, thus removing the pressure (negative) to encourage him to hold the sit position in the future (reinforcement). Essentially, to strengthen the correct behavior, an aversive stimulus is removed at the exact moment your dog offers the correct behavior.

Let's say you are out for a walk with your dog and he is walking nicely (which you should encourage using positive reinforcement), but then he begins to pull against you because he sees a neighbor approaching that he absolutely loves. He continues to pull and keeps pressure on the leash as you get closer to your neighbor. In an effort to relieve the tension, you take a couple steps toward your neighbor. The leash loosens and your dog wags away as your neighbor pets him lovingly. Several things are occurring in this scenario, but let's take a look specifically at how negative reinforcement was used in this situation. Your dog was pulling, so there was tension (or pressure) on the leash. Once your dog pulled long and hard enough, you released that pressure by stepping forward quickly. So the pressure on the leash was removed (negative) when your dog was pulling his hardest (reinforcement). You have effectively increased the chances that he will pull on the leash in the future when he wants to see someone.

Brenda Aloff refers to the concept of pressure and release as "mother nature's clicker." This means that animals naturally learn much about life through negative reinforcement because the release of pressure (or other uncomfortable stimulus) reinforces the behavior that made the pressure go away. When your dog scratches an itch, thereby providing relief of discomfort, the act of scratching is strengthened via negative reinforcement. When you get into your car and forget to buckle your seat belt, a persistent ding-ding-ding reminds you to fasten it. The ceasing of the noise the moment you snap the buckle into place reinforces the act of fastening your seat belt. When you stop procrastinating and complete an unfinished task that's been in the back of your mind for months, the relief you feel afterward negatively reinforces taking action and doing the work. These are all examples of negative reinforcement, which is part of the daily reality of people and animals alike.

POSITIVE PUNISHMENT

Positive = applying or giving something
Punishment = a consequence that *decreases* the likelihood of a behavior recurring in the future

Positive punishment consists of applying or giving a consequence in response to a behavior that is likely to diminish its occurrence in the future. Recall our example of having your dog in a sit-stay. Let's say that he is across the front yard from you, holding position, but then decides to get up and walk away. So you issue a negative marker (such as "uh-uh" or "oops") the moment his bottom comes off the ground to pinpoint the undesired behavior. You then calmly walk toward him, thus applying social pressure (positive) to discourage the act of breaking his stay (punishment). As soon as he sits down and you back away to relieve the pressure, you are applying negative reinforcement to encourage sitting. Negative reinforcement always begins, technically, with positive punishment, because you can't remove or take away something you haven't applied. The seat belt alert in your car is no exception. When the ding-ding-ding begins (positive), it discourages you from forgetting to put on your seat belt (punishment). When you finally fasten your seat belt, the sound is removed (negative) to strengthen the behavior of buckling up for safety (reinforcement).

Punishment is such a loaded word that it is imperative to remember that, in learning theory terms, it means something very different from the "punishment" we normally talk about in conversation. It does not mean harsh or abusive treatment (though it can become so if used improperly). When your dog breaks a sit-stay command, although the act of calmly and gently walking toward him will not be particularly concerning, it is still positive punishment. It is every bit as much positive punishment as when your next door neighbor catches his dog pooping in the house and whacks him on the nose with a rolled up magazine (not recommended). One instance is more obvious and one more subtle, but in sticking to *scientific* definitions, they both fit the bill.

Positive punishment is positive punishment . . . period. This specific area of operant conditioning is certainly the most divisive among professional trainers. I would propose that it doesn't need to be. What we're all looking to avoid is abuse, which can be done with *any* training tool, method, or quadrant of operant conditioning. What matters is why and how a tool, method, or quadrant is used. Plenty of people like to insinuate that the use of positive punishment is inherently abusive. This, of course, doesn't make any sense. If your friend is pestering you to go skydiving and you tell him, "No thanks. I really don't care to," you are giving him feedback (positive) to communicate your desire that he stop badgering you about going skydiving (punishment). Were you an abusive friend? I don't think so. Now, if he pesters you about going skydiving and you punch him in the face and knock him unconscious, you have entered the realm of abuse while simultaneously demonstrating a level zero proficiency in the people-skills department.

My point is that in training, everyone employs positive punishment. They may not identify it as such, but that doesn't change the reality that it is being used. I had a trainer lecture me once about training and then brag that she uses only "operant conditioning" in her training and that positive reinforcement is the "only right way to train a dog." I was utterly perplexed by her comments. Even setting aside her insinuation that only one or two quadrants comprise operant conditioning (instead of four) and that operant conditioning is all that's necessary to train an animal (when it's *built* on a foundation of classical conditioning), I couldn't get past the fact that she was at that very moment wielding a spray bottle and using it to help her manage, through the use of corrections, a group of dogs playing around her. So after weathering about five minutes of her not-so-positive attitude and the lecture she felt impelled to unleash on me, I couldn't hold back anymore and politely pointed out that using a spray bottle to stop dogs from behaving inappropriately constituted both positive punishment and negative reinforcement, which are also, scientifically speaking, components of operant conditioning. She then stood up very tall, shook her index finger at me with an "I gotcha!" look before proudly declaring, "But I'm not *training!*"

I suppose to her training happens only when she decides it is and when she has treats and is working on obedience exercises with a dog. I didn't say this to her because my purpose there was not to argue, even though she clearly wanted to. But I was thinking, *You're always training.* We are always training our dogs and they're always watching us. If we are going to do the absolute best we can for our dogs, we are wise to be completely honest and recognize that we are utilizing the various components of operant conditioning, so we need to study and fully understand all four quadrants, not just one or two. Only then can we be sophisticated, supportive, and thoughtful in applying them in the training process.

In my experience, positive punishment is most effective when used sparingly. Hitting every red light on your way across town is frustrating; hitting red lights once in a while is an expected, even essential, part of traveling the roadways. Helping your dog encounter far more green lights than red ones is what keeps training fun and allows for steady progress, which is exactly why catching your dog doing the right thing is so important. In learning a new skill, isn't it more enjoyable to have a coach who makes a big deal out of the things you do correctly (via positive reinforcement for successful attempts) than someone who is constantly identifying errors (via positive punishment for mistakes)? Think about the different bosses and supervisors you've had. I bet that the ones who got the most productivity with the highest levels of employee morale had good attitudes and leaned more heavily on positive reinforcement than punishment. That isn't to say your boss didn't reprimand you on occasion when your work was subpar, but it was not his go-to method of reinforcement.

For new skills, say, teaching a dog to come when called, I typically set up a new dog so that it is very easy for him to succeed and I can reward him and build momentum for the behavior. Once he has a high-level understanding and lots of experience with coming when called, however, I am more willing to issue a correction when he disregards the command. In the beginning of his training, I use lots of praise and treats and toys to encourage him when he comes to me when I call him, and I will likely ignore his mistakes. Once he's a seasoned veteran in the recall department, however, I like to add in some consequences for ignoring the command. Why? Because I don't want him to blow off a recall one day while he's chasing a rabbit: what if he runs out into the middle of the street and gets run over by a car? I need him to know that a recall is a command he *must* obey. I'd rather set up some controlled, low-level consequences for ignoring my command than allow him to experience someday the extreme consequence of an intimate encounter with a car bumper.

Depending on the dog and his motivation, positive punishment is administered by different means. For one dog, a stern "hey" followed by a disappointed glance from me might be enough to dissuade him from ignoring a command. For another, I might need to have a long line on him so that if he ignores a recall and runs away from me, he will get a correction when he reaches the end of it. I would never punish him for a botched recall once he came back to me. If I want him to feel totally comfortable with being together, using punishment when he arrives at my side is extremely counterproductive. He should be uncomfortable only when he's far away and choosing not to listen.

Positive punishment can be a lifesaving tool for dogs, particularly if they practice dangerous behaviors that pose a serious safety hazard to themselves, other dogs, or people. However, if it's not used in conjunction with and balanced by other training methods, it can backfire quickly and create negative fallout. Also, people normally mete out punishment when they are angry. This is not training. Positive punishment should be thoughtfully used to provide your dog with feedback about a specific decision, with the aim of getting him back on track with good behaviors you can reward.

Booby-trapping is one example of a useful way to apply positive punishment. It can prevent your dog from associating you with the correction and still accomplish the task of addressing the undesirable behavior. Do you have a dog that counter surfs whenever you turn your back? Line the edge of the counter with one-inch-wide double-sided sticky tape. He probably won't like the new sensation on his paws and will stop practicing the behavior. Credit goes to my good friend and fellow trainer Cristina Hell for sharing this strategy with me. Use your creativity and resourcefulness to come up with additional training solutions. As with all methods of training, I recommend working with a qualified trainer to develop sound strategies for working with your dog. It's absolutely worth the time and money.

NEGATIVE PUNISHMENT

Negative = removing or taking something away
Punishment = a consequence that *decreases* the likelihood of a behavior recurring in the future

Negative punishment involves removing something when your dog performs a behavior in order to decrease the prevalence of that behavior in the future. In our example of having your dog sit, simply withhold treats (negative) whenever he isn't complying with the command (punishment). If your puppy starts barking at you to get your attention, many times you can remedy this by ignoring him whenever he's being vocal and giving him attention whenever he's being quiet and polite. The idea is to let the undesirable behavior fade away for lack of attention, much as muscles atrophy when they are not used for long periods of time. Withholding a resource such as food or toys to negatively punish a behavior communicates volumes to most dogs. Negative punishment tends to work very well to shape your dog's responses when paired with positive reinforcement for wanted behaviors.

The same principle applies to people you interact with. Normally, your friend will stop telling inappropriate jokes that nobody laughs at. Without the reinforcement of laughter, he is likely to move on to something else (unless he's a real jerk and relentlessly persists, in which case you need to call him out on it). When your child pulls on your pant leg to engage you and you ignore him, over time he seeks out alternative means to solicit your attention. Hopefully, you have taught him through some form of reinforcement other appropriate ways to get your attention.

Always teach appropriate alternative behaviors. If you take something away (i.e., "don't do that"), make sure you give something in return (i.e., "do this"). Balance is a necessity; it provides clear expectations. Taking away options can create confusion for a dog that doesn't know what he should be doing instead.

For negative punishment to be effective, your dog needs to value the thing you are removing enough that it captures his attention and motivates him to change his behavior. If you withhold your dog's favorite toy to discourage him from barking, but barking at that moment is more important to him, you will need to shift gears and move to something else. It is important to recognize that sometimes your dog is absolutely unmoved by your "prizes" for good behavior because something else is perceived as more rewarding at that time. Whenever you are dealing with a behavior that is intrinsically gratifying to the dog, it is a "self-rewarding" behavior. In some cases, a dog will persist in an action because it is more rewarding to him than anything else in the world at that moment. T-bone steaks take a backseat to the activity itself. Dogs that obsessively chase cars come to mind. If your dog is practicing these types of self-rewarding behaviors, you will either need to redirect his attention or issue some form of correction. Again, professional guidance is the key to success in these instances.

Key Principles for Training and Reinforcement

It becomes obvious that if we want to make relatively minor changes in our lives, we can perhaps appropriately focus on our attitudes and behaviors. But if we want to make significant, quantum change, we need to work on our basic paradigms.
In the words of Thoreau, "For every thousand hacking at the leaves of evil, there is one striking at the root." We can only achieve quantum improvements in our lives as we quit hacking at the leaves of attitude and behavior and get to work on the root, the paradigms from which our attitudes and behaviors flow.[2]

Stephen Covey

What Lies Beneath

One of the primary reasons I don't decide ahead of time how I will address a dog's training issues is that I believe observable behaviors are a natural outcome of some internal state. I need to meet the dog first to feel out what is motivating the behavior. A dog that jumps on people has bigger issues than the jumping itself—it's rooted in a more general issue such as overexcitement. In my opinion, I do a disservice to the dog and his owner if I come in and just fix the jumping behavior. Even if I do help the dog to become more polite upon greeting people and his owner is satisfied, the dog probably isn't because we have masked the real problem. We've elicited approval from people who comment, "He's such a great dog, and so well behaved," but that doesn't mean the dog is experiencing peace within. The dog still has to live every day in a state of mind that produces unnecessary demands and stress on his system. It's analogous to treating the symptoms of a sick person without ever getting to the root cause and restoring his health.

It is important to recognize behaviors as symptoms in your dog and even more important to identify the causes that lurk beneath the surface. To apply spot treatment to behaviors in a dog is like cutting off the tip of an iceberg. The invisible but critically important mass beneath the water isn't being addressed; when one behavior is "fixed" another will pop right up behind it. I often refer to this syndrome as "Behavioral Whac-A-Mole." Treating symptoms keeps many trainers busy with work because they always have another behavior they can be called upon to address. The best trainers, however, are holistic in their approach. They work from the bottom up, and the results are Transformational. This may require extraordinary dedication and patience to see things through, but the end result is like nothing else.

Perhaps the most challenging aspect for us as owners is taking responsibility in cases where we are our dog's biggest "iceberg." They exhibit behaviors because of an unbalance we have created (or enabled) within them. It challenges us to make personal changes, not to accommodate our dogs, but to empower them. I know I have been the biggest stumbling block to some of my dogs in the past, while other times the underlying issue had very little to do with me. Either way, I want to take responsibility for as much of the situation as I can to maximize my influence and find the most fitting and transformational solution possible.

THE SECRET OF GOOD TRAINING (AND HUMOR)

Another principle to always be mindful of in training your dog is that *timing* is of the essence. If you ask your dog to sit and he does it for you, when should you tell him "yes"? Immediately, of course! The very instant his bottom touches the ground and he's in a seated position is when he should receive the verbal feedback. The treat can follow a couple seconds later. The important thing is that he receives a timely verbal marker so that he can identify exactly which behavior you are reinforcing with the food. The same goes for your negative verbal markers ("uh-uh," "no," etc.). He will grasp the information you intend to convey more clearly if it's delivered on time, and he will learn at an accelerated rate once you master the timing of your reinforcement. Dogs think in pictures, and your marker is your ticket to capturing a vivid snapshot in your dog's brain of the behavior you want to reinforce or discourage. Markers delivered a half second early or a half second late result in unclear communication of your expectations. Markers delivered right on time yield great results. So remember: timing, timing, timing!

HOW 'BOUT THEM APPLES?

Each dog determines what constitutes rewards/reinforcement for him. I personally enjoy scrambled eggs and even cooked some about an hour ago. I gave each of my dogs little nibbles, and four of my five dogs agreed with me that eggs are delicious. I'm fairly convinced my other dog perceived my egg offering as some sort of trickery. He was not a happy camper. In fact, he found the eggs rather distasteful. Just because I think eggs are good and should be a reward has nothing to do with whether or not they are to him.

The same goes for the use of punishment/corrections. It doesn't matter if I believe that shaking a pop can filled with pennies should be aversive to a dog and cause him to stop counter surfing—it matters what the dog thinks. I work with some dogs that won't do diddly squat for a treat, but they will do backflips for me if I reward them by tossing a penny-filled pop can encased in duct tape for them to catch and run around with. So have fun finding out about your dog's preferences. Step back and observe what he'll work for and what he'll work to avoid; you might be surprised by what you find.

When using training tools with dogs, some people believe that certain tools are more humane to use than others. I agree. The most humane tool to use with a dog is the tool that is most humane to use for that particular dog. Period. If I think using a head halter with my dog is humane but he hates life itself whenever I put it on him, my opinion doesn't matter, because he still hates it. If I think a pinch collar is the way to go but it makes my dog anxious and over-stimulates him, I would be wise to try something else. If I slap a harness on my dog because I believe it is a humane tool and he drags me all over town and we are constantly frustrated with each other, it would behoove me to think outside of my box and find a more humane approach for us both.

The purpose of all training tools should be to help support communication with our dogs. In choosing your tools, choose according to your dog's needs. Be absolutely certain you know why you're using a specific tool and how to use it properly. Don't get hung up on thinking your favorite tool or the one your friends like for their dogs is the best one to get the job done. Your dog might need something entirely different.

Let's say you're starting a home remodeling project. Maybe your favorite tool is a chainsaw. But you would be wise to leave it in your garage while laying new tile in your kitchen. A chainsaw simply isn't the right tool for the type of work you're doing. To use a chainsaw to lay tile would be absolute madness, just as it would be crazy to use your tile trowel to try to cut down an oak tree. Aimee Sadler always reminds her students, "If you have the right tool for the job, it makes your work much easier; if the only thing you have is a hammer, everything becomes a nail."

FINDING A TRAINER

Private training and group classes provide great opportunities for helping your dog learn and grow. A board and train is also a good fit in certain instances. Regardless of the avenue you choose, seek out a balanced trainer in your area. Talk to several and get a feel for their individual styles of teaching before settling on one. You need to be comfortable with the way the trainer works with the dogs and the people they teach. Observe a group class to get a feel for things or at least speak with them enough to get a sense of how they operate.

I have worked with some of the most famous trainers out there and unfortunately discovered a couple that seemed to have a knack for intimidation and know-it-all-ness. They were esteemed trainers, and they were very knowledgeable, but it was *miserable* learning from them because their energy was so negative despite their impressive level of skill. This taught me a valuable lesson: If a trainer makes me feel two inches tall and they have a habit of insensitively lecturing dog owners about what they're doing wrong, the dogs they train surely pick up on that negative vibe as well. My advice would be to seek out someone who will tell you the truth in a way that is supportive and constructive.

Good trainers will be honest about what needs to be done but they are also committed to providing you and your dog with plenty of encouragement as well as specific training protocols to help. You'll also want to make sure the trainer you choose is well-versed in as many methodologies as possible. There's no one-size-fits-all training approach. Each dog is unique, and, as such, has special considerations that demand a comprehensive and balanced training approach. You can search for professionals online. The IACPs Website is a great place to start.

ONE MORE THING

Always train your dog with a positive energy! Everything works better this way. I have found that my dogs would rather spend time with me when I exude a positive presence. Even when addressing a behavior in them I wish to correct, I always aim to do it so that not only do they understand the behavior is unacceptable but also I am right there to help them and they can trust my leadership. I love them and approve of them even when I disapprove of certain behaviors. While you can explain this type of concept to a child, the only way to deliver the message to your dog is with your energy. This means blending and balancing your skill of being firm, fair, personally grounded, and unmistakably upbeat and optimistic.

I frequently urge clients to cultivate and share this kind of energy with their dogs. I tell them that if they never gave Mr. Fido another treat and simply exhibited consistent, unspoken happiness in his presence, he would be more content than ever. Every companion animal appreciates being able to live and be at peace with grounded people. Now *that's* a positive way to train that has stood the test of time and worked wonders for thousands of years. Best of all, it's free and it makes you feel great too!

The Brain: A User's Guide

I consider that a man's brain originally is like a little empty attic, and you have to stock it with such furniture as you choose. A fool takes in all the lumber of every sort that he comes across, so that the knowledge which might be useful to him gets crowded out, or at best is jumbled up with a lot of other things, so that he has a difficulty in laying his hands upon it. Now the skillful workman is very careful indeed as to what he takes into his brain-attic. He will have nothing but the tools which may help him in doing his work, but of these he has a large assortment, and all in the most perfect order.

Sir Arthur Conan Doyle, *A Study in Scarlet*

If there's one thing our children could benefit from more than anything else in school it would be taking a course entitled The Brain: A User's Guide. We live in a time when education is more accessible than ever. Even people who don't receive their education on a campus can expand their intellectual prowess through online universities, and most folks have a sufficient IQ. What is generally lacking, but has been gaining ground recently, are people who harness the power of their emotional quotient, or EQ.

There are many ways of describing the concept of emotional intelligence, as well as prolific debate about what it means and questions about its very efficacy. To me, emotional intelligence is a purely conceptual model. I think of emotional intelligence as personal awareness and the ability to regulate and intentionally direct one's mind and emotions in a disciplined way to create positive outcomes. It is the essence of personal leadership. Someone with a high IQ might be tremendously well educated in the traditional sense and be well versed in history, economics, business, psychology, and philosophy. On the other hand, others with a high EQ might not be as "intelligent" as measured by academic standards but utilize their minds' power far more effectively, thoughtfully applying their knowledge and consistently translating their intentions into real-world results. Like a good doctor, they can deliver.

People who utilize emotional intelligence can think long-term. Working toward a greater good, they see value in exercising self-restraint à la delayed gratification. A person who utilizes his emotional intelligence can look beyond mere transient feelings. He would be, for example, more than willing to pass up a lucrative promotion if he believed that keeping his current title for another year would qualify him to apply for a position at another company that is in greater alignment with his purpose. This way of living requires a lot of foresight and discipline to stick to the plan, even when one's momentary yearnings are diametrically opposed to waiting.

The second half of this chapter is dedicated to presenting programs—mental models, if you will—of how to efficiently direct your mind to create desired outcomes. Again, we are going to avoid delving into deep recesses of über-scientific definitions of the mind. We are interested in simplicity and concepts we can immediately incorporate into our lives to enrich them and our dogs. What follows is a practical how-to guide. Although not a comprehensive or in-depth study of the subject, it is easily digestible and covers the essentials, so use it, enjoy it, and be on the lookout for principles that can unleash your potential.

Two Minds

Two primary branches comprise the mind: the conscious and the subconscious. To understand the difference, let's use the example of losing your keys. You would use your conscious mind to mentally retrace every step from the prior evening when you last remember having your keys; once you finally give up trying to remember where you put them, your subconscious engages and spontaneously produces the answer to their whereabouts. The subconscious mind has infinitely greater capacity for storing and retrieving information than the conscious mind. It is also intimately linked to your intuitive capabilities.

The subconscious mind is ultimately more powerful than the conscious mind. Does this make it more important? Definitely not. A person cannot directly control his subconscious mind. Its power is channeled according to how a person uses his conscious mind, which is both the gatekeeper and the programmer of the more powerful subconscious. Necessity demands, then, that those of us who are truly driven to do better for ourselves and our dogs be very selective in the thoughts we grant access to.

If someone knocked on your front door and you opened it to find a disheveled and fiendish looking character who was clearly up to no good, you would deny him access to your house, knowing that if you let him in, things could get ugly. He might rob you of your most valuable possessions or physically accost you. And yet most of us take into our minds whatever thoughts come at us on any given day. If you wouldn't let that up-to-no-good stranger into your house, why would you watch television programs with no redeeming value that glorify things like dysfunctional personal relationships destined for calamity? Why would you constantly entertain thoughts that your dog might attack another dog? Why would you spend most of your time with friends who think small, gossip, and always have drama they want to share with you?

Granting access to thoughts invites them into the sacred realm of the mind and validates their presence, so we must choose to meditate on and give attention to those thoughts that are in line with our desired life trajectory. This involves being selective about who we spend time with, what we watch and listen to, and which thoughts we entertain.

Consider what you surround yourself with, like places, people, and situations, as well as how you internalize the information coming in. No amount of water can sink a ship unless it gets on the inside. So if you are a vigilant gatekeeper, you will choose what you allow in and make sure it is of the finest quality. Of course, managing your environment to the best of your ability helps you shield yourself from unnecessary distractions and caustic thoughts.

Take responsibility for what you expose yourself to. Avail yourself of positive fellowship by being discerning about who you go to lunch with. Granted, you cannot control the things those people choose to say, and the topic of conversation might turn sour. So there are two objectives: 1) managing the information and people you surround yourself with; and 2) directing your thoughts and attention so that you are digesting the incoming information in a constructive manner.

How do you properly manage your environment and thoughts? First, set a course and direction based on who you want to become. If you are preparing to go on vacation and are clear about your destination, you prioritize what to pack. If you're going to the beach, you'll bring a towel, a bathing suit, and flip flops. You wouldn't consider packing a down jacket, snow boots, and gloves. Having a clear picture of where you're going and what you'll do when you get there dictates what you bring along. In the same way, you must have a clear picture of who you want to become and then focus your attention on things that will help you move closer to it. This means eliminating certain distractions.

You always want to have awareness of what's going on around you, but you don't need to waste valuable time and energy attending to things that ultimately have nothing to do with where you're going. Knowing what to avoid and what to ignore is a rare virtue woven into the fabric of the world's wisest people. *God, give me the wisdom and discipline to ignore the unimportant* is one of the most powerful prayers a person can utter.

Mirror, Mirror . . .

In Chapter six we will explore key tenets of ongoing personal growth. For the moment, it's critical to grasp the importance of who you *see yourself* to be. Everyone has a mental concept of who they are. Who do you see yourself to be? Consider your spiritual, mental, physical, emotional, relational, financial, and professional life, and take a few moments to consider your self-image in each of these areas.

Do you find that you sometimes base the image on how others perceive you? If so, you are not alone. I suspect all of us do this to some extent. But consider that it doesn't matter (in terms of your personal worth and potential) what others think of you as much as what you think of yourself. Do you see yourself as spiritually grounded, mentally strong, physically fit and healthy, emotionally balanced, having great personal relationships with those you love, possessing an abundance of financial wherewithal, and who adds great value to people professionally? Or do you see yourself as spiritually stagnant, mentally confused and strained, physically exhausted with health issues, emotionally drained, barely hanging on to relationships with those you should be closest to, constantly broke and having trouble making ends meet, while going through the motions at work without having any significant impact?

The way you see yourself programs the creative powerhouse of your mind (the subconscious) and therefore has greater bearing than almost anything else on your life's direction and what happens to you. Every day your conscious mind gazes upon your current self-concept—be it good or bad—taking blueprints of "who you are" and "what you do" to the subconscious. Your subconscious then constructs your life and everything you attract into it based upon those renderings. Remember the example of trying to find your keys: the conscious mind retraces your steps and gives direction to your subconscious, which later procures and produces the answer.

So the first order of business is managing your environment, which we have already discussed. The second is giving direction to the subconscious mind through the intentional presentation of mental pictures of who you want to become and *feeling* it a visceral level. The third is managing the way you internalize incoming information as well as stored information. Let's look at these areas of mental programming next.

Once you set a course for your subconscious mind to follow, it automatically begins filtering out unimportant information so that you can focus on only what is necessary to create your desired outcome. It explains the common phenomenon encountered whenever you learn a new word; you believe that you "never heard it before" when really you have heard it a thousand times but filtered it out of your awareness. And now that you have learned the word and brought attention to it, you consistently notice it popping up in conversations. Similarly, who you see yourself to be brings attention to certain personal characteristics and goes about strengthening them over time. If you see yourself as someone who gossips, you'll hear a bunch of it. If you see yourself as someone who engages in only constructive discussions, the gossip surrounding you will tend to be filtered out, or at least become background noise, because your mind is oriented toward information of a different content.

An old axiom says, "What you resist persists." That's why if a person on a diet keeps telling himself, "Don't eat junk food," he is bound for failure. The subconscious mind ultimately thinks in terms of pictures, so that little word *don't* gets lost in the shuffle as the brain is daily bombarded with pictures of the very junk food he wants to avoid. His subconscious then goes about making that picture of eating junk food come to pass, and next thing he knows he's feasting on Ho Hos.

Let's run a quick experiment. Whatever you do right now, do not think about or picture a centaur . . .

How did that work out for you? My guess is that you immediately—if for only a fleeting second—pictured a centaur in your mind. Once the conscious mind requested it, the subconscious retrieved it. The only possible exception to this is if you were not familiar with what a centaur is, in which case your mind is primed and will be much more apt to hear about or see centaurs in the future. The suggestion has piqued your interest and you may even do an online search to learn something about them.

The complimentary axiom to "What you resist persists" is "Whatever you focus on expands." The person who wishes to stop eating junk food must work *with* the subconscious mind by telling himself to eat *healthy* foods. This will set his mind into motion with a focus on becoming more educated about what foods are healthy, where he can buy them, and the various options for cooking and preparing these foods. This type of mental directive will eventually yield the desired result, *assuming* he continues to focus his attention on eating healthy foods as opposed to avoiding junk food.

So in setting course to experience the life you dream of having, program your subconscious in the proper direction by deciding where you want to go, and then focus on only those things that will help you get there. If you want more joy and peace, orient your mind toward such things and you will experience them with increasing frequency. If you want to experience drama and despair, watch the news constantly and spend lots of time listening to friends who always have something to complain about. This principle works. The only question is, will it work for you or against you?

Relating focus back to the concept of attention, it may be useful to think of your attention as a flashlight of sorts. Whatever you focus that flashlight on expands and illuminates. Although awareness is always the first step in growing yourself so that you can define the present reality, attention is about focusing your mental, physical, and spiritual energy in a specific direction so that you can get where you want to go. If, for example, you are out with your dog on a hike and encounter a tense situation that brings fear to your mind, you have two choices: focus on the fear or focus on specific actions you can take to mitigate the danger. The former will entrap you and position you as a victim of the situation, while the latter will open up possibilities and keep you in a solution-oriented mind-set.

A very simple way to keep focused on solutions as opposed to problems is through the proper use of questions. Proper questions empower you and put you in the driver's seat. Proper questions have a positive tone to them.

- How can I help my dog feel more confident in this situation?
- What resources are available to me to accomplish this task?
- How can I help my family members feel more valued and appreciated?
- What are the potential benefits that can come to me as a result of this layoff?
- What lessons can I glean from this situation, despite its challenges?
- How can I earn my son's respect?

- How can I improve my ability to stay calm in the midst of life's storms?
- What would I have to do or believe to feel better about myself?

Contrast the preceding questions with one like: "Oh my God, what am I going to do about this debacle?" Such a question has a negative, defeated ring to it. It directs the mind toward the problem and will produce vastly different answers from your subconscious than a solution-focused inquiry. Asking yourself questions *will* change your life. Asking the *right* questions produces the best quality of answers, allowing you to create the life you desire. Shifting perspective is powerful. As Wayne Dyer puts it, "When you change the way you look at things, the things you look at change."

Intimately related to the concept of impeccably using your attention, one other very important subject warrants a dedicated section of its own: How you think about and remember your successful and unsuccessful attempts in any task you engage. Before we get to that, however, let's revisit a concept we have already touched on, namely, that outcomes cannot be directly controlled and trying to control them is a direct path to personal frustration.

Performance is king. If you are a salesperson, you cannot control whether you make a sale—that is an outcome. You *can* control the quality of your effort and focus your mental energies on the process. People who dominate their fields are always masters at "losing themselves" in the flow of the process. Great singers, dancers, actors, and other performing artists cannot produce a mesmerizing show (outcome) because too many factors are out of their control (lighting, sound, musicians, etc.), but they can immerse themselves in their craft moment to moment, which provides the best opportunity to captivate their audience. World-class athletes and Olympians engaged in competition cannot afford to waste their attention worrying about coming in first; too many variables are outside their control, and trying too hard is one of the greatest performance killers. Athletes who consistently appear at the top of the leaderboards are those who manage their thought processes and keep their minds clear of all things during competition . . . well, all except one: unwavering attention upon the quality of their performance.

This leads us to consider, once again, that when we work with our dogs, we cannot control their behavior (outcome), but we can control the quality of our effort and keep the mind free from useless distractions such as worry, as well as those dangerously appealing vixen sisters named Wishin' and Hopin,' which render us passive and powerless. If you focus on performing well when training your dog by providing him with timely and quality reinforcement, even if the outcome doesn't match up with what you'd envisioned, you can be completely happy with the performance you gave and be at peace, knowing that you left nothing on the table. And as you make a habit of properly applying your attention and fully-immersing yourself in the quality of your effort, it begins to change how you think about yourself. Impeccable performance starts to become characteristic of you as a person. This leads us to consider the irrefutable importance of the next topic: how you internalize success and failure.

The Blessing of Forgetfulness

Many people could turn around their self-images and lives to a more powerful end if they would learn the simple concept of forgetfulness. As we've extensively discussed, outcomes cannot be directly controlled. Forgetfulness functions the same way. It is accomplished indirectly through proper focus.

Let me state it simply: Focus on your successful outcomes and refuse to linger on those that are unsuccessful. There's not a person in the world strong enough to overcome the negative impact of beating themselves up constantly. It's just impossible. Acidic environments do not foster growth. The environment or situation you're currently in may be acidic and negative, but your mind can be oriented to weather the storm and come out stronger and more empowered.

Let's face it, we all experience failure more than success, particularly when we are learning a new skill. That's one of the reasons there is such a high attrition rate among new students across all disciplines. Let's say you are new to the world of dog training. Maybe you just got your first dog and have begun training him with some basic commands, like sit, down, stay, etc. There is no question that, because all of this is new, you will experience more "failed" attempts than "successful" ones. Step one to experiencing more success as a trainer is to have a clear idea of what great training looks like. Visualization is important here. Similar to the way you need a complete picture of what a puzzle is supposed to look like when it's all pieced together, you need to build a mental concept for what an intended action looks like when it's done properly. Once you have a clear picture in mind you can practice the new skill and have confidence in the direction you're headed.

So if you are training your pup using a verbal marker of "yes," and you have a definite picture of what proper timing looks like, and yet you're delivering your marker late ninety-nine times out of a hundred, you should focus solely on the one time you got your marker exactly right. It's the only instance that matched your mental picture, so put your attention right there and keep it there. It makes no sense to focus on the ninety-nine botched attempts, because you'd only present that warped picture to your subconscious, and you don't want a repeat performance of anything but that one time you got it right. Remember, "What you resist persists." Replay in your mind over and over the one perfect performance. Give yourself pats on the back and refuse to ruminate over any failed attempts. This is good use of the principle that says "Whatever you focus on expands." You have to see success as your normal state. No one sees Thomas Edison as a failure because he made 10,000 "unsuccessful" attempts before he invented a viable light bulb, and neither did he. If he didn't see himself in his mind's eye on the path of success during the process of inventing, he never would have had the staying power to move past thousands of failures until he reached his "normal" state of success once again.

If you've had a streak of subpar performances, don't get off track. Stick to the basics and use visualization to watch yourself executing the skill with precision. Watch it again and again. Bring in not only the visual aspects but also the emotional and kinesthetic ones as well. *Feel* the sensations produced in your muscles and the flow happening in your mind when you do it right. Also, experience the way it feels emotionally afterward to have performed the task perfectly. After you've rehearsed this picture multiple times, go back and do the activity. You will find that proper visualization and bringing attention to successful attempts steepens your learning curve. I would be willing to bet money that Thomas Edison used his own version of this principle through reminding himself after every single attempt to create a light bulb what the finished product would be like when he got it right.

One reason visualization is a time-tested technique for accomplishing stellar performances is that the subconscious cannot distinguish between actual experiences and those that are vividly imagined. The same regions of the brain are stimulated either way. Through visualization, the subconscious receives messages just as it would if you had physically performed the activity. So if you are learning a new skill or perfecting an old one, visualization is the most reliable way to consistently "experience" peak performance. You can always imagine doing something exactly right. The value of actually practicing the skill is that you are building the neural pathways and muscle memory in your body. Obviously, visualization and practice are both absolutely necessary.

If you are learning a new sport, for instance, you must be disciplined in training your body so that you have the physical resources to draw upon to create a great performance—that's a given. Where most athletes, even elite ones, experience breakdown, however, is in their *mental* games. Choking under pressure is a psychological performance issue, not a physical one. Therefore, we realize that learning to execute a skill with precision can be accomplished sooner and more consistently if we use visualization, and we support ourselves and our progress by giving attention only to our best performances.

These principles are closely related to how we should think about reinforcing our dogs. We should focus on all the right things they do (and it's more than we usually give them credit for) and minimize attention directed toward wrong behaviors. Dogs thrive on encouragement the same way people do. So when your dog makes a mistake and you have to correct it, hold in mind the picture of your ultimate goal. If your dog counter surfs, the goal isn't to have him stop this unwanted behavior; it's for him to keep all of his paws on the floor when he's in the kitchen. And if you correct him for counter surfing, do it quickly and move on. Your focus should immediately shift toward the next opportunity you have to encourage him for getting it right. Say he walks through the kitchen a couple minutes later, looks up at the countertop, pauses, thinks, and then walks away. Praise him like crazy! Minimize his mistakes and bring attention to his good behavior. Over time, it will start to become "normal" for him to do the right thing.

If you feel like you are constantly telling your dog no, you might have a focus problem. Orient your mind to have greater awareness of the things he does right, and you'll start to notice a different side of your dog. Keep in mind that your dog desires your attention. So if his good behaviors go unnoticed and unrewarded, he'll lose interest and begin practicing the only behaviors that get him attention: that's right, all the bad ones you don't like. If you simply reverse that process, you will immediately benefit from a greater relationship with a dog that is more respectful and mannerly.

Be a person who seeks out the best in yourself, your dog, and other people, and then be intentional about pointing out and nurturing those standout qualities. Know that the human mind will naturally gravitate toward the negative. Whereas cynicism requires no effort and is a natural byproduct of an idle mind, finding the good in dogs and people is a precious quality. People who possess it are intentional about what they focus on. It doesn't just happen. They focus on the good in life and it expands. They attract more of it over time, bringing out the best in themselves and others, and they experience the best that life has to offer. Strive to be that kind of person. It's a choice, and you can make it today.

Cultivating cooperation and bringing out the best in our dogs and ourselves is a choice.

Picture Perfect: Your Novipsum

Pavlov's dog is a lot smarter than Pavlov would have us think.
I think the only difference between us and that dog is that the dog
actually believes a reward naturally follows the ringing of the bell,
and we believe rewards are a matter of chance. If we would
observe the synchronistic events in our lives carefully, we would
see the pattern and perhaps we too would believe. Maybe then we
would ring the bell more often and, believing, we would have our
rewards.[3]

Pete Koerner

Most of us have a concept or mental picture of what success looks like. It is different for each of us because we all value different things, but we do have a template for success, however vague it may be. What does your success picture look like? Take a minute to close your eyes and view it before reading any farther.

Whatever elements comprised your picture are specific to your personal vision, but a far more important question is embedded here: Were *you* in your picture? Aha! The answer to that question is of the utmost importance. Most people have a picture of success, but they're not anywhere to be seen when they should be front and center.

Your full potential can be accessed only if you see yourself in the right light, because if you can't envision something, it's impossible to create it. Of course, you need a level of natural aptitude in addition to skill developed via concerted effort in whatever you endeavor to succeed at. But assuming those pieces are in place, the only thing that can stop you is having a warped perspective of who you are and what you can become. Zig Ziglar, in his book *See You at the Top*, pointed out: "You cannot consistently perform in a manner that is inconsistent with the way you see yourself."[4] The way you see yourself is your achievement thermostat: If you move too high above the baseline through exceptional performances or too far below it with dismal ones, your subconscious is activated to make adjustments and return you to your "normal" state.

It naturally follows that to raise your capacity for achievement, you must change the way you think about and see yourself. This mental concept or picture is what I like to refer to as the *Novipsum*, a term I coined that is a combination of the Latin words *novum* (meaning "new") and *ipsum* (meaning "self"). Utilized properly, this tool empowers the user to program the subconscious with a definitive and purposeful positive direction. Everyone uses this tool; *how* it's used is what separates the wheat from the chaff. Since we have already alluded to the concept of presenting the right pictures to our subconscious so that we yield the right results, let's specifically look at how to program your *Novipsum*.

Make a list right now of the most important areas in your life. List the top priority areas first and then work your way down. These areas might include your spiritual life, your family life, your relationships, causes you believe in, your purpose and design, your career, your physical and athletic pursuits, skill sets you would like to expand, etc. List each of these areas on paper in bullet format, and next to each item write out a description of how that area would ideally look in the future. You'll also want to script timelines for reaching specific goals (short-, medium-, and long-term) and write out action plans that will help you stay on target. We will look at how to incorporate specific goals shortly, but for now understand that the main purpose of a *Novipsum* is to create a new self-image, as goals are only achievable to the extent you see yourself as capable of manifesting your desires.

For example, if you desire to increase your productivity at work, you could write:

Work: I am the top producer in my department each month. I am regularly recognized for my outstanding performance. I receive extra promotions, time off, and other favorable benefits as a result of my efforts. I continually look for ways to improve the quality of my work, and I am the best at what I do—it's just normal for me.

If you want to capitalize on your ability to train your dog, you might write something along these lines:

Dog Training: Walking my dog and giving him appropriate outlets is part of my normal routine. I am a great leader and I have a phenomenal dog. Every day I work with him and help him to be confident, balanced, and secure. I set aside time daily to train him. I am a wonderful trainer and am the exact right person he needs to help him experience the best life possible. When I train him, I am confident, dependable, and consistent in my reinforcement, regardless of the obstacles we face. We have an awesome relationship.

It is vital that each of these areas is described in the *present* tense because it implies that you are already on your way to becoming that person. It opens up possibilities in the now and expands your belief. It keeps you pointed in a positive direction. And since you can't rise above any limiting beliefs you have about yourself, you must begin the process of replacing them with beliefs suitable for the new you.

Throughout childhood, every person naturally acquires a set of beliefs about life. Some of them are deliberately chosen, but far more often they are suggestions absorbed from our environments that we just accept. It takes a lot of effort, and is frightening, to question those beliefs and assumptions once they've been incorporated into our—false—identities (the ego). If they're a part of us, we are compelled to defend them and find evidence to support them. Any evidence to the contrary must be rationalized away to justify our beliefs and protect our covetous egos. This is a power-draining predicament.

I am not saying you should abandon your beliefs. I'm advocating pure connectedness with your true identity as revealed through the wisdom gained from the exercises in Chapter one. I'm also promoting an honest and candid audit of the beliefs you hold. Did your parents tell people "We're not a very artistic kind of family," or tell you that "Dogs are dangerous animals that can't be trusted and can snap at any moment"? Do you and your coworkers harbor feelings of resentment and suspicion toward upper management? Through suggestion, you may have passively accumulated these beliefs and given them a place in your life. Can you see how these beliefs could lead you to dismiss artistic inklings, be untrusting and fearful of dogs, and bitter toward people in management positions? How could you ever freely explore your capacity for artistic creativity if you have a subconscious belief that you aren't good at it? How could you possibly overcome your lingering distrust of dogs without usurping a belief your parents installed in you? And how on earth do you expect to land an upper management position at your company if your underlying belief system sabotages your every effort?

Make a list of beliefs, sayings, and sentiments you have or were told about important areas of life like spirituality, travel and adventure, marriage relationships, children, the wealthy and the poor, health and fitness and body image, people's relationship with animals, and any others you can think of that are relevant to you. Once you've written them out, identify every limiting belief, every idea and concept that naturally narrows the field of "the possible" or harbors a negative tone, however subtle it may be. It can be difficult to let go of ideas that have guided us our entire lives, but as warriors, we must be willing to give up everything we are to become what we were created to be. We must have the courage to take hold of new beliefs that serve us better.

Jesus said, "No one pours new wine into old wineskins. Otherwise, the wine will burst the skins, and both the wine and the wineskins will be ruined. No, they pour new wine into new wineskins" (Mark 2:22 NIV). In the same way, we have to be made anew (our minds transformed) in order to receive the fullness of life's blessings. If we hold on to our old, stubborn ways of thinking, believing, and viewing the world, even if great things come our way, we will have no way to receive them. We will either repel them, they will repel us, or we will actively fight against the very things that we need the most but are not equipped to handle.

It is impossible for an overweight person who believes genetics make people fat to lose weight and keep it off. A person who thinks people are naturally mean-spirited will have a hard time opening up to others. Someone who believes rich people are greedy will never experience wealth, because it goes against who they think they are and what they believe. But what if those same people shifted perspectives? What if the overweight person accepted a new belief that proper diet, exercise, and lifestyle are the most important factors that determine whether a person is fit or fat? What if the guy who believes people are vindictive internalizes a new belief that people are generally well-intentioned and forgiving? What if a man who believes that money is for the corrupt and the hoggish changes his mind to see money as a force for good and rich people as being typically generous?

We must understand that we do not have to be conscious of these beliefs for them to impact us. Someone who was warned by his mother when he was young with the saying "A moment on the lips, forever on the hips" will be psychologically and physically affected by that attitude unless it is brought into conscious awareness, dealt with, and replaced. The impact these unconscious beliefs have on us cannot be overstated. They determine which doors of opportunity are open to us and which remain closed. We build our lives based on them, much like a builder follows a blueprint to create a home. By having conscious awareness of our beliefs, we can actively select those most fitting for the life we've always wanted to live. So examine your blueprint and erase any beliefs that are impediments to progress. Replace them with new ones that support your efforts and are consistent with your dreams and desires. When your convictions are congruent with your passions, your power will be unleashed.

The next element to incorporate is visualization itself. For me, this means that I memorize the affirmations on my personal list and spend time every day (morning works best for me) repeating the proclamations silently while visualizing myself as the person who is the complete embodiment of each. My visualization is very vivid, even visceral, as I picture my *Novipsum* and the presence I naturally project as a result of being that person. I get to where I step into each role as I work my way down the list so that by the end of that daily practice, my subconscious has a crystal clear picture of my *Novipsum*.

This is a perfect place to introduce a couple of important considerations and practices to maximize your effectiveness. Cultivating deep conviction that a desired reality is already yours is a prerequisite to outward manifestation, and belief an absolute must if you wish to see the creative process through. Infusing the process of visualization with gratitude demonstrates belief, because appreciation is something you naturally express for things already *in* your life. I would also very politely yet adamantly recommend that you practice meditation (see Chapter one) prior to engaging in your visualizations. During meditation your brain waves (measured in cycles per second, or hertz) will slow, which results in less distortion of the messages you send to your subconscious. Remember, the subconscious is the powerhouse of the mind and accepts whatever makes its way through, while the conscious mind is the "filter." Having a filter is incredibly important, especially with the barrage of messages that come your way each day. Believing and acting on everything you see and hear would be disastrous.

The problem this presents is that your conscious mind, if engaged at the wrong time, will sabotage your desires. It will scoff at your affirmations and tell you over and over why "That won't work." By the time your visualizations and prayers make their way through all the fog, they are peppered with doubt, unbelief, and logic about how impossible and unrealistic your dreams really are. This renders them ineffectual. But if you will meditate prior to practicing your affirmations and visualizations, thus minimizing conscious interference, you will be amazed at how what you meditate on will come to pass in your life—and perhaps much sooner than you anticipate. Progressive muscle relaxation exercises combined with meditation can help you access more powerful states for cleanly impressing desired messages upon your subconscious. Information about these techniques is readily available online.

How often do you visualize the perfect walk with your dog? If you've had a rough go of it lately, perhaps the simple practice of daily affirmation and mental rehearsal will create a better experience. It certainly can't hurt. Can you see yourself walking with your well-behaved, relaxed friend right at your side? Can you feel the leash draped softly over your fingers? Can you hear the light jingling of your dog's tags as you walk peacefully through a crowd? Can you feel the sense of ease, living in that moment?

All of these principles are intimately linked to goal setting but distinct in that the creation of your *Novipsum* is more about who you *are*, whereas goal setting is about what you accomplish. Specific ways of acting and patterns of behavior are associated with the *Novipsum* (it's normal for a confident person to act confident). I like to incorporate specific goals with my practice of *Novipsum* affirmations and visualizations by placing them at the end of the appropriate category. For example, a salesperson could tag something on the end of his affirmation, such as "I won the regional sales competition this year." A swimmer might add the following to his affirmation: "I placed first in my age group at this July's swim meet for the 200 meter freestyle."

As previously mentioned, goals can do more harm than good if they are overemphasized. A couple chapters from now we will touch on why personal growth should receive greater emphasis than goals themselves. For now, realize that thinking about, stressing about, and obsessing over goals usually leads to missing them altogether. Too intense a focus applied in the direction of a specific goal (outcome) will cause you to try too hard and deteriorate the quality of the work you're doing. It diverts your attention and energy away from the actual effort, so always keep your focus on performance and proper execution of the task at hand. Be the absolute best you can be at what you do, and accomplishment of set goals is a natural consequence. If you focus primarily on goals, however, you may overlook the importance of personal growth and progress, thus negating the possibility of achievement.

Personal goals should be defined, specific, and measurable, as well as broken down into long-term, medium-range, and short-term goals. They need to be daily and actionable with a definite time frame for completion, and they need to be written down. But above all else, be careful not to let them trump your reverence for the process. Meticulous preparation followed by masterful execution that is guided by exquisite control of your mind is the essence of excellence, and it is only through the *process* that your character is fortified, not by reaching the end goal.

To focus your attention on the outcome—particularly the day of a competition for athletes—saps energy. Stop thinking and start doing. After all, accomplishing a goal is predicated upon executing a great performance. The purpose of incorporating the visualization of goals is to set direction and see yourself as capable of accomplishing them. Once you are in the throes of the competition, let your subconscious mind take over. Instead of trying really hard, enter into a state of flow, with every bit of your attention directed into the feel of the activity. Conscious thought during a performance leads to doubt, fear, and negative self-talk. When your conscious mind tries to take over and think about the situation, project itself to the end, or wrestle with how it can escape the stress, remember to shift your focus back into your body and stay 100 percent present-minded. It's the perfect time to remind yourself to "Breathe-See-Feel."

I recently watched a movie, *Edge of Tomorrow*, starring Tom Cruise and Emily Blunt. Cruise's character, Lt. Col. Bill Cage, is a military officer who is unexpectedly thrust to the front lines of war, despite the fact that he has never been in combat. He is killed in battle but then wakes up and is "reset" to the prior day. This loop continues over and over, much like he's in a video game where he plays, dies, and goes back to the beginning of the level, each time learning something new and getting a little bit closer to his goal. He meets Blunt's character, Rita Vrataski, who is a venerated war hero and used to be caught up in the same loop as Cage, able to remember the events from previous repetitions. They need each other to succeed, and Vrataski has lost her ability to remember what happens once they die, so she depends on Cage to find her again each day and bring her up to speed so that together they might find a way through the carnage to victory.

In studying the importance of knowing when to *think* with the conscious mind and when to *do* with the subconscious mind and the body, *Edge of Tomorrow* gives a perfect illustration. Every day Cage meets up with Vrataski and they prepare for battle by recounting what they learned prior to reset about the positions of the enemies, as well as how to maneuver past obstacles and best position themselves to make it farther than the day before. This is when the thinking, planning, and strategizing are done: before a situation is actually engaged. The pair then sets out warring against aliens and carrying out their plan. When moving through the fight, they are present-focused, very much inhabiting their bodies and engaging their subconscious. Planning while in the throes of fighting simply takes too much precious time, so they must lean on their intuition and carry out their plan with attention focused solely on action. Each time they die, they reset, find each other, utilize critical thinking to come up with a game plan, and then set thinking aside so they can execute their plan with complete awareness, becoming more impeccable as warriors with each repetition.

At the end of the day, disciplining our minds, directing our focus, and mastering ourselves is the ultimate victory we continuously realize as we immerse ourselves in the journey of life. We do not fret when things don't go our way, because every outcome allows us to learn and adjust. We don't see things as good and bad, because we know that everything works together according to a greater plan for our lives. We welcome each day with gratitude and stay open to what comes our way instead of insisting that things go our way. We stay grounded and trust our inner guidance system. And we win by abiding in our Source and letting go.

Letting Go

When trying to remember a person's name, have you noticed that it almost never comes to mind until you stop trying to remember it? That is because it's only when you've released a directive to your subconscious mind that it can do its work. Your conscious mind runs interference if employed when the subconscious mind should be running the show. Since you obviously can't make yourself stop thinking, place your attention instead on a task that needs your conscious attention. Rather than trying to remember the person's name, shift gears and think about your upcoming schedule to prioritize the items you need to complete over the next several days. This releases the name-retrieving task to your subconscious.

In practice, take time every day to envision and affirm your *Novipsum* as a present reality, and after you have gone through all the items on your list, simply move on and go about your day. It is the subconscious mind that powers the process, so it must be presented with information from the conscious mind and then that information must be consciously released.

This act of letting go is often the last thing standing between a person and his or her desires. There's just no way for the conscious mind to accomplish a task that is strictly subconscious in nature. The subconscious mind is a trustworthy worker, so it is best to assign it a task, move on, and let it do its work. This counterintuitive concept can be very difficult to stomach for people who are controlling by nature, but the tighter we hold on, the better the odds we will lose our grip. Letting go and trusting in the process not only makes life easier, it also helps us obtain the results we want much faster.

So here is the breakdown of the key ingredients we must include in our "desire obtainment" recipe:

- (1/2 cup) Supportive belief system
- (1 cup) Consistent visualization of a properly con-structed *Novipsum*
- (1 tsp) Affirmations and a distinct release to the subconscious
- (2 tsp) Focus on personal effort and flow; not on controlling outcomes
- (3 *heaping* TBSP) Attention given to any personal successes along the way

You can use this recipe to sharpen your skills in the workplace, become a more confident and outgoing person, or build a fantastic marriage. The sky is the limit.

Tracking Progress

The last component of these processes we will examine is certainly not the least important: Make sure you have a system for measuring progress so you can track it. If you make record keeping a habit, you can isolate what works and stay grounded.

Tracking results over a period of time is the only way to systematically evaluate what works for you. The way I train dogs is not the way you train them, at least it shouldn't be. We all operate from the same set of principles, but we are each uniquely gifted and equipped, which means our best work comes as a result of operating from our strengths. I think you'll find, as I did, that when you train in a manner that plays to your individual strengths, you will be markedly more effective. Authenticity is the hallmark of true greatness. Authenticity is accomplished by combining the best of what you know (different techniques, methodologies, and strategies) and applying it in a way that stays true to who you are as a person.

Record keeping allows you to see results in black-and-white. As you incorporate new tactics into the way you train your dog, it will help you zero in on those that provide the greatest benefit. It would be futile, after all, to train your dog only one way. There must be some room for creativity; otherwise, you become dogmatic in your training and force your dog to fit within the confines of your training plan instead of fitting your training plan to the needs of your dog. Keep a progress journal in which you record any changes made to your training plan, as well as specific outcomes observed as a result of using the new techniques.

There is often a huge gap between how well we think we're doing and how well we're actually doing. This gap gets wider whenever we fail to track our progress. It's just human nature. There's a scene in *The Matrix Reloaded* where the character known as the Architect tells the principle character, Neo, "Denial is the most predictable of all human responses." We fake ourselves out when we fail to hold ourselves accountable with an objective system of measurement. That may be acceptable to the vast majority of people, but it is uncharacteristic of a warrior making the effort to read and apply the principles of Transformational training to his life. We simply cannot afford to indulge denial and miss out on capturing our potential. We are seekers. We are hunting for those things that create positive transformation in ourselves and in our dogs. We avoid the pitfalls of denial and delusion and keep ourselves honest with essential record keeping to monitor progress in each key area of life we are working to improve.

Neuro-Linguistic Programming

Neuro-Linguistic Programming (NLP) is a field of psychology that studies the "mental maps" successful people use to yield outstanding results. NLP is built on the premise that the fastest, most efficient way to duplicate the results of an expert in a particular venue is to study the way he operates psychologically while applying himself to his work. How does he mentally prepare himself? What questions does he ask himself before beginning a task to make sure he is ready to begin? How does he employ self-talk (internal dialogue) to focus on his task? What mental pictures does he see? How does he construct them? How does he transition from preparation and thinking (conscious mind) to entering flow and doing (subconscious mind)? How does he mentally process successful and unsuccessful outcomes? When does he make necessary adjustments, and how does he know they're necessary? How does he construct his criteria so he knows when the job is done? There are myriad more questions one would want to ask of an expert in order to develop a template and begin programming one's own mind, and NLP is a much more expansive field than we will touch on here. However, we will examine some critical components of NLP that can help us understand how to use our minds more effectively.

The first and most obvious way to increase your proficiency at any skill is to study people who are already highly proficient at it. One of the greatest benefits of mentoring with great people is that their attitudes will rub off on you. The opposite is also true; spending lots of time absorbing the attitudes of negative and inept people (despite whether or not they're "good people") will create a shift in your attitudes and thoughts, and you will experience similar negativity and ineptness. The proof is in the pudding: Write out a list of your five closest friends. Then record next to each of their names how much money they make. Add together the yearly income of those five friends and divide by five. The average of your friends' salaries will likely be very close to yours. This is good news if you are exactly where you want to be financially, but not such good news if you aren't. If you want to prosper, step out and establish relationships with people who are prospering. You don't necessarily need to distance yourself from old friends, but you will definitely need to add some new ones. As Albert Einstein wisely pointed out, "You cannot solve a problem with the same mind that created it."

Transformational change begins within. Is there an area of your life you'd like to improve its quality? Great! Immediately begin to study some people who are effective in that area, because what's going on inside them is what's producing the results around them. If you want to become better at training your dog, find a well-balanced trainer with whom you can study and work with. If you want to have a better marriage, establish friendships with couples who have great marriages, so you can learn what the happy couples know. The worst thing you can do is to hang out with other people whose marriages are falling apart and then learn their opinions and undesirable ways.

If you cannot build a direct relationship with those you would like to learn from, study them from a distance. Attend a seminar. Read books, articles, and blogs they have written. Study audio and video presentations. Develop a hunger for knowledge. Realize that your philosophy about life directly affects your results in life. The word *philosophy* is the synthesis of two Greek words: *phileo*, which means "love," and *sophia*, meaning "wisdom." Philosophy, then, is the love of wisdom. When you hunger for wisdom you will find ways obtain it. And if it feels like you're spinning your wheels and getting nowhere, be patient! Consistently seeking wisdom will eventually open doors to you, often in the form of people who possess what you want and are willing to share their insights.

Life is like a search engine. It will eventually give you exactly what you are looking for. Make sure you are looking for the right things in the right places. One of the best ways to do that is to get in the hip pocket of folks who have already been where you want to go. Then it's your job to find out how they think. Pick their brains and then model your way of thinking after their proven psychological strategies. You'll also need to be the type of person who gives—not one who just takes. Cherish the people who help you grow, and find ways to serve them. This is how you bring in the balance.

Also realize that everything you've experienced in life has a place in your mind. It is permanently stored in the subconscious. Granted, certain experiences may lie in the deepest of recesses, and you will never consciously recollect them, but they are undoubtedly there. They are mental "residue," in a sense.

What, then, is the difference between two people who have a similar life experience and upbringing who go through a traumatic event and yet one of them disintegrates while the other finds meaning and goes on to lead a full and happy life? While the answer is surely multifaceted, there is a single, specific ability the second person would have unquestionably employed more skillfully. You guessed it: the power of focus and attention.

The quality of our focus and attention affects the way we mentally and emotionally digest information. From a NLP perspective, it boils down to how we assign meaning to our life experiences. Are the great experiences of your life in the forefront of your mind, or do the negative experiences dominate your memories? The way you mentally code information about your experiences will profoundly affect your life's direction.

Take the next few minutes to perform a couple of exercises. First, recall a past experience that is one of your all-time favorites, something that makes you happy just thinking about it. Now, close your eyes and relive that moment. Remember what sensations you were feeling in your body. Focus on what thoughts were going through your mind. Make sure you vividly recall sounds and any significant scents that contributed to the experience. What were you looking at in that moment? What colors did you see? Relive this moment as lucidly as possible.

How do you feel after reliving the experience? Note that the way you recall the experience has a lot to do with the emotional impact it has on you. The more you allow yourself to become immersed in the experience again, the more you are willing to lose yourself in it, the greater the impact. Recalling the situation from a first-person perspective (as opposed to watching yourself from a distance), makes it feel closer and more vivid. Brighten the surroundings and see the colors in all their brilliance; you might find it has a greater impact on you. If you increase the volume of the sounds or place greater focus on the internal sensations you felt, what kind of an effect does that have? Experiment with recalling the situation multiple times. Each time focus on a different element. You will find that certain triggers increase the intensity of the memory's impact. Once you have identified these triggers, you can focus on them whenever you recall pleasant events.

Unfortunately, it's easy to get tripped up by recalling unpleasant past events, particularly if they are vivid memories. One simple way to diminish the negative impact of bad experiences is to change how you encode and remember them. This isn't about denial of their occurrence; it's about stripping them of any paralyzing power they have over your mind. First, recall the experience in its fullness and develop awareness of particular elements within the memory that trigger intense negative emotions. Take a couple minutes now to recall a moderately negative past experience and develop awareness of its emotional triggers. In some situations the trigger might be the sight of someone's face. In others it's hearing what someone said. In any case, find out what those triggers are.

How do you feel after reliving the experience? Probably not awesome. That's okay because you're going to move through it. Notice I said *through* it not around it. Close your eyes again and begin to change some things about the memory. Up close, personal, vivid mental pictures; clear and crisp auditory memories; intense physical sensations: all of these things produce intense emotional responses. That is how you should code positive experiences. Negative experiences can be softened by doing the exact opposite. View your bad memory from a distance, as if you are a detached, far-off, third-party observer. Change the quality of the picture so that you see it in black-and-white or simply shades of gray. Make it a little out of focus. Lower the volume of any sounds, and experiment with changing the pitch of people's voices. If people's voices are high-pitched, does that intensify the emotion of the memory, or soften it? What happens if people's voices are slow with an Eeyore-like quality? Experiment with changing people's accents. What happens if you change the size of the environment so that everything but you is itty-bitty? What if, during the replay of the memory, you feel a mellow energy slowly moving through your body, like a cool breeze on a warm sunny day? There are endless ways to alter the impact of memories. It's not about erasing them, but rather controlling the way you remember them so they don't dominate you. The important thing is to use the quality of your focus and attention so that memories work to your benefit.

If your dream is to be a great singer and you know you have the talent, you had better find a way to deal with the memory of your father telling you when you were young, "You are never going to be great at singing. It's just not in you." If it has been negatively affecting your mind, you need to recode that memory. You will also need to increase the intensity and emotional impact of your successes and memories of the times you received encouragement from friends, teachers, and loved ones. Be sure you determine the tone and direction of your mind, for, in the end, whatever dominates your thought life will make or break you.

Putting It All Together

When choosing how to best train your dog, you first need a solid understanding of the various modes of communication you have at your disposal. There are lots of options. You can pull from the categories of classical conditioning as well as operant conditioning. Within each realm lies a vast array of training applications that you can use to help your dog; everything from creating new associations and altering old ones to utilizing various combinations of reinforcement to establish new behaviors.

Since we all use positive reinforcement, negative reinforcement, positive punishment, and negative punishment in our interactions with our dogs, become a student of these principles so that you can learn how to use them in the most supportive and appropriate fashion possible. Be sensitive to the needs of your dog as an individual, because no one training methodology is appropriate for every dog and situation. Take into consideration many factors in developing your training plan and remain flexible in your approach. As your dog and situations change, make necessary adjustments and be mindful to change your game plan to meet the current and most relevant needs of your dog.

Many tools and techniques are available to you, so many the combinations are endless. No doubt more tools will be developed in the future. Instead of getting lost in a sea of tools and becoming overwhelmed by information about different techniques, view things in the light of overarching principles. For instance, you might see a man walking his two dogs—one dog wearing a harness and the other a pinch collar—that both spot a squirrel and begin to bark. Their owner changes directions and walks away from the squirrel, which places pressure on the leashes (positive) to stop them from barking at the squirrel (punishment) and redirects their attention by going a different way. Despite that one dog is on a harness and the other on a pinch collar, the same *principle* of positive punishment is being used. Techniques change but principles never do. Understanding the principles of training allows all techniques and tools to be understood in simple terms.

When training your dog, remember that behavioral problems always have an embedded source. The root of a problem is what you aim to remedy as opposed to behaviors that are merely symptoms of the primary issue. The reinforcement you give your dog needs to be delivered at the right time so that there is clarity about what is being reinforced. Select tools that are most beneficial in helping your dog learn. What works for one dog may not work for another, and what worked at one time for a dog may not work today, so change your training methods accordingly. When rewarding your dog, make sure to use something that *he* perceives as rewarding. If he likes playing tug as a reward for a job well done instead of food, adapt your approach and play tug instead.

Above all, have a positive presence with your pup. Being moody around dogs only creates confusion and insecurity in them. Being balanced and predictable in your energy, however, gives them the courage to try new things and engenders trust. When working with your dog, seek out opportunities to reward good behavior. Focus on what's right, and when you have to address mistakes, maintain a positive presence with the sole purpose of getting your dog back to rewardable behavior as quickly as possible.

Of all the sophisticated tools available, the human brain is atop the list. It is divided into two realms: the conscious and subconscious. The subconscious mind's job is to take each of us in the direction presented to it by our conscious minds. Therefore, be deliberate about which thoughts you choose to entertain. Whatever you focus on expands, so manage your environment to make sure it is a healthy and positive.

Be discerning about the people you spend time with as well as what you listen to, watch, and think about. Not to do so is to drift through life like a ship without a sail, being controlled by the waves and currents of life. If you don't determine your character, the world will. Since charting a course begins with knowing where you're going, tear down any negative and limiting images and beliefs you hold about life and yourself, and put up in their place positive pictures of who you aim to become and where you want to go. Thoughtfully direct your focus and attention toward those things that can move you in the right direction.

When you are confronted with problems, focus you attention on finding constructive answers. Ask yourself questions that presuppose solutions, and the subconscious mind goes about finding them for you. Then apply your efforts to the task at hand, all the while remembering that you cannot control outcomes, only the quality of your performance. The locus of your attention should be impeccable execution.

When training your dog, lose yourself in the *process* instead of wasting precious energy and focus fretting about outcomes and results. You can think, evaluate results, and strategize about refining your process after the work is done. Understand that there is a time for thinking (conscious mind driven) and a time for doing (subconscious mind driven and physical/somatic). Continually pursue mastery of both. The timing of when you engage each will be determined by whether you are in a planning phase of an activity (use the conscious mind to think) or the performance phase (use the subconscious mind and engage the body).

Once you know what you are striving for, what a desired finished product will look like, hold that picture in your mind, constantly referencing it as you work toward its realization. Present it to your subconscious mind and utilize visualization and affirmations while also habitually focusing on successful performances and refusing to ruminate over failed ones. When you fail, be grateful for having the opportunity to extract important lessons from the experience but don't relive the moment over and over. Replay and focus your attention on the times you get things right. In this way, you will begin to see success as your normal state and something that is within your grasp.

Your *Novipsum* is a concept of what success looks like for your life. It is the ultimate person you want to become. Actively construct this picture and put yourself right in the center of it, because it simply cannot be a vague notion or a picture you are not associated with. List the most important areas in your life and then write out a description of your *Novipsum*. Read the description daily while seeing and feeling what it is like to be inside the skin of that person. After this daily task is completed, practice the act of letting go, thus releasing the image to your subconscious, and then track your progress through record keeping. Record information about specific outcomes you experience in key areas related to your *Novipsum*, as well as any changes made in your techniques or approach. This keeps you grounded in reality. You can now systematically evaluate the effectiveness of different methods you use. Charting your progress (or lack thereof) helps by providing objective information. Reflect on this information and evaluate the soundness of your techniques; it is the platform you stand upon and the vantage point from which you strategize your future courses of action.

Your progress in life can be catapulted forward by studying people who are already masters at what you are working toward. Examine how they think and adopt similar attitudes. Observe and ask questions and be diligent about programming your mind to mirror the beliefs and thought processes they utilize. This practice compresses time, allowing you to progress at an accelerated rate. Seek out people who are spiritually, mentally, emotionally, relationally, financially, professionally, and physically where you want to be. This requires you to actively pursue relationships with a number of people and to invest in resources like books, videos, seminars, and audio presentations. Investing in personal growth pays lifelong dividends and allows you to be a greater contributor to those around you.

As you grow to understand how your experiences and memories have contributed to who you are, you can become all the more intentional about how you code and recall past events. Vividly remember positive experiences from a first-person perspective. See everything as close up, vibrant, and bright. Recall each sensation with as much intensity as possible and magnify the elements that trigger the most powerful positive emotional responses within you.

With unpleasant or painful memories, become aware of the elements that trigger negative emotions and then recode them to soften the impact. You can do this through dissociating (recalling the experience from a third-person perspective) and seeing everything as far off, dull, and dim. Experiment with changing the visual aspects of the memory as well as the auditory and somatic. Recode the experience in such a way that it neutralizes the negative emotional impact.

Practical Application Exercises Related to the Mind

For Your Dog:

1. Take a completely neutral stimulus (object, sound, etc.), one your dog does not have any particular association with, and then have fun by creating a new association with it. For example, let's say your dog loves fetching tennis balls, and whenever you reach for the shelf where you keep his tennis ball, he spins a quick circle before sitting down and waiting expectantly to play his game of fetch. For the next week, add the neutral stimulus of running both of your hands through your hair right before you reach for the shelf to grab his tennis ball. Eventually, simply running your hands through your hair will cause him to spin a circle and sit down in front of you. In this example, you would have effectively taken a neutral stimulus (the running of your hands through your hair) and created a conditioned response in your dog (excited anticipation manifested as spinning a circle and sitting down). The particular stimulus used and the new association you develop isn't important. The importance is that you go through the process of creating a brand-new association for your dog. Have fun and be creative with this exercise. It's a kick in the pants if you do it right.

2. In each of the four quadrants below, list at least two examples of how you have used the particular principle of operant conditioning in working with your dog. If you aren't sure, spend ten minutes training your dog, making a conscious effort to be aware of how you reinforce or discourage the different choices he makes. Then come back and fill out the table below.

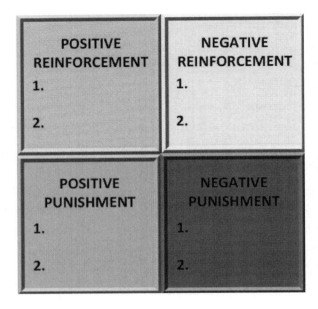

POSITIVE REINFORCEMENT	NEGATIVE REINFORCEMENT
1.	1.
2.	2.
POSITIVE PUNISHMENT	NEGATIVE PUNISHMENT
1.	1.
2.	2.

3. Take a video of yourself doing a training session with your dog. Review the video and observe the way you handle your dog. Is your timing accurate? What tone do you use when issuing commands, markers, praise, corrections, etc.? Is your demeanor calm, excited, frustrated, happy, etc.? How would you characterize the energy you are sharing with your dog? Are your body movements smooth and clear, or herky-jerky and frenetic? Do you look confident, or worried? Is your body relaxed, or holding tension? If you are using a leash, notice when there is tension and when it is loose. Review the video a second time and focus your attention on your dog. How does he respond to the information you are providing? Does he look confused and concerned, or curious and happy? What seems to connect with him and engage him the most? Use the information gathered from this exercise to fine-tune your handling skills.

For You:

1. Your conscious mind is an evaluation tool that has a past-future orientation. Your body and intuition are present-moment entities. The timing of the use of each is critically important if you want to maximize your effectiveness. Your conscious mind is the great preparatory wizard that sets the stage. Your subconscious and intuition, along with your body, are the players onstage the moment the curtain opens. This exercise is about channeling your attention properly to increase the *quality of your performance*.

   Choose a basic task, preferably one that requires giving some thought to planning but is fairly simple, like putting a new plant in the yard or going to the grocery store and picking up fresh fruit. Next, plan out the basic execution of the task with your conscious mind. Anticipate what you will need to bring with you as well as specific actions you will need to take to complete the task. Also decide upon a specific ending point to the activity so you know when you are done, such as when you reenter your house.

   Once you have finished this first step, transition to the second by standing still and taking several deliberate deep breaths. This will help you redirect your attention from your conscious mind into your subconscious mind and body. Finally, you'll enter into step two by taking some kind of physical action, anything from reaching for your car keys to walking toward a coat closet. You are now engaging the present-moment vehicle of the subconscious mind and the body itself.

   Once you initiate this second step, your task is to *keep* your mind on the activity. If you start to "think," remind yourself to stay present by silently repeating Breathe-See-Feel as often as necessary while performing the task. After you reach the predetermined end point of the activity, review the experience, thus reengaging your conscious mind. This is the time to reflect on the task and evaluate the experience as well as any lessons you learned—a debriefing, if you will.

How was the quality of the experience affected by staying present and drinking in every detail of each moment? How did engaging your body and intuitive mind feel? Were you surprised by how difficult it was to keep your attention in the here and now?

2. This next activity is an easy-to-do, two-day exercise. Your prep work before starting is to select an area of your life you would like to improve. Once you have done this, you will start the first day of the exercise by asking yourself "What can I do to become better at _____?" All you need to do is ask yourself the question in a quiet place with all of your attention focused on the question, and then release it to your subconscious mind and move on with your day.

Keep a small notebook with you on day one and record any answers your subconscious mind presents. Do not evaluate them logically; just write them down. This is an intuitive process and will therefore not always make sense to the conscious mind, which is intellectually driven and naturally skeptical. At the end of the day, sit down with your list and pick out two or three simple and realistic action items from your list.

On day two you will arise, revisit the desired improvement area you selected on day one, and tell yourself that you are improving greatly in that area, while visualizing what it will look and feel like as you apply yourself to performing specific actions from your list. For this one day it is critical that you are willing to set aside pride, doubt, and hesitation. You must visualize yourself as someone who is experiencing quick and significant improvements in the area you have chosen. Put yourself in the picture and see it as normal, if even for just that day, for you to be great. Meditating prior to your visualization will make this easier. Don't try to force it. As a matter of fact, don't try at all, but remind yourself in the morning, at noon, and again in the early evening of your set intention and let your actions naturally follow.

At the end of the second day, make a list of your observations about how the exercise affected your mind-set, emotions, and actions. How did it feel to try on a new self? If you liked it, realize that you can continue on that path, provided you are willing to be disciplined in the daily practice of seeing yourself in a new light and acting accordingly until it becomes natural for you and you begin to say, "That's just who I am."

3. This is a journaling exercise. Depending on your personality, this will either fit you like a glove or take focused effort to stick with it, but either way it is an invaluable exercise and takes place over the course of only a couple hours at most, so anyone can do it. The example below goes into some detail to help illustrate the exercise. The primary steps are as follows: 1) select an activity; 2) choose specific aspects of the activity to bring attention to; 3) record observations as well as some type of measurable result (score, time, etc.); and 4) review the results as revealed through your record keeping and evaluate which items specifically affected your performance in a positive or negative way.

Choose an activity to perform that you have some kind of experience with. Due to the nature of the exercise, a physical activity such as a sport may lend itself best. Let's assume that you are a bowler. Go to your local bowling alley and play at least three games. Have a separate score sheet for each game and decide on exactly what you plan to focus on. Some examples might be: the overall angle and positioning of your torso as you approach the lane to take your shot; positioning of each shoulder relative to the other throughout each phase of your approach and release; the flexion of your hand and wrist on your bowling arm; the cadence and depth of your breath throughout the preparatory and action phases of your shot; what comprises your self-talk; what thoughts are going through your mind; where your eyes are looking and how wide or narrow your focus is; how much of your overall focus is dedicated to—and being diluted by—irrelevant details about your surroundings and the people around you, etc.

Since there are ten frames per game, take your score sheet and divide the games up into smaller, two-frame chunks. Put a bracket around each two-frame group, and below that list a specific item you would like to bring attention to. For the first frame of each group you will focus your attention on *awareness* of the selected item. For the second frame of each group you will focus your attention on *tweaking your technique* in that area. If you focused on awareness of your breathing the first frame and found that your breathing was relatively shallow, you could consciously focus on using a steady, deep breath for the second frame.

For each set of two frames you will have a different area of your technique you will focus on. Before moving to the next set of two frames, come back to your score sheet and record not only your score but any observations you made about how changing your point of attention or technique affected the experience.

Do this for the first two games played and then take a ten- to fifteen-minute break to rest and evaluate the results. How did each focal point affect the feel of your game and your score? Take the focal point that made the biggest positive difference in your score and spend the entire third game focusing on that one item: one frame observing yourself and being more aware of subtle movements; the next frame focused on improving the quality of that aspect of movement. Record your results and repeat until the third game is complete. You will begin to see in black-and-white which areas, when focused on, give you the most bang for your buck.

Chapter Five

Look at That Body

It is the pervading law of all things organic and inorganic, of all things physical and metaphysical, of all things human and all things superhuman, of all true manifestations of the head, of the heart, of the soul, that the life is recognizable in its expression, that form ever follows function. This is the law.

Louis Sullivan

It is an axiom of nature that form follows function. This relates back to the topic of Chapter one on design. If you were in the desert of a foreign land and happened upon what looked like some type of tool but weren't sure exactly what it was for, you could study it's form—the material it was made from, the shape and density, etc.—and make some inferences about its function and how it might best be used. With respect to the body, this principle is undeniable.

Dogs (purebreds especially) are physically equipped to do the job they were bred for. Dogs bred for retrieving purposes, for example, are built differently than dogs bred to warm the laps of royalty. Everything from the thickness of a dog's coat to the shape of its head to the positioning of its eyes to its stature is influenced by what it was bred to do.

Take the Komondor for instance. This fascinating breed lays claim to one of the most unique looks in the canine world. These dogs stand around thirty inches tall, weighing over one hundred pounds, with an all-white, dreadlock-like braided coat that alone weighs in the neighborhood of fifteen pounds! The Komondor's appearance is part and parcel to the function it was bred for, namely to guard flocks of sheep from predators such as wolves and bears. They are incredibly protective, and should the sheep they are guarding be threatened, this well-camouflaged beast will emerge from the flock to surprise the intruders with a very unceremonious greeting, driving the predators away or attacking them to ensure the sheep are protected.

The Komondor: a stunning example of form following function in the canine body.

In a more general sense, all dogs share some common characteristics. They all have eyes, ears, tails, and such, and each part of a dog's body is used within the context of canine communication. Dogs cannot speak, at least not the same way people do, so they skillfully use their bodies to do their talking. Their bodies can give us clues as to what they are thinking, and if we pay attention to their physical needs, we will also see that we can do much to ensure they stay healthy and fit. From general fitness and skin health to promoting relaxation in the body, we have the responsibility to be informed owners and great caregivers for our dogs. Since dogs communicate so much through their bodies, the more in tune we become with their needs in this area, the stronger our relationship will become.

In educating ourselves about caring for our dogs' bodies and health, we would be remiss if we neglected our own. We are all busy. We all have work to do and deadlines to meet and family obligations to fulfill. Everyone on this magnificent planet shares one common variable: We're all given twenty-four hours each day. Imagine giving two individuals a million dollars each to do with as they please. They will inevitably spend or invest the million dollars very differently, and the manner in which they allocate the funds will determine the extent it benefits their lives and the lives of others. Similarly, how people choose to spend or invest the twenty-four hours they are given each day is what separates them. Since the gift of time is far more precious than any sum of money, being good stewards of the time we are given is of the utmost importance.

Taking care of your body requires time. You may say, "That's just it; I don't *have* any time." But remember, we all *have* the same number of hours in a day. Realize that no matter who you are and how busy your life is, someone else has a heavier work load, a larger family, and more extensive physical challenges yet still manages to stay fit and maintain balance in his or her life. I find it helpful to seek out stories of such individuals, because it inspires me and gives me the will to move forward when I see someone with greater challenges who is making things happen despite her circumstances. I've had brief bouts of feeling sorry for myself because I experienced some type of setback or injury. But then I'd read about a person like Bethany Hamilton and have a complete shift in mind-set.

You may be familiar with Bethany's story. From a young age she loved surfing. At age thirteen, while waiting to catch a wave, a tiger shark attacked her and bit off her left arm. She lost more than half of her body's blood by the time she reached the hospital. Fast-forward a year. Bethany was not just back on her surfboard, she was surfing in national competitions. At the time of writing this, she is ranked and surfing on the pro circuit. Wow. Reading about someone like that changed my attitude about what was possible in my own life and eliminated excuses I had about overcoming my own challenges.

Taking good care of your body, just as in other aspects of life, requires letting go of excuses and becoming creative in planning your twenty-four hours. In his book *The Magic of Thinking Big*, David Schwartz dedicates the entire second chapter ("Cure Yourself of Excusitis, the Failure Disease") to the topic of eliminating excuses from one's life. Humans are incredibly resilient and can overcome most anything. One thing a person cannot overcome, however, is an excuse they refuse to let go of. How many people do you know who constantly make excuses and whine about what happened to them ever get ahead in life? I don't know any either.

You may be wondering why I've devoted a chapter that solely focuses on the body. Because it's impossible to let any aspect of the mind-body-spirit continuum crash and burn and still maintain a balanced life. Our dogs' bodies need to be in balance, as do ours. Taking care of one's body is not selfish; it's one of the greatest acts of giving. When we take care of our bodies, we have more energy, more confidence, and we add more years to our lives and life to our years. It is fundamental that we can't give what we don't have, so we must develop balance in our lives if we hope to share it with our dogs and other people.

Form and Function in a Dog's Body

What Does That Mean?

Have you ever had someone say something ambiguous to you, something that made no sense, was out of context and left you asking, "What does *that* mean?" I'm sure we all have, just as we have all watched our dogs do something that made no sense at the time. We knew they were trying to tell us something—that there was some important underlying message—but we just couldn't sort it out. So how do we begin to do that? We learn how to listen to what they've been saying all along.

Clearly, people rely heavily on verbal messages when communicating with each other. While this makes perfect sense for human-to-human exchanges, it is the least natural mode of conversing for dogs. Dogs are talking all the time but with very little vocalizing. In fact, vocalizing is the last and least used mode of relating to their world and to others. By the time a dog is vocalizing (barking, growling, snarling, howling, etc.), they are usually at the end of their rope, because all of their other attempts at communicating have gone unheeded or been ignored. As mentioned earlier, dogs have a much greater portion of their brains dedicated to the olfactory (scenting) and visual senses than they do to the auditory region. So while it's our natural tendency to want to talk to our dogs, it is helpful to keep in mind that their native tongue is different from ours. They communicate first and foremost with what Cesar Millan refers to as the "universal language of energy."

The language of energy transcends the boundaries of species and is the most authentic way to communicate with your dog. It is an intuitive process that requires some practice to get in touch with, but it is 100 percent worth it. The exercise from Chapter three of spending two days without talking to your dog should have been a great start. You feel such a wonderful connection with your dog when the two of you are functioning on the same wavelength and engaged in conversations without a word.

One of my favorite things to do is go hiking with a large pack of off-leash dogs. Feeling that undeniable, strong, silent connection between all members of the pack communicating so effortlessly is a profoundly peaceful experience. Just having the sun shine down on us as the wind makes its way through the grass and trees, listening to the rhythmic symphony of panting dogs and pitter-patter of footsteps as we move along the trail, and watching so many individual dogs come together to work as one unit with the pack changing directions and shape-shifting like a flock of birds . . . there's nothing quite like it.

If you haven't done so recently, spend time just walking with your dog, somewhere off the beaten path, somewhere quiet and remote enough that you can experience moving together and enjoying each other's company without all the disruptions of your neighborhood. Once you've reconnected at this level, you are ready to move on to communicating at the next level: through observing the way she uses her body. Think of her whole body as one big puzzle and each body part as a piece of that puzzle. Her tail is one piece, her eyes, ears, and legs are others. Many individual parts are working together, and it is good to become familiar with how dogs can use each segment of their bodies to relay different messages. For instance, the particular way your dog arcs her body and shifts her weight when approaching another dog tells the other dog much about her intentions and can either engender friendship or start a fight. Having knowledge of what these different approaches looks like can help you translate the conversation.

While a study of the intricacies of canine body language is certainly beyond the scope of this chapter, you should know some basic principles. Many of them you are probably already in tune with, but it's always good to review. Watching dogs interact in a group setting can accelerate the learning process because you can see the "call and response" style of their communication. Following are some of the most salient principles for reading canine body language:

- **Know what "normal" looks like.** In teaching federal agents how to detect counterfeit bills, the agents receive intensive instruction in what *authentic* bills look like. Once they know precisely what a normal bill looks like, it is easy to detect variations and identify fake paper money. In the same way, once you know what canine body language typically looks like, you will be able to identify when something is off. This is a crucial skill to develop, because in a real-time interaction between dogs, you may not have time to put your finger on exactly what's wrong (like you would if you have the benefit of video footage you can slow down and view multiple times), but you can see if something doesn't quite look right and redirect or interrupt the interaction. The most normal and healthy interactions between dogs are characterized by the following:
    o They lack facial and body tension—there's looseness in the body.
    o They approach each other with "bent" bodies; there's a curvature of the spine instead of a rigid, arrow-like or straight-on approach.
    o A curious nose: dogs want to sniff each other front and back (first name and last name).
    o The eyes are nice and "soft," with plenty of blinking and avoidance of direct eye contact.
    o Play is characterized by plenty of breaks. The dogs may shake off (like they do when they get wet), sniff the ground, look away from each other, or otherwise disengage momentarily

before resuming play. This keeps the energy of the interaction from escalating too high.

o Dogs tend to role-play (playfully rehearse) different life scenarios. They may initiate a game of chase, with one dog being the prey and the other the predator. These roles can, and often do, switch. The play is mutual and the dogs keep it that way, without allowing it to become too serious or life-like beyond each other's comfort levels.

o Posturing or mounting behaviors are generally used minimally and short in duration. There should be a lightness and jovial feel to the play, regardless of the specific body language.

o Any corrections the dogs give each other are proportionate responses to unwanted behaviors. The other dog respects and heeds the correction, and then play resumes.

o Play naturally includes some longer rest periods when the dogs just "hang out" or lie down and relax.

- **Watch the other dogs.** Be aware of how other dogs act and feel around a new dog. Their reactions to her can tell you much about her intentions. Dogs are far better judges of other dogs' energy than we humans are, so we should look to them for guidance when trying to get a "read" on another dog. Do they seem relaxed around the new dog? Do they seem worried? Do they want to play with her?

- **A wagging tail doesn't tell you anything.** The notion that a happy dog wags her tail is a very dangerous myth. Dogs can wag their tails when they are happy, anxious, aroused, excited, content, or right before they attack. Don't just focus on the tail; it can be very misleading.

- **Don't jump the gun.** People have a tendency to jump to conclusions and interfere with interactions between dogs way too much. Normal, stable dogs are able to skillfully interact with each other, diffuse tension, and resolve conflict. People who overmanage dogs' interactions create tension, prevent the dogs from communicating naturally, and can even cause fights to happen. Constantly interfering and telling the dogs what to do prevents them from learning to respect one another's cues. That's all fine and dandy, except that when the person isn't around, the dogs won't have the necessary social and "listening" skills to safely manage the interactions themselves. The result? The dogs end up in fights when people's backs are turned. Other people are too hands-off and have an overreliance on letting the dogs "work things out." This is less often the case, but it's not any healthier.

- **Be aware of breed and individual differences.** When evaluating the body language of a dog, take into account any idiosyncratic tendencies she has. For instance, bully breeds (bulldogs, Boston terriers, pit bulls, bull terriers, boxers, mastiffs, French bulldogs, etc.) generally present a forward and direct approach for greetings. People frequently perceive this as being aggressive when, in fact, it is very normal. Then you have a dog's individual personality quirks and play style to account for as well. In addition to having a general knowledge of overall canine behavior and body language, make sure to get to know each dog you interact with as an individual and learn what normal looks like for her.

- **See the forest.** The most important principle with respect to body language is to look at the whole picture. As previously mentioned, each part of a dog's body is like an individual puzzle piece. Keep in mind that you must put all the pieces together to get a clear picture of what a dog's overall communication is at any given moment. In other words, don't get hung up on any one or two pieces of body language, because you won't be able to see the forest for the trees. Step back and take a look at the bigger picture. It's a far more accurate indicator of what's actually taking place.

- **How does that make you feel?** I have watched a lot of video footage of dogs interacting with other dogs, people, and their environment. I have been astounded at how useful watching video can be at helping me pick up on details of a dog's behavior and body language I didn't notice at the time. I have been equally astounded at how misleading video footage can be. Videos miss out on the most crucial component of all: the energy of the dogs. Some very tenuous situations involving dogs don't look like that big of a deal on video, because a video captures only the audio and visual aspects of behavior but misses the overall vibe at that moment. So if you are trying to evaluate your dog's body language and you just can't get a read on her, make sure you are in tune with the underlying energy she's sharing. It can help you fill in the gaps and decipher her intentions.

Commit these principles to memory and put them into practice. They are indispensable tools for anyone wanting to understand dog-speak in a greater way. For an in-depth study of the subject, I highly recommend Brenda Aloff's book, *Canine Body Language: A Photographic Guide*. It is a comprehensive, fun, and an easy to understand must-read you will reference again and again.

Tell Me Where It Hurts

A benefit of treating humans with physical maladies is that they can tell others where they are experiencing discomfort. Dogs cannot do this, at least not verbally, so it is up to us to know what normal looks like for them and to explore any deviations from it. We should be aware of subtle changes in our dog's body, energy, or behavior, as many dogs are quite stoic when experiencing pain. This makes perfect sense when you think about it: Dogs are a social species whose well-being is dependent on the overall health of the pack, and a dog that shows weakness can become a target because she threatens the group's stability. A dog is wise, then, to downplay any type of physical ailment that might draw unwanted attention to herself.

One of the least desirable things that can occur within our dogs' bodies is the development of chronic tension. Tension in the body is natural if it is temporary. For example, it requires a certain amount of exertion and tension to exercise and play. However, it is not healthy for a dog to hold that tension for extended periods of time. Tension is not normally associated with positive social interactions, because healthy social behavior between dogs requires that pack members are at ease with one another. It's very difficult for a dog to be stiff in body and feel at peace at the same time, but chronic tension is a reality for many dogs, especially those who aren't psychologically stable and are easily thrown off if something in their environment changes. Lack of healthy exercise and mental stimulation, as well as imbalances of the mind, body, and soft tissue damage or disease can all cause sustained stress and restlessness. The key is to find ways to promote relaxation in your dog's body. An array of options are available.

The following list highlights a few specialty modalities for physically treating the body. Remember to always confer with your veterinarian to determine appropriate options for your particular dog. Similar to training methods for dogs, all therapeutic approaches can be beneficial when paired with the right dog at the right time for the right reason when balanced with other complimentary forms of treatment to provide comprehensive care. Your veterinarian should be your first point of contact with any health-related issues your dog is experiencing. She can make specific recommendations based on your dog's complete medical history and individual needs, and she can refer you to local specialists when necessary. (Remember: Consider the skill level, credentials, demeanor, and energy when selecting a professional in any field related to your dog's health.)

In today's world, it is easier than ever to find practitioners in the veterinary field who are holistic in their approach and have extensive knowledge stretching far beyond traditional medicine and modalities. As with finding a balanced trainer who has experience utilizing an array of training methods, it is a good idea to find a vet who is balanced in her approach, has many tools at her disposal, and treats each dog according to her individual considerations and needs. Many veterinarians have experience in the practices of acupuncture, homeopathy, essential oils, herbals, chiropractic care, and more.

Dietary considerations are also of great importance to your dog's health. Her nutrition supplies the building blocks her body uses to conduct everything from blood sugar and hormone regulation to maintaining healthy immunity and building tissue. Weekly, I have dogs brought to me because they have purported "behavioral problems" that are not behaviorally rooted. Instead, they are issues related to imbalances in the body and mind created by poor nutrition. A dog's behavior is a function of her overall psychological, emotional, and physical well-being. Training issues aren't always training issues. Sometimes, there are more pressing needs, such as making sure a dog is nutritionally sound. Dogs, and people, that feel well tend to act well. When the body has what it needs, it can better cope with environmental stressors and ward off all kinds of sicknesses, both physical and psychological. It makes no sense to compartmentalize things like nutrition, training, behavior, and fitness, because they are all interrelated and mutually dependent. While I won't delve into specific dietary recommendations due to the extensive nature of the subject, I encourage you to do plenty of research in this area, because if your dog's diet is wrong, nothing else will work properly. A great place to start gathering more information is Wendy Volhard's Website: www.volharddognutrition.com. For decades, Wendy has advocated for and developed balanced natural diets for dogs. Not only a consummate expert in the fields of canine training and nutrition, she is a remarkably friendly, kind, and generous human being, whom I feel very blessed to know.

ACUPUNCTURE AND ACUPRESSURE

These therapeutic treatments have been successfully used to help dogs overcome a variety of ailments, including anxiety, muscle fatigue and tension, neurological damage, as well as assisting in pain management. They involve either placing small needles (acupuncture) or applying pressure (acupressure) in specific locations on the body to release tension or to stimulate nerves and blood vessels in different areas. Sometimes lasers are used to stimulate these points as well (laser therapy). These treatments help balance the flow of energy within the body. Acupuncture and acupressure are considered alternative forms of treatment. However, many veterinarians trained in traditional Western medicine also incorporate these therapies into their practices, so make sure to inquire about them to learn if they might benefit your dog.

CHIROPRACTIC

Imbalances in your dog's body can cause extreme discomfort. Chiropractic treatment involves making specific adjustments to the dog's joints to restore normal alignment within the body, especially along the spinal vertebrae. The practitioner typically uses her hands to manipulate the spine and joints, opening up neural pathways that have been blocked due to misalignment or impingements caused by trauma or chronic overuse. If you think of the spinal column of a dog that is out of alignment like a water hose with a kink, removing that kink helps restore the flow. Likewise, correcting spinal misalignment or impingements increases blood flow and oxygen delivery to areas of the body that have been deprived. Chiropractic treatments can reduce pain stemming from pinched nerves and open up the lines of communication between different regions within the body.

MASSAGE

Canine massage is a broad category encompassing many techniques and specialized practices, but the overall benefits of this hands-on work have been widely demonstrated and recognized. Most techniques are the same as those used in human massage therapy but adapted to accommodate for differences in dogs' physiological and structural makeup. There are applications for everything from injury prevention and muscle tension release to increased oxygen delivery and toxin excretion. It is a powerful modality for creating and maintaining better balance in and throughout the body's systems. In watching a dog undergo a massage treatment, it is easy to witness immediate benefits, most notably the relaxation it creates within her body. The expertise, comfort level, presence, and energy of the therapist working with your dog have great bearing on the efficacy of the treatment itself. Seek out the best for your dog. Your veterinarian can point you in the right direction and refer you to a trusted local professional.

HYDROTHERAPY

Dogs benefit from having access to water, whether it's for recreational purposes or for therapeutic reasons. Water therapy is often used for post-operative rehabilitation, or for dogs that have neurological challenges or injuries. It is also a great option for dogs that need to exercise, but arthritis or other physical limitations prevent them from high-impact activities such as running or walking. Dogs can do low-impact exercise by swimming in a pool or walking on a water treadmill. These activities help release energy while also strengthening muscles, ligaments, tendons, joints, and increasing overall balance and coordination. Best of all, these activities are fun and engaging for the dogs and help build trust between the dog, the therapist, and the owners.

PHYSICAL THERAPY

This is a broad category that encompasses a range of therapies designed to support dogs that are post-operative, injured, have neurological issues, or are struggling with disease. Physical therapy can include stretching exercises to increase a dog's range of motion in her joints, balance exercises to promote joint stability and reduce muscle imbalances (therapy balls and balance boards are often used here), and a wide spectrum of other exercises that can help increase strength, coordination, concentration, and even help those "pleasingly plump" dogs shed some extra pounds. Because dogs yearn for exercise and can experience depression when they are too weak to engage in physical activity, physical therapy can help restore mobility and give them a new lease on life.

What Do You Want to Do Today?

One of the fastest ways to your dog's heart is to give her the opportunity to do something she loves. You have many choices of enjoyable activities you can do with her, and not only will she have fun, but it will keep you moving as well. Every dog has favorite activities, just as kids have favorite sports. Find out what your dog loves to do and you have found something that she not only delights in but also gives her a sense of purpose and keeps her healthy and active. Below are a few ideas of fun activities you can try. Pull up some videos of them online for a closer look.

- Skijoring: If you live in a colder climate, try skijoring! In this sport, you cross-country ski while your dog helps pull you along.
- Sledding: Sled dogs at work are a sight to behold. They are enthralled with their task, and it's a great adventure for you as well.
- Obedience: Obedience work, when done right, is enjoyable for you and your dog. Not only will it get you both up and moving but it helps your dog learn skills like focus, manners, self-control, and it teaches you how to more clearly communicate with her.
- Rally: This is obedience work with less focus on competition and precision and more on teamwork and having fun in a relaxed environment.
- Agility: Agility work requires you and your dog to maintain a strong connection and to be on the move together. It can be a great confidence builder and is

especially well-suited to dogs that are high-energy, athletic, and love a good challenge.

- Hiking: What better way to explore the great outdoors, get some fresh air, and experience the benefits of exercise?

- Frisbee: Disc dogs are very impressive to watch, indeed. Do you have a dog that is superfast and loves to jump and catch things? This might be just what you've been looking for.

- Dock diving: If your dog loves to run and jump and would relish the opportunity to leap into a pool of water, dock diving could be the perfect fit.

- Freestyle dancing: Do you love to dance? Does your dog enjoy movement and learning new tricks? This combination of choreographed movement and trick training is tons of fun.

- Flyball: If your dog has exceptional drive for tennis balls, consider Flyball. She'll get to run on a four-dog relay team, jump over hurdles, snatch her tennis ball from a box, and sprint back to you for her favorite reward.

- Weight pulling: If your dog is a tugboat on walks, why not give her a sporty outlet for her pulling instinct? Weight pulling competitions are impressive to watch and are fun for the dogs, too. Once she has an outlet for her pulling, she'll be more fulfilled and less inclined to take it out on you when you go for walks.

- Schutzhund: A combination of tracking (scent work), obedience, and protection, this sport offers great variety, and with supportive training produces dogs that are in love with the work itself.

- Ring Sport: This shares some commonalities with Schutzhund training but with a wider gamut of performed skills. Ring Sport requires tremendous dedication, and demands an exceptional level of drive, discipline, and control throughout competition. Ring Sport includes many skills, including retrieving, bite/protection work, obedience, and jumping over hurdles and high, vertical walls.

- Herding: The name says it all, but experiencing it is something else entirely. "Pure joy" is one way to describe what your dog will feel while she instinctually directs the movement of a group of sheep, cattle, or even ducks.

- Treibball/Urban Herding: If you think your pup would love herding but you don't exactly have a flock of sheep waiting at the ready, Treibball might be a perfect fit. Your dog will learn to move large exercise balls into a goal that looks like a soccer net.

- Search and Rescue: This can be performed at a recreational level, professional level, and everything in between. If you like to make a difference and your dog loves to track, look into the possibility of doing search and rescue training.

- Nose Work: A fun extension of traditional tracking and detection work, this is an increasingly popular training option for dogs. If your dog is good at using her nose and you want her to learn to focus, nose work can be a godsend. It is especially suited to older dogs that do not have the mobility they once did or that can't see or hear very well. One thing's for sure, they can still use their noses!

With so many options, how do you choose? I recommend immediately looking into a couple of the above listed activities that jumped out at you in any way. These activities are great bonding opportunities and very fun to do. Do a little research online. Find your dog's bliss. You may just find yours as well.

Training Your Body

Work It Out

I have found that most people consider working out to be drudgery on many levels. While I understand this viewpoint and used to operate from it, I am here with good news: It doesn't have to feel that way. Working out, when approached and structured the right way, can be fun, relaxing, spiritually enriching, a great stress reliever, and something you look forward to every day. Doesn't that sound like a better way to go? Let's look at how we can work to make *that* our new normal.

Most everyone has some kind of physical activity they naturally enjoy doing. It might be running or cycling or hiking or kayaking. The challenge with some of these activities (such as hiking and kayaking) is that unless you live in a place like the mountains, having your favorite activity as your mainstay will not allow for enough consistency in your exercise regimen. Even if you can do it every day, mixing things up will help you avoid excessive repetitive motions that can lead to unnecessary stress, fatigue, and injury.

I challenge you to do some form of exercise at least five days a week. Most people need to expand their options to integrate greater diversity into their physical outlets. If you love hiking but make it up to the mountains only on the weekend, you will want to build in some variety so you can be more consistent throughout the week. Search the Web for suggestions. You can also look at your local gym and rec center schedules to see what group classes they offer.

You do, of course, need to consult with your physician before beginning any exercise program. But assuming you are cleared for activity, incorporate it into your life very slowly at first, gradually increasing levels of duration and intensity over time. Physical activity might consist of gardening one day, walking or jogging another, resistance training the next, going on a short bike ride at lunch the next day, stretching exercises another, and rounding out the week with a light swim. Exercising consistently throughout the week (i.e., five to seven days a week for ten minutes at a time) is far better for your body, mind, and spirit than going on a ten-mile hike once a week (although a ten-mile hike is a great one to throw into the mix). Exercise is like eating: Doing a ton of it all at once and hoping it will last you the rest of the week is unrealistic and unhealthy. Consistency is the key!

If you look into your options, you may be surprised by the variety of clubs and meet-up groups in your area, where people do community walks, runs, bike rides, etc. If those aren't available to you because you live in the boonies and ten-foot snow drifts are everywhere, numerous in-home fitness devices are readily available. If you have trouble staying motivated to work out alone, get creative and make a game of it by using a fitness app on your phone and set goals to work toward. A lot of these apps can be integrated into social media and shared with friends who are also doing their own workout programs. Getting ample exercise is very doable if you're willing to drop your excuses and get moving. If you're *not* willing to do away with excuses, I have no good suggestions, because there isn't a solution for unwillingness. One of the most common excuses for not exercising is the tendency to want to do it 100 percent or not at all, which is obviously unrealistic for anyone in the world other than professional athletes, and so it becomes a convenient way of excusing oneself from such an impossible task. Remember: You don't need to do it all. Just do *something*, and do it *today*.

You Wanna Race?

*Until one is committed, there is hesitancy, the chance to draw
back—Concerning all acts of initiative (and creation), there is one
elementary truth that ignorance of which kills countless ideas and
splendid plans: that the moment one definitely commits oneself,
then Providence moves too. All sorts of things occur to help one
that would never otherwise have occurred. A whole stream of
events issues from the decision, raising in one's favor all manner
of unforeseen incidents and meetings and material assistance,
which no man could have dreamed would have come his way.
Whatever you can do, or dream you can do, begin it. Boldness has
genius, power, and magic in it. Begin it now.*

Johann Wolfgang von Goethe

I remember intensely disliking running for the first ten-plus years I did it. I wouldn't say I "hated" it, because I don't like that word, but it was something very close to hate. Very close. Running was something I did to "get in my cardio" and stay in shape. It was a necessary evil. Drudgery, I tell you, drudgery.

One day in 2008, I got a crazy idea that maybe I should run in the Bolder Boulder, a local annual 10K race that attracts 50,000-plus runners, walkers, and wheelchair racers of all ability levels. I thought, *I'm already running close to three miles sometimes. I bet I could train up to running a little over six by late spring, and I might as well get something out of all this work I'm doing.* This not-too-well-thought-out impulsive decision became a huge blessing. I trained for the race three days per week for several months; nothing exceptionally difficult, taxing or intense. I just ran. I also began to toy with the idea that maybe I could come in under sixty minutes. And then about a month later I thought that maybe, just maybe I could do it in under forty-five minutes.

This mental shift in my approach to training because I knew a race was coming up didn't make the training any less painful, but it made it hurt so good. At least now there was some kind of purpose to running, and I also knew I didn't want to show up on race day unprepared, so I trained consistently. I soon noticed that I was doing a lot less eye rolling during my workouts. Suddenly it wasn't about getting it over with anymore. It was about focusing my attention in the moment and making the most out of the run. If I started whining in my head about how hard a run was, I could get myself back on track much easier by simply thinking about the up-coming race.

Well, race day came and I was super nervous. The electricity from the crowd of runners around me was pretty exciting, though. The starting gun went off and I was on my way. People had lined the streets to watch and cheer us all on, and it was very motivating. My headphones blasted music all the way to the finish line, which I crossed in just under forty-five minutes from the time I started.

What happened next caught me totally off guard. A wave of emotion hit me hard. I can't really describe it, but for those of you who have given your all in competition, you know what I'm talking about. Having laid it all on the line, feeling proud of all the training that went into making that effort possible, as well as being around other like-minded people with stories of their own struggles, it was very overwhelming for me. I was also one of my favorite experiences.

After that day, and after ten-plus years of disdain for running, it all changed. Something clicked. Running was now enjoyable. Something I never thought possible, believe me. The reason I share this story is because it points to an important principle: In the words of Ray Bradbury, sometimes we have to "jump off the cliff and learn how to make wings on the way down." The day I signed up for that race and committed myself, I put myself on a course that led me to enjoy exercise, and it became about so much more than the race itself.

If you find yourself in a similar spot, where exercise seems like a drag, I encourage you to sign up for something. If you hate running and walking but you do it anyway to stay in shape, grab a friend or two and go out on a limb by signing up for a 5K run/walk. Commit to some kind of conditioning schedule that will have you ready on the day of the race. You could focus on many smaller goals while working out, from a time you want to complete the race in, to just finishing the race, or simply enjoying a morning outdoors walking with your friends. Make sure to get involved with something that gives you a target to work toward. It's one of the best ways in the world to change a negative perspective and get moving.

The following year after the first race I ran in, I got a little overzealous in my training (I am just a little bit, barely, *slightly* type-A) and injured my knee. I was bummed because I really wanted to do the race again, but the knee pain was pretty bad. *Well, I thought, I'm not going to let all my conditioning go completely out the window.* I had to find an alternative form of exercise. The stationary bike was out because it aggravated my injured knee, so I eventually bit the bullet and decided to take on my arch nemesis: swimming.

When I was just a wee tike, my dad took me to swim lessons—the kind where the overall goal is to teach you how not to drown. I did manage to learn at least that part, but even that was a real stretch. I also had an incredible phobia about being in water and panicked every time I went to a swim lesson. Twenty years later when I got into the pool at the local rec center, I had the distinct pleasure of feeling it all over again. I had never had a formal swim lesson on how to do anything but float and "doggie paddle," so I managed to teach myself some version of a freestyle stroke and kept myself in shape until my knee could tolerate running again . . . and then I got out of the pool as fast as I could.

About a year before writing *Transformational Dog Training*, I decided to give the pool another shot to add some variety into my training, which at the time included running, resistance training, stretching, and occasionally yoga and rock climbing. I hired a coach for a few private lessons to help me swim with proper form, instead of the sloppy version I had taught myself. One of the first thoughts I had that first day back in the pool was, *What the heck am I doing swimming again? This totally freaks me out. Am I crazy?*

I think part of why I did it was that I hated the idea of being controlled by my fear. I wanted to master it instead. I'd seen so many friends letting fear dictate how far they could go; I just couldn't imagine living that way. So instead I jumped into the deep end and got some help from swim coach Bob Bowman. "Wait a minute!" I hear you saying. "That's Michael Phelps's coach." Yes, that's true, but it's a different Bob Bowman we're talking about here. Long story short, Bob not only taught me how to swim better, he taught me all four competitive strokes and gave me lots of encouragement along the way.

I was happy with the progress I had made, and swimming was somewhat more enjoyable, but it still felt the way running once had: like an obligation. So when Bob told me I was ready to join a Masters team, I jumped at the chance before I could talk myself out of it. I knew I had to leap off the proverbial cliff again by getting involved in swimming in some organized way if it was ever to become an activity I genuinely liked to do. So I joined a team in the town where I live. It was a bit of a shock—and simultaneously an honor—to be in the pool with awesome swimmers, most of whom had been swimming since they were little kids, and many who also competed in high school and college. Some of them had even been to the Olympic trials. And then there was me—the guy who was afraid of water.

Little by little I built up my skill and endurance enough to keep up with a few of them, and soon I was competing. My first competition was the Colorado Masters State Championship four months after I joined. Being at that meet made me feel massively underqualified and humble, but I also experienced raw excitement and pure joy. The following year, my team won the State

Championship, and I took first place in the 50-yard backstroke. I didn't do any sports in high school or college, so winning and being part of a winning team was a very special experience and one I will never forget. Years ago, I never would have dreamed I'd be at competitions with people who had been to the Olympics. Today I genuinely love to swim, and my fear of the water is long gone.

My story won't be like yours, but I hope that in sharing mine, it might encourage you to try some new things and get more active. You may already be right on track with taking care of yourself physically. If that's the case, congratulations and keep it up! Staying fit and healthy can be a fun, lifelong journey. I once had an employee whose grandfather rode a stationary bike every day for at least a half hour, followed by a half hour circuit workout with weights, until he passed away at ninety-four years of age. Now that's a man who knew how to make consistent exercise a part of his life. I figured if he could do that, I could certainly fit some kind of physical exercise into my daily routine as well. Never have there been so many activities, clubs, and classes available to keep people active and healthy. Take advantage of what's available and have fun with it! Plus, when you take care of yourself, you have the energy to give into the lives of those that you love.

You Look Like You Could Use a Little Om

Om (sometimes written as "Ohm," which is a bit closer phonetically) is a chant, sound, or vibration sometimes employed during Yoga classes. The significance of Om is deeply embedded in various cultural and religious traditions, but the sound is easily recognized. It is generally used in Yoga classes to help quiet the mind and shut out any outside distractions people may be preoccupied with. Regardless of how you feel about Om or Yoga and any of the funny looking poses you may have seen people doing in a studio, I highly recommend taking at least four or five

Yoga classes. It doesn't matter if you are a fitness Nazi or pretty close to sedentary. It doesn't matter if you are as flexible as Gumby or you haven't touched your toes since you were a baby. Find a place with a certified and experienced instructor and sign up.

Why? Because it is one of the very best ways to help develop body awareness. This may not strike you as especially important, but let me assure you that it is. Knowing your body is a must. Knowing how to move and balance and integrate your body and mind is a must. Yoga is just a fun way to learn this indispensable skill. It is also very challenging, and concentrating on the movements as you flow between different poses is demanding physically and psychologically. It requires your full attention and helps you understand the virtues and necessity of fully operating in the present moment.

The first time I went to a Yoga class was, shall we say, "interesting." I felt kind of silly, to be honest. If I caved to my ego's ploys I would have skipped class to go pump some iron at the gym. That would have definitely been more comfortable for me and had more of the cool factor for sure, but I kept my resolve and entered the Yoga studio instead. There was such a mixture of people in the room. One gal moved into poses with incredible ease and was crazy flexible. She looked like she was a Cirque du Soleil performer. Then there were the rest of us: people of every age, shape, size, and ability level, which was much more variety than I had experienced in any of the other group fitness classes I had taken in the past. At first I was a bit intimidated and afraid of looking like a fool in front of others. That all dissipated once we got moving. I soon realized that everybody was focused on performing the movements and maintaining balance and breathing, and there just wasn't any way to do that without directing all of one's attention into the activity.

One thing that struck me the most was how much Yoga emphasized both breath control and an awareness of *how* I was breathing. It also helped me understand cycles and the crucial balance between of tension and relaxation and how to apply just the right amount of each at the right time. I learned of some specific imbalances in my body and muscles that had been compromising normal day-to-day activities as well as athletic pursuits. I also gained a deep appreciation for how an activity can be incredibly strenuous and profoundly relaxing at the same time. I found Yoga to be the perfect training ground for learning to handle pressure, stay in the moment, and work through stress instead of trying to escape from it.

Yoga can help you develop and balance your breathing, strength, coordination, and capacity for maintaining focused relaxation.

The prospect of Yoga can be intimidating if you are a beginner, but let me assure you: It is totally worth it. Like most things you fear, once you have enough information and begin to slowly immerse yourself in the practice, the fear you once had and the inhibitions begin to melt away and you start asking yourself, "What was I so worried about?"

Make sure to find an experienced and certified instructor who shows genuine interest in helping you find just the right fit based on your lifestyle and ability level. There are different forms of Yoga, variations within each form, and also mixtures of styles. You can find the right avenue with the guidance of a professional. Give it a try! I can't think of a better and quicker way to learn so much about how to intentionally use your body while strengthening your mind and teaching it how to operate effectively under pressure. You'll also develop a greater understanding of how to effectively integrate your mind and body.

What Did You Say?!

If any stumbleth not in word, the same is a perfect man, able to bridle the whole body also.

James 3:2 (ASV)

I thought it would be a good idea in this chapter about the body to "say a word" about words. It's very interesting to me that people live like they speak. People who have positive direction and are moving forward in life speak entirely differently than people who are stuck in a rut. People who understand the creative power of their words are thoughtful about what they let come out of their mouths. They realize that words have the power to bless or to curse. One text says that the tongue "has the power of life and death" and it goes on to explain that each of us will, essentially, eat our own words. Since we're looking at the body in this chapter and examining how things such as exercise and diet affect it, it's appropriate to explore how our "word diet" affects our bodies and overall natures.

The importance of proper speech is a common thread woven throughout religious and philosophical literature of all persuasions. Scientifically, the region of the brain associated with speech and the formation of language (called the "Broca's Area") is also associated with the planning of movement and action. Certainly, the words we choose can come back to bite us or bless us. Our words and our destinies are inextricably intertwined. The importance of choosing our words wisely cannot be overstated.

One of the simplest ways to help yourself use words properly is to think before speaking (like Mom always told you) and ask yourself two questions: "Do I want what I am about to say to come true and continue to be the case in my life?" and "What do I want my future reality to be?" Words have creative power and set the direction for times ahead. So if you forget to ask yourself the previous questions and proceed to tell your spouse that she doesn't love you anymore, don't be surprised if one day that becomes the case. You may think you are cleaver because you "saw it coming all along," when in reality you set the stage for it to come to pass. Similarly, if you feel like a cold might be coming on, saying that you are catching a cold is in no way helpful. You are aligning yourself with the future reality of sickness instead of health and vitality.

In Don Miguel Ruiz's book *The Four Agreements*, based on the Toltec tradition, the entire first agreement is an urging to "Be impeccable with your word."[1] That one quintessential phrase embodies this principle perfectly. While most people speak the way they do as a reaction to their circumstances, those who subscribe to the idea proposed by Alan Kay that "the best way to predict the future is to invent it" are highly intentional in choosing their words. They speak of negative situations, feelings, and thoughts as things of the *past*, and they set the tone for the *future* by describing it in ways that open the doors of progress, possibility, and prosperity.

For instance, I didn't grow up in a family with a ton of money. Despite that lack of money was a familiar condition of my environment, I made up my mind very early never to think of or refer to myself as being poor. I thought of myself as someone whose natural state was one of prosperity and abundance, and that is what I spoke about, not necessarily out loud, but in my internal dialogue. In my mind's eye, I was a naturally prosperous person who was temporarily experiencing money challenges. If I had spoken my way into agreement with my circumstances, I would have negated the possibility of ever experiencing financial abundance, and even if I had acquired a lot of money by some stroke of luck, my lack of impeccability in the speech department would have created a self-image inconsistent with someone who has money. The result? It would have been short-lived and the money would have disappeared about as quickly as it had shown up.

When you elevate your expectations and speech, you are "casting your bread upon the water," as the saying goes, and when the tide comes in (you never know exactly when this will happen, which requires faith and steadfastness on your part), a curious thing happens: You get back what you cast out, but it comes back multiplied.

Be aware of and intentional about your self-talk as well as the way you dialogue with others. Our words are powerful and certainly impact people around us. In speaking to one another, our minds translate words into pictures, so part of the impeccable use of words is refining our speech so that it best conveys our intended messages in such a way that when that picture is presented to the conscious and subconscious mind, it is constructive and clear and creates greater connection and understanding.

The opposite of impeccable speech is gossip and judgment. Gossip isn't talking about others. It's when we say things about them we would never say in front of them because the content of the message is designed to disparage them. Judgment isn't disagreeing with a person's actions or specific choices. It's when we assign a label to them ("inconsiderate," "dishonest," "bad parent," etc.) regarding their character or heart, things that no one other than God can truly see.

Judgment is often rooted in jealousy, although the ego is pretty good at disguising it. We might speak poorly of others and try to cast a negative light on them because we feel slighted (entitlement mentality) because of something they have that we don't. So to make ourselves feel better, we condemn what they have or do to justify the way we live our own lives. That's a tough pill to swallow, and I know from experience that the ego is pretty crafty at covering its tracks, but it's a good idea to question our motives—not the motives of others, but *ours*.

It's enlightening and liberating when we are honest and aware of why we do and say things. Casting gossip and judgment out onto the waters has a way of bringing back those very issues we accused others of having into our own lives with ever increasing frequency. By contrast, impeccable speech builds up people and has the power to inspire and enrich our lives while creating positive change around us.

Are You Going to Finish That?

This question alludes to two key areas of life. The first is the area of dietary habits. I know that I'm not the only person out there who is passionate about food, and I can assure you that I've asked my fair share of friends if they were going to finish the food on their plates . . . 'cause if not, I'd love to do it for them.

The second area where this is a fitting question is in the case of tasks we take on. Some people finish what they start and do what they say, and then there are those who give it the good ol' college try, which translates into botched attempts. Let's look at both scenarios. We'll begin by touching on dietary habits first.

Let Your Food Be Your Medicine

The spirit is willing, but the flesh is weak.
Matthew 26:41 (NIV)

Dietary balance is a key and necessary component to achieving overall balance, not only physically, but emotionally and psychologically as well. The way we eat profoundly impacts our ability to physically recover from exertion and is the means by which we fuel our efforts. It also influences the way we feel. If our diets are on point, our bodies will operate efficiently and we will have plenty of energy. When we have plenty of energy it is easier to maintain emotional stability and think clearly. Having a diet that is off track is like trying to running a car on cheap fuel. It bogs down and corrodes the engine, sapping the car of its power, and making it impossible for it to run efficiently.

Two categories of people come to mind who almost never neglect their bodies with insufficient diets: athletes and expectant mothers. Athletes can't afford to let their efforts wane. They need to support peak performance on every level. Expectant mothers are careful about supplying ample amounts of essential nutrients to their babies to avoid consequences that come with dietary neglect. But all of us need to renew our commitment to improving our diets. We need to get past the cop-out of "I know I need to eat better" followed by the *but* and the litany of excuses. Everybody can improve their diets in some small way today. I find that most people know what they need to do; it's simply a matter of deciding to act. Small actions count, and, in the end, it's the summation of our small daily decisions that make us who we are. Being impeccable in thought and action in the moment is, after all, the single thing we really need to master in this life. If you are having challenges with your diet and want to make it better but are truly at a loss for what to do next, consult with an experienced professional to get some guidance.

I used to work in the field of strength training and conditioning for both athletes and the general population. It involves a considerable focus on proper dietary habits. Although I had a sufficient understanding of what a healthy diet consists of, for years I struggled with finding the right fit for my body. Implementing a lot of the conventional wisdom and the most current information about eating properly had limited effectiveness and frustrated me. I was a high energy person and still getting a lot done, but I felt like my "engine" was constantly running on low-octane fuel. As a result, I had to grind out a lot of my work day-to-day, and it had a negative impact on my mind and emotions. I worked to have a great attitude and have balance in my life, but it seemed my efforts were being stifled at every turn. It's challenging to have a good attitude when you don't feel right.

Finally, I saw a naturopathic doctor who ran several tests to determine what foods I might have sensitivities or allergies to. When the tests came back from the lab, it revealed that a lot of the "healthy" foods I had been eating were actually causing inflammation in my body. My gut was also in need of repair. Long story short: I adjusted my diet in accordance with my individual needs. Once I did so, a lot of the things I'd been struggling with in terms of my mood and energy fluctuations began to diminish, and I finally felt the way I should have been feeling all along. I also needed less sleep, and the sleep that I was getting was replenishing for a change. My frustration began to fade as my body and mind were finally able to keep up with my spirit. I experienced a whole new level of vitality.

Although I am not going to provide specific advice about what your nutritional plan should look like, I would definitely encourage you to get it sorted out if you haven't already. If you're like me at all, you just can't afford to continually lose time, money, and energy by not supporting your system properly. Get some qualified guidance in this area. You deserve to feel well, and if you'll invest in yourself the payoff will be huge. Resolve to take care of your body and your body will take care of you!

IF AT FIRST YOU DON'T SUCCEED, STOP TRYING

The world would be a better place if people stopped trying. I can't think of many other things that give people, especially children, such misguided ideas about how to approach life. Have you ever seen someone straining, *trying* to do something, who was consistently effective? No one comes to mind for me. I see several challenges with the notion of trying that warrant analysis. Let's explore some of those issues and then discover a few more empowering ways to position ourselves.

The first issue is that when someone says, "I'm going to try to do it," it implies a high probability of failure. The very way their words frame the challenge is a form of self-handicapping. Self-handicapping is when a person essentially makes excuses before she's even engaged a challenge, so if things don't go well, at least she has a predetermined out. If your friend tells you that she's giving a presentation at work but is not sure how well it will go because she hasn't been sleeping great, she's practicing self-handicapping. Since she hasn't been sleeping great, if anything doesn't go quite as planned during the presentation it's okay, because she's already voiced concerns about a roadblock that will prevent the presentation from going smoothly. If it ends up going fantastic, she has even more to brag about: Despite not getting much rest, she still hit it out of the park. What a cleaver maneuver the ego has devised to hedge its bets. There's a built-in cushion in case failure occurs, but a pedestal is waiting to exalt the ego if success is the outcome.

So now we've arrived at the next issue: success and failure, both of which describe an escapism mentality, since they are after-the-fact judgments about an outcome. People want success and they strive for it, and there is nothing wrong with experiencing success. The problem is that when a person's energy is so focused on success, her mind-set undervalues the journey and wants to escape the effort and get to the end result, which robs her of the opportunity to learn from the process. If she does succeed, she'll celebrate; if she fails, it's a blow to her ego and she'll punish herself. Punishment could be as subtle as dealing with a general sense of discouragement or as severe as active self-chastisement.

Whenever you "try" to do something, it automatically introduces tension into your system. The issue isn't settled (if it were, you would *do* instead of try), and the natural byproduct is a lack of total commitment and general angst about the task you are trying to perform. This is a disempowered stance from which to launch your efforts. Your mind and muscles become rigid and tense as they brace against the challenge. But great performances are all characterized by the ease and flow that accompany a focused effort, which is relaxed and simultaneously strenuous.

Performing a demanding task can and should carry a graceful ease. We have all experienced this at times when the boundary between self and an activity melt away and we become a part of the effort. We still feel strain and sometimes pain, but we experience oneness with the effort also. We're not trying to escape the situation; we're living right in the middle of it. Success and failure aren't even on our radar, because we are interested in using our attention impeccably by focusing on the quality of execution. When the task is over, we see the results as an *outcome*. This information provides us with valuable feedback and helps us better direct our future efforts.

When you are truly present, you can meet the needs of the present. Thinking about the outcome siphons precious energy and attention. Focusing on the now makes all of your energy to meet the challenge available to you. When you're trying, you're bracing against the activity, hoping that things go well—a defensive and powerless position. Focusing on an outcome during an effort is like chasing a mirage. Not only is it exhausting and futile but also out of your control and cannot be grasped, but the *moment* can. When you commit to doing something, you're giving the best of yourself to the challenge; all of your gifts and talents and attention and energy are available to you. That's how things get done. *Doing* creates a meaningful effort and facilitates learning and the gaining of wisdom.

Trying creates frustration and is the long road to learning a skill, because it focuses the mind on the goal, blinding us to all the subtleties in our performance we need to focus on to learn so we can rise to meet the challenge. But what if you don't know whether or not you can do something? How can a person just decide to "do" something, thinking that will magically make it happen? These are the wrong questions. "Trying" focuses the mind on outcomes: success and failure; "doing" focuses the mind on total commitment to fully immerse oneself in the process, purposefully directing energy and attention into action. "Trying" puts a person in the position of a victim, subject to an outcome that is out of her control; "doing" puts a person in a state of power, whereby she is responsible for her effort. So, if at first you don't succeed, stop trying and start *doing*.

Putting It All Together

As you think on Louis Sullivan's quote from the beginning of this chapter, about form following function, consider that the way a dog's body is designed and the way your body is designed provide clues as to what activities suit each of you best. All bodies are designed to be active and *move*. Experiment with some of the activities listed in the beginning of the chapter—obedience, agility, skijoring, etc.—and find some fun energy outlets to share with your dog.

Become a skilled observer of how your dog communicates with her body. Does she hold tension or have imbalances you need to address? Have you consulted with your veterinarian on options for releasing that tension, healing lingering injuries, and managing pain? Since dogs can't tell us where it hurts, we have to watch for clues.

In your dog's interactions with other dogs, be mindful of the principles of canine communication: Know what normal looks like so you can spot any deviations from it; watch other dogs and their responses to her; keep in mind that a wagging tail doesn't mean jack; don't jump the gun and interfere needlessly in dog-to-dog interactions; be aware of her individual and breed considerations that make a difference in her personal communication style; see the forest by stepping back and looking at the whole picture; and if you get stuck and you're not sure what you're looking at, get in tune with the energy of the situation by asking yourself "How does it feel?"

In balancing your own body, appreciate its value in the overall picture of having balance in your life. Consistency of physical activity is a prerequisite to experiencing ubiquitous personal harmony. Realize that even though you may have occasional days when you don't feel like working out, you can get to a place where your normal state is that of genuinely looking forward to exercising. If you feel like you have to constantly drag yourself out of bed and it takes forever to get yourself psyched up, look into joining a team or club, finding workout partners who will challenge you, or by signing up for a future event that will add motivation and focus to your training efforts today. Enhance your body awareness by taking several Yoga classes; they will help you better understand the interplay between breath and movement and will also help you pinpoint weak areas and imbalances within your body that you were not previously aware of. It's also the perfect venue to expand your ability to handle stress effectively.

This is a great time to revisit the principle "Whatever is in the well comes up in the bucket." How impeccable is your speech? The words you choose are a reflection of what's within. Are things like gossip and judgment and defensiveness coming up, or do your words encourage others and express love and a positive expectancy about the future? People live like they speak. Our words carry the power to create a wonderful future or one full of sadness and regret. The choice lies solely with each of us. Like the North Star guides sailors in the ocean to where they want to go, impeccable speech helps us chart our course in life and keeps us heading in the right direction. By contrast, improper speech casts up storm clouds, obstructing our view, stirring up troubled waters, and blocking our way home. And remember, what others say about us isn't the critical factor. What matters is what we accept, internalize, and speak about *ourselves*. We should also pay it forward and speak life and encouragement into others, but it is ultimately up to them to come into agreement with what's spoken and align their speech with it if their desires are to come to pass.

Become a doer. Get "try" out of your dictionary and experience life at a new level. Direct your full attention into the moment and the quality of every effort. Immerse yourself in each activity you do; be intentional about enjoying the journey as you go through the process. Learn everything an experience has to teach you, and realize that in any arena, if you master the process, the results will take care of themselves.

Be sure to have a diet that supports your efforts. Your nutrition fuels your body and undergirds mental and emotional balance and strength. Good fuel promotes good performance; great fuel promotes great performance.

Practical Application Exercises Related to the Body

For Your Dog:

1. Select an activity from the list at the beginning of the chapter. Look into a local club or training facility where you can take your dog and attend at least one class. Oftentimes, trainers are more than happy to have you try a class, or at least sit in on one and observe so you can get a feel for it.

2. Sit with your dog for five to ten minutes and look over her body. Start at her nose and work your way to her tail, making sure to check things like how clean her ears are and if you notice anything on any other part of her body that seems off. Gently maneuver her limbs to make sure they are nice and loose. Make note of any areas that cause her discomfort or joints that seem stiff. Look at her teeth; are they clean? What about her paws? Are there any abrasions or sores between her pads? If you find anything out of the ordinary, reach out to your vet, particularly for any lumps or bumps you find, or any discomfort or painful areas. And, of course, stay safe when handling your dog if she shows pain or intolerance to handling in general.

3. Pull up an online video of dogs playing in a group. Closely observe how they use their body language to communicate with one another. Notice as many subtleties as you can, things like weight shifts and how they use blinking or averting their gaze to avoid direct eye contact. Pay attention to any instances where a dog communicates, without growling or snapping, that she is uncomfortable with an approaching dog. Pay attention to the way dogs indicate with their bodies that they would like to engage in play with

each other. Also note the role any humans in the video play and how their interactions with the dogs affects the communication for better or worse.

For You:

1. Sign up for several Yoga classes with an experienced instructor and go to them.

2. Make two short lists. The first should consist of three physical activities you can do this week. Then block off time in your calendar to do them. Make it realistic and make it a priority. If it's truly a priority you will get it done.

   The second list should consist of three to five specific steps you can take this week to improve your diet and nutrition. Pick a couple of the easiest to implement items and integrate them into your life this week. Again, make them realistic. Selecting absurd dietary changes will not help your cause, because you won't follow through. Do something simple, but do it.

3. Keep a sign on your desk at work for the next week that simply says WORDS. Use this as a reminder to be conscious of the words you use. I promise, it will cause you to change the way you speak, and changing how you speak will elevate the quality of your thoughts and your daily interactions. Send out only words consistent with what you would like to see happen in your life.

Chapter Six

Growth, Adventure, Gratitude, and Peace

Security is mostly a superstition. It does not exist in nature, nor do the children of men as a whole experience it. Avoiding danger is no safer in the long run than outright exposure. Life is either a daring adventure, or nothing.

Helen Keller

Our dogs possess a high level of mastery in a few additional areas that are of utmost importance. In this chapter we will become students and sit at the paws of our dogs and learn from them to transcend old, stagnant, and uninspired ways of being. Our dogs can teach us many things, but we will focus on a few key areas to round out our study of Transformational training. These focal points are personal growth, adventure, gratitude, and peace. Let's start with adventure.

It's the stuff that movies are made of, stories with characters we celebrate for having the courage to go out on a limb and leave the safety of what is familiar and comfortable to venture out into the great unknown. Our appetite for adventure is so embedded in the core of who we are that if we are not partaking in our own, we will satisfy the craving vicariously through movies, music, video games, our friends, spouses, or our children. Security, as Helen Keller so rightly stated, is a superstition, an illusion. We are not as safe as we tell ourselves we are. At any moment we could encounter danger or death, whether we're on the couch or skiing in the backcountry; whether we're watching reality TV or carrying out a daring endeavor; whether we're too scared to risk exposure or brave enough to be vulnerable and take a chance.

Most folks want both safety and adventure, which is why couch cushions all across America have well-established circular depressions. I'm not pointing fingers. I enjoy comfort as much as anybody else. But what I also know is that if we stay in what's comfortable too long, it becomes a prison instead of a place of replenishment. I am absolutely convinced that the soul longs for novel experiences embedded with elements of danger and uncertainty that show us what we're made of. It is one way we connect with our essence. To deny ourselves this opportunity is to deny our very natures, and if we push it down long enough, we become broken, lacking purpose and wondering deep down, *Do I even have what it takes?*—a haunting question that needs an answer.

At any given point in life we are operating from one of two positions: one born of fear that keeps us retreating and clinging to safety; or one born of love that propels us forward into the unknown. In many traditions, including the Toltec tradition, the latter position—born of love, a thirst for knowledge, and moving past what is known—is taken only by those with the courage to honor their natures. We call these people warriors.

The warrior title is not just reserved for the soldier. It is for those with the courage to challenge and cast off the parts of themselves that lack authenticity to become seekers of greater truth. Warriors enjoy comfort like anyone else but cannot dwell there very long because they feel and answer the call within: the call to arms. They are drawn to unknown realms and give themselves wholeheartedly to any challenges; they choose their battles wisely and commit fully. They know, unlike most others, how to find and fight from a place of inner peace, despite the dissonance and disorder of the chaotic world surrounding them. They are grateful for their challenges, for they provide opportunities to grow as a person, to expand their influence and power, and to face and conquer their fears.

Within each of us is a warrior lying in wait who yearns for adventure and freedom, yet few are brave enough to summon him. Joel Osteen, in his book *Your Best Life Now*, made a statement that's been etched in my brain ever since I read it: "It's not what you have in you; it's what you're getting out."[1] Think about that. What's buried within you doesn't mean a thing until it is awakened and brought forth. What good is potential if you can't, or won't, bring it into being? What good is raw talent if it isn't refined by tests and trials? And what good is having the heart of a warrior if it's never stirred up to give rise to a new way of living?

Some answer the warrior's call while they are young, others in their middle or old age, and, sadly, many people never do. It doesn't matter what your age, sex, race, creed, or situation is. Respond. Today. No one can answer for you. It's a personal decision and a bold one at that. It certainly doesn't make life easier, but it will make you come alive. It will help you abolish limiting beliefs, find a greater source of power, and overcome obstacles instead of wishing they were easier to deal with. Remember that warriors walk by faith—faith in a greater calling and faith in oneself. They know that adventure cannot be tamed and made safe, so they don't waste energy and attention trying. Instead of getting caught in the grips of fear, they access their love of knowledge and step out into the unknown, where all great learning and adventure takes place. Being a warrior is not a technique; it is a way of life, a way of seeing and thinking—an attitude.

I haven't said anything about how this all relates to dogs because adventure is second nature to them. A balanced dog, and especially a dominant one, is bold and courageous. He is not reckless or rash; his wisdom prevents him from rushing into dangerous situations for which he is totally unprepared. However, he does not shy away from challenges that carry healthy levels of risk. He meets them head-on with much wonder, joy, gratitude, and the stability that can only come from having inner peace.

He has much to teach us if we will allow him to, which is the theme of this final chapter. My challenge to you this week is to deliberately embark on an adventure by doing a new activity you are totally unfamiliar with, or by exploring a place you have never been. While you're at it, take your dog with you and pay attention; he'll remind you how adventure is done and keep you focused on the journey.

Which Way Should We Grow?

Truly happy people seem to have an intuitive grasp of the fact that sustained happiness is not just about doing things that you like. It also requires growth and adventuring beyond the boundaries of your comfort zone. Happy people, are, simply put, curious... Yet curiosity—that pulsing, eager state of not knowing—is fundamentally an anxious state... Curiosity, it seems, is largely about exploration—often at the price of momentary happiness. Curious people generally accept the notion that while being uncomfortable and vulnerable is not an easy path, it is the most direct route to becoming stronger and wiser.

Todd B. Kashdan and Robert Biswas-Diener[2]

One of the best things about training your dog is how much it can help *you* grow. Dogs are naturally curious and relish the opportunity to engage new experiences and expand their horizons. Being in tune with the present, they perceive the subtlest details of each experience, which accelerates the rate at which they obtain knowledge. Compare this with the experience of a typical human who is preoccupied with a specific goal (outcome), while lingering in the past and worrying about the future. Only a miniscule amount of his attention is left available to help him learn and develop. He would benefit greatly from expanding his awareness and keeping his mind in a quiet and receptive state.

Programming your mind for continual growth requires developing a hunger for knowledge and having a present-minded orientation. This opens you to what an experience can teach you. Goals are great to have, no doubt, but people who are highly goal driven often miss out on the best life lessons. Anytime a person is goal driven, his mind is programmed toward a specific outcome, placing the emphasis on the end result instead of personal progress. He is more concerned with what he gets than what he becomes. This lack of focus and attention on the process prevents him from experiencing the richness of the moment and teaches him to value accomplishments and titles over personal growth. What a shame!

In the end, it is the warrior who focuses on the steady and deliberate expansion of his skills as he engages his challenges, seeing them as teachers instead of mountains to be conquered, who reaches the summit. He reaches it not by straining hard to reach the top but because he relishes every moment of the adventure. He learns each lesson his challenges have to teach him, which expands his wisdom and strength so that reaching the mountain summit is an unavoidable result of his process-oriented work ethic.

The martial art of Aikido places a heavy philosophical emphasis on seeing one's opponent as a teacher rather than an adversary. That is exactly the kind of mentality that creates a lifelong learner. I challenge you to change your mind-set, if you haven't done so already, to view the obstacles you face as your greatest teachers instead of thorns in your side.

Aikido also encourages students to garner a complete and courageous commitment to engage opponents, despite the danger posed, if a more peaceable option doesn't exist. Once a warrior is in the throes of combat, there is absolutely no room for doubt or anything other than a total, uncompromising embrace of the process of combat. The aim of the Aikido discipline is to blend with and redirect the aggressor's momentum to gain the upper hand and diffuse the attack. In the same way, you can choose to engage challenges fully, staying flexible and assimilating new information on the fly. This enables you to flow with the situation and redirect obstacles to develop solutions and discover new opportunities.

When we work with our dogs, it is tempting to become frustrated by recurring challenges or training plateaus, but these are our greatest teachers lying in wait! They are opportunities to show our dogs compassion and patience while building our own perseverance and teaching us to stay focused on the journey. One of the most common training mistakes we make with our dogs is trying to get them to do too much too soon. When teaching our dog to stay, we issue the command and proceed to take three steps away from him when we should start by slightly leaning our weight back on our heels and then reward him for staying. The next time, we simply lean our weight back a little farther and reward him for staying again. About twenty repetitions later we can take a few steps backward. Baby steps are the way to go.

Gradual approximations are easy for our dogs to learn (as opposed to quantum leaps) and remind us to appreciate the value of the process. We get into trouble when we get greedy and try to skip steps to get to the "goal" quicker. This week, teach your dog something new, a trick or task, and write out a plan that includes detailed steps you'll go through in teaching it to him. Be sure to teach him the new behavior gradually and systematically. Think in terms of hundreds of repetitions/steps instead of dozens.

Dogs naturally go with the flow and aren't constantly in a rush to get everything done. People . . . not so much. What comes naturally to dogs is something we must intentionally train ourselves to do. We have to develop within ourselves patience and consistency, two of a warrior's greatest assets. A warrior knows that the greatest progress is made by compounding effort over time. Gaining wisdom and insight is more important to him than any individual goal. He appreciates the value of outcomes and avoids falling into the trap of labeling them as successes or failures. In this way he keeps things in proper perspective and uses the information provided by specific outcomes to learn, grow, and adjust his approach as necessary. It's like the classic tale of the rabbit and the hare: slow and steady wins.

Goals are most reliably obtained when our primary focus is on *growth*. And growth can't be rushed; there is an optimal rate at which it occurs. When this natural pace is disrupted, either by being rushed or stifled, we get out of balance and bad things start to happen. Goals are important because they provide direction and motivation, but intentional focus on the process is what develops our wisdom, character, and power. It's the individual who values growth over goals that masters his craft and outperforms others in the long run.

Where's Fido?

We don't stop playing because we grow old; we grow old because we stop playing.

George Bernard Shaw

I think most of us have had the heart-stopping experience of having our dogs escape the yard. Maybe he dug a hole under the fence or jumped over it, or maybe we just left a gate open. However it happened, each and every moment that passes is a scary one, particularly if we live in a busy neighborhood with lots of traffic.

While this may not be a fun experience for us as owners, we can learn something from it. For me, this type of behavior in a dog can present itself for a number of reasons, but there is one common underlying motivation: the natural urge to explore. Balanced dogs are curious creatures. They're not content to hang out in their own backyards forever. They have an undeniable inner prompting that keeps telling them, in effect, *There's so much more out there. I need to venture out and see what I've been missing.*

Dogs were built to roam, migrate, explore, and be daring. They are willing to let go of what feels good and comfortable and safe so they can break out into new frontiers. I think one of the reasons it's so easy for them to do this is because they aren't plagued by the same complexities of the human psyche that cause people to worry, fret, rationalize, and justify a million reasons why they shouldn't do something. Dogs know how to *live*. They see everything in a fresh and new way (just think about the scenario of leaving the room and coming back in ten seconds later and having your dog excited like he hasn't seen you for days). Dogs aren't content to just exist, either bored by monotony or paralyzed by their fears. Then why should we be content to go through life that way?

As long as we have breath in our bodies, we have a choice to either thrive or merely survive. Adventure doesn't have to mean going on some dangerous expedition deep within the jungles of Central America (although it will for some people). Adventure is, like so many other things, a choice. Anytime we step over the line of our present comfort zones, an adventure is waiting on the other side. For warriors, there is no other way to live. They can't be common people, for that wouldn't be true to their nature. They *need* to experience adventure. This internal drive propels them beyond the limits of what they thought they could do, and they come to know themselves better as time goes on, while those around them become progressively more disconnected from their true selves as they age.

Warriors know their conscious minds will always tell them that they shouldn't venture out, but they also know that their conscious minds are cowards in the midst of adventure. They know that staying in their comfort zones would only hold them back from their potential and from knowing their true selves. So they make a conscious decision to consistently grow by stepping outside their comfort zones to engage new undertakings. Knowing how to direct their minds while in the midst of a challenge allows them to stay present-focused and efficiently process fear and stress. The outcome of the new experience is impossible to predict with any great degree of accuracy beforehand, because they are in uncharted waters. But one thing's for sure: If they stay curious and give themselves to the challenge fully, they will never be the same. They will have expanded their wisdom by bringing the new experience within the known realm. They are willing to let go of everything they are to become something more.

If you have seen the 2004 movie *The Village* by M. Night Shyamalan, you may remember the character Lucius Hunt being asked why he's not afraid when everyone else in the village is. He simply replies: "I do not worry about what will happen; only what needs to be done." The lesson we take away from the film is the realization that we end up creating our own monsters and surrounding ourselves with self-imposed fear, and we cannot stay safe by keeping danger out, for it causes us to contract, stay ignorant, and practice the denial that hurts us more than anything. Fear always stands guard at the cusp of personal progress, and we must learn how to systematically dismantle fear and move forward despite its presence. There is nothing quite so liberating as connecting with our love of adventure and casting off the restraints of a mind bound by fear in the animated pursuit of our personal destiny.

I'm Home

Do you stay in a state of gratitude or are you always looking for more?

Dr. Wayne Dyer

Dogs have to be the best greeters on earth. Coming home to a dog that is genuinely happy to see you is a wonderful feeling. By nature, dogs are masters at unconditional love. People have a harder time with this but are very good at giving their dogs unconditional affection, which creates more behavioral issues than anything else I know of. But I digress . . . Dogs are tremendously grateful creatures. They always seem to appreciate what life has to offer.

A dog will see a stick in the backyard and think he just won the doggie lottery. His unbridled joy as he prances around the lawn makes us smile. He'll trot over with it, as if to say, "Aren't you proud of me? Look what I brought you!" If we throw the stick for him, he will bound after it and bring it back time after time. When he's tired from playing, he'll rest next to us, giving kisses to show his gratitude. Dogs are so good at finding everything that's right with life.

I met a dog a couple days ago that came to hang out with my pack. Through some degenerative issues in his spine, he eventually lost all his feeling in his back legs and has a little wheelchair to support his back end while he propels himself with his front legs. That little guy runs around with the biggest smile you've ever seen on a dog's face. He is really fast, and even if he flips his chair over so he's upside down, he'll just flip back over and carry on. He is a picture of perpetual happiness and has such a zest for life. It was a powerful example of resiliency and gratitude for me, and I was very grateful for the opportunity to meet him! I could go on and on with examples of how dogs naturally express gratitude, but I know you can come up with plenty of your own.

When a person is focused on the blessings in his life, he tends to attract more of them. While it is so easy to look around and see everything that's wrong with the world and missing from our lives, it takes intentionality and effort to focus on what we do have. We must remind ourselves that what we focus on expands. Sometimes it requires laser focus to keep our attention on what we want. This also relates back to responsibility and utilizing our resources the best way we can. As an example, if I'm behind schedule and have only ten minutes to wrap things up instead of the thirty minutes I was planning on, I would be wise to focus my attention on being grateful for the ten minutes I have. This is an empowered mind-set, because I'm focused on the fact that I have ten minutes instead of zero, and I can think of ways to best use that time. If I were to focus on the twenty minutes I "lost," that I was "entitled" to, it would set me up to feel like I somehow got cheated, and that negative attitude would soak up valuable attention that should be directed into meeting the needs of the present.

When our dogs show us gratitude, we feel good. Showing gratitude has a way of lifting our spirits and the spirits of those around us. People and dogs love to be appreciated. To appreciate means to increase in value, so when we are grateful we are literally increasing in value whatever we are grateful for. As that value continues to increase, we begin to see blessings surrounding and overtaking us. Gratitude is a decision, just like adventure. It's a choice our dogs make and show us every day, from the little things to the big things. It's part of why we love them so much and is an indispensable character trait for anyone who wants to be filled with our final topic of discussion: peace.

Let Me See Your Peace

Never be in a hurry; do everything quietly and in a calm spirit. Do not lose your inner peace for anything whatsoever, even if your whole world seems upset.

Saint Francis de Sales

Success isn't measured by money or power or social rank. Success is measured by your discipline and inner peace.

Mike Ditka

Take a balanced dog on a walk and observe him; take him for a road trip; show him how to wade into a stream; go hiking in new areas; watch him meet and play with other dogs; and watch him curl his body up in the shade of a tree after all of it to rest for a while. What is the one common theme you will see in him time after time?

Peace.

It pervades everything he does. Even when he takes on new challenges he manages to maintain it.

Peace can be temporarily experienced even by an unbalanced dog if circumstances line up and result in an environment that suits his liking. This kind of peace, however, is temporary. It cannot be sustained and is totally dependent on manipulating circumstances to provide comfort. True peace is experienced only by stable dogs. It comes from within and is not subject to the ever changing currents of life's circumstances. It is that quiet inner confidence a dog has that allows him to embrace whatever life brings. If our dogs do not seem to be at peace—save for the times they are at home or in situations where they are totally comfortable—we have some work to do. After reading this book and putting the principles into practice, both you and your dog should be well on your way to a more tranquil way of living.

The greatest task of a warrior is to create peace within. This means that his mind, body, and spirit must all be healthy and in sync. The journey of the warrior requires him to have a strong spiritual foundation, else it caps his potential and limits him to what only his mind and body can accomplish. Most everyone believes in the realm of the spirit, despite that we have different takes on what it consists of. Regardless, if we neglect the spiritual dimension of life, it is impossible to have perfect peace, because peace is *rooted* in the spirit.

For me, having strength of spirit is supported by spending time in prayer and meditation—in experiencing God's presence. It means practicing silence. It means reading the Bible, books on spirituality, and listening to empowering messages that add depth to my understanding of it. It means practicing my craft and being in the flow of working with dogs and helping them find balance, while helping their people foster those same qualities. It also includes listening to music, watching movies, and spending time outdoors—there's something profoundly spiritual about being silent in the midst of nature and connecting to the field of infinite potentiality in God's presence. These are ways in which I find it easiest to connect to my power source. Your spiritual disciplines may look completely different from mine, but the important thing is that you place proper emphasis on keeping spiritually fit. I find that when I am in alignment at the level of the spirit and function from that place, life has a certain flow to it, which allows me to stay in peace; and when I begin to step outside of that and function primarily from my mind or body, the wheels begin to fall off the wagon.

We might be housed in flesh and blood, but we are spirit at our core. Operating from that place first and then moving out into the mind and body holds things in proper order and keeps us connected to our true source of power. The mind and the body are exhaustible entities; the spirit is inexhaustible and doesn't tire. Your spirit is timeless, keeping you connected to the present. It is not consumed by past regret or worried about your future. Greatness originates here. When your spirit is well nourished and you ensure that your mind and body are connected and on the same wavelength, energy and power will flow freely. If you are out of alignment (and have good self-awareness) you will know; it feels like having all of your power suspended behind a dam while you're stuck downstream in your mind and body. A trickle of power slips through, but nothing like what's available if only you will tap into spirit and release the floodgates.

There is a natural order to things, and it is impossible to rearrange and conquer that order. When you are aligned with your purpose, have balance in your life, and are functioning from a place of love, you can experience peace no matter what is happening around you. Circumstances may not be pleasant, but as a warrior you don't fret when things aren't going your way. You recognize that life has many detours, and a change of direction doesn't mean that you've missed your destiny. For you, this is part of the adventure of it all; the twists and turns add to the wonder of the journey itself. You live an inspired life because you know many paths lead to the summit. You've embraced a way of being that dogs show you every single day: You stay present; you stay curious; you stay in touch with your intuition; you are bold and courageous; you keep your peace and are ever hungry for adventure.

Notes

Chapter One

1. Marianne Williamson, *A Return to Love: Reflections on the Principles of A Course in Miracles* (New York: Harper Collins, 1992), 190-191.

Chapter Two

1. Eckhart Tolle, *The Power of Now: A Guide to Spiritual Enlightenment* (Novato, CA: New World Library, 2004), 12–13.
    2. Ibid., 189.

Chapter Three

1. B.M. Kavoi and H. Jameela, "Comparative Morphometry of the Olfactory Bulb, Tract and Stria in the Human, Dog and Goat," *International Journal of Morphology*, 29(3) (2011): 939–946.
    2. Gavin de Becker, *The Gift of Fear* (New York: Dell Publishing, 1999) 72.
    3. Donald J. Trump and Robert T. Kiyosaki, *Why We Want You to Be Rich* (Rich Publishing, 2006), 40.

Chapter Four

1. John Maxwell, *Put Your Dream to the Test: 10 Questions to Help You See It and Seize It* (Tennessee: Thomas Nelson, Inc., 2009) 176.
    2. Stephen Covey, *The 7 Habits of Highly Effective People* (New York: Free Press, 2004), 31.
    3. Pete Koerner, *The Belief Formula* (Georgia: Bell Rock Press, 2007), 191.
    4. Zig Ziglar, *See You at the Top* (Louisiana: Pelican Publishing Company, 2005), 54.

Chapter Five

1. Don Miguel Ruiz, *The Four Agreements: A Practical Guide to Personal Freedom*, (San Rafael, CA: Amber-Allen Publishing, Inc., 1997).

Chapter Six

1. Joel Osteen, *Your Best Life Now: 7 Steps to Living at Your Potential* (New York: Hachette Book Group, 2014).

2. Todd B. Kashdan and Robert Biswas-Diener, "What Happy People Do Differently," *Psychology Today* (August 2013): 53.

About the Author

Brian Bergford is a Certified Dog Trainer (IACP-CDT) and member of the International Association of Canine Professionals. He has done extensive work as a dog behavior specialist and is the owner of Altitude Dog Training and Uptown Dog. His expertise is the interplay between dog behavior and human psychology.

Brian earned his degree in Psychology from the University of Colorado, taking particular interest in neuroscience, psychopathology, clinical psychology, and the principles of human psychology and personal performance. His passion for helping people and dogs drove him to expand his knowledge base by studying the principles of Canine Psychology and Behavior as well.

Having studied a wide spectrum of training applications, his experience working with many different training methodologies allows him to develop creative training solutions—solutions that are most appropriately suited to meet the needs of the individual dog and family. Brian is a Volhard Dog Nutrition consultant, and this additional specializ-

ation in nutrition and holistic health modalities adds greater depth and sophistication to his insight about canine behavior.

For more information on Brian's training, seminars, clinics, or related services, visit www.altitudedogtraining.com.

14143301R00159

Made in the USA
Middletown, DE
18 November 2018